Cracker-Boy

Cracker-Boy

A History of Plantation America:
1607–1865

By

James LaFond

With Lynn Lockhart

Dedication

Dedicated to the runaway children of Plantation America who became frontiersmen, Indians, pirates and otherwise avoided the unmarked grave of a slave, and to Mary Kay Krogman, for bringing long-discarded lives to light.

Dust Cover

In this in-depth survey of Plantation America, the author brings to light the conditions of life for the millions of forgotten and dismissed Americans, many of them malnourished child slaves, who were literally planted as human cattle in a pristine land in a desperate bid to transform it into a taxable mercantile garden. Such facts as the holding of Chinese and Southeast Asian slaves in Maryland in the early 1700s and the frequency with which runaways stole from their masters or were shackled are illuminated in this chronicle of the Actual Plantation America, which should put forever to rest the venerated lie of Colonial America.

Introduction

...in reference to Seisures, that when the Governour shall have carryed off & taken to himselfe, the Estates of Tobacco, Cattle, Servants &c as hee does (which are the stock upon the Place) of what value or consideration the bare Acres can be of to his Majestie.

-Samuel Wiseman,

Writing for:

Herbert Jeffreys

John Berry

Francis Moryson

March 27, 1677 from the Plantation of Virginia (Wiseman p107)

This massive volume, comprising over 100 runaway slave advertisements, as well as original texts from the ancients and from the Colonial, better described as the Plantation, period, is a treasure born from one man's relentless curiousity, and revealed by his sweeping understanding of history.

Slavery was not invented in North America, it has always been a vital element of any civilization, only hidden from us now by the abundance of petroleum, offshore manufacturing and subtle changes in employment arrangements. Hereditary slavery was perhaps somewhat innovative, attributable to the relatively abundant food and soft working conditions that allowed slaves in the Plantations to increase in number, rather than die in their labor, as the numberless multitudes have through history.

In this volume you will read the enticements and warnings issued to those who would risk travel to the New World, descriptions of runaway slaves and other associated property, and see a simple statistical analysis of runaways advertised in Maryland. Thousands more runaway listings remain to be analyzed and many original texts remain to be unearthed, even as the effacement of unfree European labor in North America is a fait accompli, and the enshrinement of the uniqueness of African Americans' suffering is nearly so, as discussions of present-day working conditions in Asia are subordinate to the claims of the One True Slavery.

As the editor and contributor to this book and the Plantation America project, I have located original sources online (where possible, URLs are given in the Bibliography), transcribed texts, and supported the author in the herculean work of restoring and revising the history of this nation, the kernel of greatest and most powerful civilization, for better and for worse, ever to bloom and wither on this earth. James LaFond has named the nameless dead, uncovered the buried tracts, and given voice to the silent servants and slaves, here he gives their descendants the opportunity to understand and preserve their true history.

-Lynn Lockhart

Contents

Ancient Threads

Slavery is the oldest civilized economic system and must not be thought to have originated in early modern America. As an introduction to the concept of slavery, below are articles on ancient servile traditions.

'I Am Brown'

A Young Bride's Wedding Night Plea (Rossiter)

Three parties sing in this processional song:

The Maidens
"You are deservedly adored."

The Bride
"I am brown—"

The Maidens
"Rather lovely!"

The Bride
"Oh, disdain me not for being brown;
Because the sun has looked upon me.
My mother's children disdained me;
They made me mistress of the fruit garden;
But my own garden I have not kept.
Tell me, my love, where do your flocks rest at noon?

Why should I be pale as the veiled in mourning,
Roaming among the flocks of your companions?"

Solomon
"I have compared you to the Pharaoh's chariot
steed..."

***

Apparently, the groom compared her favorably, for
the song paeans sensuously on for pages.

The fact is, through a recent review of the
over 200 pieces of period art depicting women of
European, Middle Eastern, North African and
Amerindian races, I have noted that women are
consistently depicted as being lighter of skin than
their men, unless he is a holy man or an enthroned
king, avoiding the staining gaze of the sun from
behind their tapestried walls. There is little doubt,
based on explorer accounts and the accompanying
and inspired illustrations, that Europeans of the Age
of Discovery were noted for their pallid
complexions due primarily to their habit of
remaining heavily dressed year round and residing
indoors as often as possible.

Worldwide, the beauty standard for women,
from antiquity through the 1800s, was one that
valued lightness of skin, indicating her youth, as
evidence that the woman did not toil out of doors,
that her father had been able to afford her shelter
from lowly chores and that her hands would be

smooth and her face free of wrinkles into her middle years.

Even among the Ugandans, their queens, lying in state within their large houses, fed, oiled, bathed and rolled over by their train of maidens, were notably lighter than the common women who worked under the sun.

'Laws Kept by the Indians of New Spain'

A Comparison of English and Aztec Slave Laws

The most trivial thing, at this point in our inquiry of Plantation America, is to speak of "whites" or even "Europeans" and also of "Indians" and "Native Americans" as groupings of humanity that made sense to those people to whom we refer. By Indians of New Spain, the understanding was that these were speakers of related languages and practitioners of related religions living in what is now Central America—people who were, or had recently been, living under the rule of the Aztecs. Likewise, the slave laws of what would eventually become the United States were entirely English institutions with their roots in biblical laws put down in Leviticus, Nordic thralldom and Feudal serfdom. In other words, the cultural package brought to these shores by English planters were a layering of ancient Israelite, Romano-Briton and pagan Nordic customs.

According to the standard narrative, American Indians never held slaves in bondage and were not able to survive as slaves, but wilted like summer flowers in winter. However, actual historic records indicate that all native societies practiced slave-holding and that where agricultural surpluses permitted, mass slave-holding societies soon grew up, just as they had in the Old World of Biblical Testament.

I find it useful to compare Aztec and English law, for the Aztecs are the most reviled folk of the ancient Americas, with even passionate Amerindian advocate Ron West pointing out some of the dehumanizing aspects of their culture, and because Anglo-American institutions formed the basis of the system we now live under in the postmodern United States of America.

Below Find Aztec Slave Laws with English Correlations

Sourced from *The Pre-Columbian Mind* by Francisco Guerra, M.D., Ph.D., D. Sc. 1971, Seminar Press, London, page 22.

Aztec Law: A son who gambles away his father's estate, if a chieftain, is secretly strangled; if an ordinary man, is sold as a slave.

English Law: In English law, either man might be sold for his crime, the law being paramount over honor. Only Royalty escaped debt crimes under English law.

Aztec Law: If one stole a fishnet, he paid in cloth. If he was destitute, he was sold as a slave.

English Law: Thieves were either hanged or sold into slavery.

Aztec Law: If one stole a canoe, he paid for it with an equal value of cloth or was sold into slavery.

English Law: Thieves were either hanged or sold into bondage.

Aztec Law: If someone had use of a slave girl before she came of age, he became a slave.

English Law [Virginia & Maryland]: This was not a crime under English law unless the rapist [a slave girl had no sexual agency and was not permitted to willingly give her body, only the consent of her master made sex legal] was himself a slave, in which case, his term was extended.

Aztec Law: If a man sold a girl at the market place for clothing and then wished to go back on the deal, he lost the deed to the slave girl.

English Law: A slaver could not be enslaved for any lapse in ethics, unless he was found to be culpable in selling a slave while in conspiracy with that slave in order to abet his escape, thus defrauding the purchaser.

Aztec Law: If an orphan was sold by relatives, the judges fined the relatives and bought back the slave and freed him.

English Law: There was no recourse for wrongful sale of a person. In fact, when King George of England took up the cause of Jemmy Angelsey, who had been sold into slavery by his uncle, the courts blocked the King's petitions and Jemmy saw no restitution before his death, the institutions of debt and slavery being sacred above God in English law. Indeed, many underaged slaves were sold into bondage by older sisters, older brothers or by a widowed parent. Any English parent or guardian of a child or youth was permitted to sell that person into bondage with no restrictions. Indeed, what the Aztecs saw as a crime was, among the English, regarded as a useful allocation of labor resources.

Aztec Law: If a runaway slave sold himself to another owner and was later found, his new owner lost out.

English Law: In this matter, English and Aztec law agreed, with the new owner being regarded as not having researched his purchase, at the least, and possibly guilty of fraud. Luring away the slaves of a competitor was a common habit among 17th century Virginia planters.

Aztec Law: If a slave girl was impregnated by a man who did not own her, the man who impregnated her became a slave if she died in childbirth. However, if she delivered a child, the child was freed and given to the father.

English Law: In Catholic Maryland, Anglican Virginia and Quaker Pennsylvania, the rapists of slave girls were absolved from all guilt, [in Maryland and Virginia] the woman was whipped after delivering the child, her servitude was extended and the baby was sold by the church wardens [in Virginia] to live as a slave for 31 years and given over as a slave to the mother's masters in Pennsylvania until age 21. Maryland law is unclear, other than that the mother is to be tied to a post and whipped after safely delivering the child.

One must cite Aztec law, in this instance, as being far more humane than English law.

Aztec Law: If someone sold a child as a slave [as most children were sold out of England] and afterwards it was recognized [as with Peter Williamson and Jemmy Angelsey], all involved became slaves, one given as a slave to the duped buyer and one to the mother of the slave.

English Law: There was no statute for the punishment of kidnappers and slave traders under English law. Rather, goalers were literally licensed as freelance slave traders in Plantation America, at liberty to abduct and sell any undocumented [unowned or not bearing freedom papers] person. Indeed, Peter Williamson, when publishing a pamphlet back in Scotland exposing his childhood abduction and sale, was himself jailed and put on trial. Kidnapping of children of a certain age was technically illegal, but such crimes are not known to have been punished.

Aztec Law: Murders committed by poison were punished by the poisoner being beaten to death, except if the victim were a slave; then, the murderer was sold into slavery [which marks slavery as a living death in the eyes of the Aztecs]. This law was almost identical to ancient Babylonian law, which placed higher value on affluent persons than upon wronged slaves.

English Law: No killer of a slave or servant in Plantation America was ever punished worse than being barred from buying more slaves. Again, Aztec law placed more value in the life of a slave than did English law.

Aztec Law: The thief who stole sacred relics from a temple or broke into a home was made a slave for the first offense but hanged for a second offense.

English Law: According to the testimony of James Revel, this Aztec law was almost identical to the English practice, with his more experienced gang mates being hanged for the same crime for which he was sold.

A Heroic View of Slavery

I declare and ordain as free and quit of every obligation of captivity, subjection, and slavery, my captured slave Enrique, mulatto, native of the city of Malacca, of the age of twenty-six years more or less, that from the day of my death thenceforward forever the said Enrique may be free and manumitted, and quit, exempt, and relieved of every obligation of slavery and subjection, and that he may act as he desires and thinks fit.

-Ferdinand Magellan, June 19, 1519

Magellan also willed Enrique 1,000 maravedis.

The heroic view of slavery, expressed by Magellan in the will above, occupies the moral ground halfway between the primitive view of slavery encountered among Eastern Woodland Indians, who typically used slavery of militarily able men and boys as a trial period between capture and adoption, and the idea of plantation chattel.

In societies where warrior culture is important, total masculine reduction and invalidation of the owned person is not common.

Even in a massive chattel society like Rome, since there was high value placed on martial spirit, slaves who made the warrior grade could be permitted to live on and serve as gladiators and bodyguards rather than simply be degraded like the chattel of the Early Modern Age. Even in savage Morocco, slaves such as Thomas Pellow might be elevated to warrior status and even command.

But in Protestant societies of the Early Modern Age, where every soldier was an expendable slave to be dressed up, paraded and shot, masculinity stood as a barrier to total domestication and the breaking of the captive soul, such that by 1800, legal action was being taken in the United States to limit the ability of a grateful owner to release his slaves from bondage. Even George Washington was foiled in his plan to release his black slaves by the disloyalty of his wicked widow.

James LaFond

'The Unfortunate Boys'

Pages and Apprentices at Sea in the 1500s

Sourced from *Over the Edge of the World: Magellan's Terrifying Circumnavigation of the Globe*, Laurence Bergreen, 2003, pages 103–112.

On December 20, 1519, on the never-sleeping swells of the Atlantic Ocean, the Sicilian ship's master of the tiny *Victoria*, the first vessel known to have circumnavigated the globe, was strangled on the orders of Ferdinand Magellan for the crime of sodomizing a little boy—a page or cabin boy by the name of Antonio Ginoves. The boy would later drown, either thrown overboard or jumping due to the ridicule of the crew.

All pages were between 8 and 15 years of age.

Pages were of two types: First, the sons of families of some means—it being understood that if they were loyal and efficient they might find some favor in the cruel world—who had the duty of keeping time by the use of large hour glasses and calling out the hour, a function crucial to navigation and religious observances and which consigned them to a sleepless life.

The other pages were "unfortunate boys," orphans, or other poor children kidnapped on the streets and waterfront and pressed into service, where they were treated exactly like a boy would be treated in a modern prison. These boys were tasked with scrubbing the decks, hauling waste buckets and other menial chores.

Just above the pages in station were apprentices, 17–20-year-old youths who had the most dangerous duties, such as reefing and unfurling sails in high winds. Apprentices, also known as grumetes, hauled on hawsers, the capstan and other devices that moved the heavy masts and cargo. They were the most likely to be punished, beaten and locked in stocks and had the unenviable task of shaving the legs and trimming the toenails of their masters.

Pages and apprentices were slaves, plain and brutal.

The Newlander Conspiracy

Besides I say that those who suffer themselves to be persuaded and enticed away by the man-thieves, are very foolish if they believe that roasted pigeons will fly into their mouths in America or Pennsylvania without their working for them.

-Gottlieb Mittelberger, *Journey to Pennsylvania*, 1755

The modern American has been taught that there is no such thing as a conspiracy and whole-heartedly believes that no two men have ever worked in concert to best a third, that no two lions have ever stalked a zebra together, that no three hyenas have ever worked together to relieve the lions of their kill.

If the reader who finds this book, despite the very real efforts to suppress it, would rather believe that men have never met in back rooms to decide the fate of nations, that mobsters have never conspired to do ill to their fellows, that the two men who tried to waylay me on December 7, 2017 just happened to be accidentally next to each other when they both decided independently and without cooperation to attack me; if that is the kind of world you are interested in remaining in, then don't read this book. However, if you want to know something of the evil foundation of our misrepresented nation, then starting with Gottlieb Mittelberger's account of the mass human trafficking of Germans to 18th century Pennsylvania is a good start.

James LaFond

'Against the Soul Traffickers'

Extracts from Gottlieb Mittelberger's *Journey to Pennsylvania in the Year 1750 and Return to Germany in the Year 1754: Containing Not Only a Description of the Country According to Its Present Condition, But Also a detailed Account of the Sad and Unfortunate Circumstances of most of the Germans That Have Emigrated, or Are Emigrating to That Country*

Special thanks to Tennessee Keith for providing this incredibly valuable book for my study. I was wrapping up this volume when I received Gottlieb's book. After a perusal of it, I decided to use it as a source for *Paleface*, as Pennsylvania was White-Indian central for 150 years. Indeed, Mittelberger writes in detail about the natives and the wildlife, including a creature he calls a monkey, which was certainly a raccoon. However, since the few white-slave narratives we have were of children, the information concerning the process of their bondage, their transport, the Middle Passage and their eventual sale tends to be wanting.

As a literate adult and a pious Christian who served as a minister on board the ship of horrors, he took the Middle Passage on as an organist, contracted through an agent by a consortium of leading citizens to teach music and German at a Philadelphia-area church. Mittelberger was the cream of the servant class, who had been promised all the things that modern academics tell us were effusively given to all Caucasian servants in Plantation America. Mittelberger voluntarily sold himself to a group of honorable men to fulfill a three-year obligation of service as a schoolmaster. But in his book, which was begged by many of his fellow suffering German slaves in Pennsylvania to be written as a warning and protest against the horrid condition they had been trafficked into, Gottlieb relates the horrors of German–American servitude, an arrangement that, on the face of it, appeared to be even better than that suffered by so-called indentured servants from the British Isles. In his heart-rending rendition of suffering, which equals in horror anything reported from African slave ships, Mittelberger describes in very real and practical terms how a contract to serve a Pennsylvania master for three years was, more often than not, a death sentence.

Mittelberger addressed his book to his Sovereign German Lord, Prince Carl, Duke of Würtemberg, and took it upon himself to inventory the Germans who had been trafficked into

Philadelphia in the four years of his stay from October 1750 through July 1754. Mittelberger noted 20–24 ships every autumn arriving with German immigrants in Philadelphia, depositing 25,000 souls over four years. On his return to his homeland, he received a letter [most likely from the honorable Captain Diemer] stating that 22,000 Germans had been trafficked into Philadelphia that very autumn and that so many were sick that they had to sell their children and then linger like zombies, burying one another as they perished from the effects of the savage Middle Passage, which was intentionally extended for sick human freight.

In five years, 47,000 Germans were trafficked into Philadelphia, at the very time that most runaways were Irish. In 1727 and 1728, 5,000 Irish and 2,500 Germans had been trafficked into Philadelphia. According to Mittelberger, roughly a third of those shipped perished. If we take low median yearly human inventory for Philadelphia at 5,000 sold and 1,000 lost in transit from 1700 through 1775, and then again from 1784 to 1799 [it being impossible to figure shipment rates during the Revolution], we can arrive at a low conservative estimate for the souls swallowed by the Atlantic on the way to Pennsylvania at 80,000 and those processed in [roughly half of whom perished in bondage] at 400,000.

The greed of one province in Plantation America easily consumed a half-million European souls in the 1700s alone.

Thank you, Tennessee Keith.

'Eyes of a Rational Man'

Esteemed Reader, from the Publisher of Gottlieb Mittelberger's *Journey to Pennsylvania*.

Carl Theo. Eben, the editor of Mittelberger's tale of soul-trafficking of Germans into Pennsylvania in the 1750s stated that the lack of stylistic literary convention and direct exposition and that Gottlieb is not a writer by trade is "a gauranty of his sincerity, not to mention the fact that he writes for the most part as an eye-witness."

The publisher enthusiastically declares the book to be a valuable supplement to European knowledge:

"What the author narrates with simplicity and without ornamentation of the various Europeans and American savages...[is] of such a nature that thinking readers will be glad to perceive in it a special mingling of the European and American climate, of the customs of the Old and the New World, and of civilized people living in part in natural freedom."

This statement betrays a very real sense among immigrants to Plantation America that contact with the uncultivated world and uncivilized people had wrought a hybrid society.

However, the editorial voice does not neglect to point out that the purpose of this book was to save tens of thousands of Germans from being misled into a cruel bondage and taken forever from their Fatherland:

"...the fate that awaits **most**[1] of the unfortunate people who leave Germany to seek uncertain prosperity in the New World, but found instead, if not death, most surely an oppressive servitude and slavery."

---

[1] My emphasis. A review of Mittelberger's account indicates that virtually all of the Germans shipped to Pennsylvania were lied to, defrauded and very often ruined physically in a naked attempt to get ahold of their children, who could be enslaved for 2–4 times the term of the parent. It seems certain also that roughly half of all Germans shipped to Pennsylvania died during the three legs of the journey, most during the Middle Passage.

'His Employers'

Gottlieb Mittelberger's Freedom Paper, from
Journey to Pennsylvania

Before this document, the English translator
provided verification that Gottlieb had been
transported onboard the *Osgood,* William Wilke,
Captain, and that he took the oath of allegiance on
September 29, 1750, according to the Pennsylvania
Archives, 2nd Series, Vol. XVII, p. 324.

What follows is an indication of the firm
form of privatized social control in Quaker
Pennsylvania, as, it will be noted, a consortium of
leading citizens must first pen a freehand pledge
that Gottlieb had served his time and was free to go
and that this was witnessed by two persons, perhaps
a notary and a colonial official, though the function
of these two persons and whether or not they were
government officials is unknown—though in the
absence of titles, it seems they were free agents.

Below are the contents of this rare document:

Whereas the Bearer, Mr. Mittelberger, Music Master, has resolved to return from this Province to his Native Land, which is in the Dukedom of Würtemberg in High Germany; I have at his Request granted these Lines to certify that ye above nam'd Mr. Mittelberger has behaved himself honestly, diligently, and faithfully in ye Offices of Schoolmaster and Organist, during ye Space of three Years, in ye Township of New-Province of Pennsylvania, etc. So that I and all his Employers[1] were entirely satisfied, and would willingly have him to remain with us. But as his Call[2] obliges him to proceed on his long Journey; we would recommend ye s'd Mr. Mittelberger to all

---

[1] Mittelberger had the good fortune of not shipping with his wife and child and of selling himself to three leading citizens.

[2] It is noteworthy that the unnamed agents who arranged Mittelberger's passage to Pennsylvania— thereby defrauding him in numerous ways—attempted to convince him, once back in Europe, to return to Pennsylvania, claiming that his wife, child and relations had shipped to Philadelphia. See *The Newlanders* (next chapter). Suspecting that this was a ruse intended to send him back to the Plantations in order to suppress news of the plight of Germans in their homeland, Mittelberger trusted a letter from his wife, indicating that she would never make the trip without him and made it home. For Mittelberger returned as a missionary for the many doomed souls who asked him to go back to Germany and let their people know of the evils that awaited the immigrant.

Persons of Dignity and Character; and beg their Assistance, so that he may pass and repass until he arrives at his Respective Abode; which may God grant and may ye Benediction of Heaven accompany him in his Journey. Deus benedicat susceptis ejus & ferat eum ad amicos suos maxima prosperitate.

Dabam, Providentiae Philadelphiae Comitatu Pennsylvania in America, die 25 Apr. A.D. 1754

John Diemer, Cap.[3]

Sam. Kennedy, M.D.

Henery Pawling, Esqr.

T. Henry Marsteller

Matthias Gmelin

Notes

---

[3] Captain Diemer was the savior of the upper-class Germans who had been defrauded and may have been instrumental in spiriting Mittelberger's wife and children back to Germany, which did not require such a document, which indicates that when the Captain, the Doctor and the Lawyer, members of the evangelical Lutheran St, Augustine's Church in Province, purchased Mittelberger for his three years of service, that said purchase freed his wife and children from the bondage that awaited the dependents of all folk of the uneducated classes.

Mittelberger had the good fortune of not shipping with his wife and child and of selling himself to three leading citizens.

'The Newlanders'

Evil Agents of Immigration

As described by Gottlieb Mittelberger, the *newlanders* were German or German-speaking Dutch agents who solicited people to immigrate out of Germany into Pennsylvania, where they were told many opportunities awaited. All immigrants were encouraged to bring their families and elderly persons were sought for immigration in hopes that their children and grandchildren might come. In the case of well-to-do or educated immigrants, they were induced to pay for passage ahead of time. This money was pocketed by the agent as his finder's fee. This agent, or newlander, often pretended to be travelling to Pennsylvania but would switch ships and disappear with the transport fee.

Passage on board the ship was hence not paid. Once the immigrants arrived—those that survived the slave ship conditions—they had to pay for their passage with money at hand, all of which had usually been spent in the three months awaiting the Middle Passage, as 36 customs checks were done in various European ports, exhausting food and money that might have been brought on their persons. Monies deposited for safe keeping with the agents had been pilfered.

Below are some quotes from Gottlieb's account, concerning these agents:

...the fatalities which I suffered to and fro... and the evil tricks of the newlanders, which they intended to play me and my family, as I shall relate hereafter, have awakened the first impulse in me not to keep concealed what I knew... the wretched and grievous condition of those who travel from Germany to this new land, and the outrageous and merciless proceedings of the Dutch man-dealers and their man-sealing emissaries; I mean the so-called newlanders, for they steal, as it were, German people under all manner of false pretenses and deliver them into the hands of the great Dutch traffickers in human souls.

...even princes and lords, might learn how they had fared, to prevent other innocent souls from leaving their fatherland, persuaded thereto by the newlanders, and from being sold into a like slavery... how long it takes to get there; what the journey costs[1], and besides, what

---

[1] It is an astonishing fact that people were defrauded, by the tens of thousands, into spending their life's savings to journey to a new world in search of wage work or

hardships and dangers one has to pass through; what takes place when the people arrive well or ill in the country; how they are sold and dispersed; and finally, the nature and condition of the whole land. I relate both what is good and evil...

There is another case of a lost ship that has probably never been made known in Germany... nothing was ever heard of it except that a notice was afterward sent from Holland to the merchants of Philadelphia.[2]

...such old people followed them, trusting to the persuasion of these newlanders that they would be better provided for."

These men-thieves inveigle people of every rank and profession... [they] take them to Rotterdam or Amsterdam to be sold there. They receive their from the merchants for every person of 10 years and over, 3 florins or a ducat; whereas the merchants get in Philadelphia 60, 70 or 80

---

setting up a business, and then be sold as slaves! Some of the immigrants, the poor, with no passage money, would be expecting to be sold, but the large number of families and the fact that even members of the German nobility were sold at auction in Philadelphia, indicate a broad-based campaign of disinformation. This would be like buying a time share in Thailand and then being bought by a brothel owner or a lumber mill.

[2] One defrauded noblewoman sent her gentleman son to recover the money and he was never heard from again.

florins for such a person, in proportion as said person has incurred more or less debts during the voyage.

Frequently these newlanders say they have received power-of-attorney from some countrymen or from the authorities of Pennsylvania to obtain legacies of inheritances...

never forgetting to display their money before the poor people, but which is nothing else but bait from Holland and accursed blood-money.

...these thieves often remain in Holland with the [entrusted] money... so that the poor defrauded people, when they reach the country, have no other choice but to serve or sell their children, if they have any, only to get away from the ship.[3]

Below, Mittelberger, after discussing the censorship and rewriting of letters back to Germany, writes:

While in Pennsylvania, I myself heard such men-thieves say that there were Jews enough in Holland, ready to furnish them for a small consideration

---

[3] For every member of a family that died during the Middle Passage, survivors would have to sell themselves for additional contracts to pay for the passage of the deceased. Ideally, three generations of a family would be shipped together, with the 50% casualty rate therefore ensuring that the youngest surviving family members could be sold on deck as virtual lifetime slave laborers.

counterfeits of any seal, and who could perfectly forge any handwriting.[4]

If I had believed those seducers of the people, and had returned to England and America, not only would this account of my journey not have been published so soon, but I should, perhaps, never have met my family again in this world.

---

[4] The great banking houses of Holland, which dominated the African slave trade, were owned by Sephardic Jews. However, there is no definitive evidence in Gottlieb's account that he suspected that the trafficking of his countrymen was a Jewish initiative but only that Jews were involved in the documentation process, which was a criminal activity. Other than that, the only evidence that trafficking in German souls was conducted by Dutch Jews was his mention of "great Dutch traffickers" and "merchants" which could be taken to indicate the Sephardic banking houses. The extensive discussion of "great merchants in Holland" on pages 42–43, as well as the fact that these merchants had conducted an extensive, international fraud in Würtemberg, even obtaining physical descriptions of his wife and child, getting her signature and assigning false berths on a ship to Philadelphia, strongly suggest that these agents were heavily networked in Germany and had direct control over transatlantic slave shipping.

'Like Herrings'

Gottlieb Mittelberger's Middle Passage

Mittelberger's experience forms the basis for this account, though he supplements it with experiences of many of the Germans he met in Pennsylvania.

After the Germans had been stalled for nearly three months in Germany and Holland, forced to spend their money and eat their supplies, they were finally loaded onto great ships in Rotterdam or Amsterdam. Some children were killed in boarding accidents. Once on board, each passenger was assigned a 2-foot-wide and 6-foot-long space on the wooden deck. This was the same space given to Africans, with the difference being that the Africans were chained, which made their lot more miserable, and that they were restrained, which prevented smaller and ill folk from being crushed by rolling people when the ship pitched violently. At certain points—days on end—the decks crammed with people were masses of rolling, puking, pissing bodies. Most children under five failed to survive these conditions. Pregnant women, not having enough room to spread their legs and give birth, were heaved out through portholes to sink among the swarming sharks which trailed the ships doggedly, as at least one body was thrown from every ship every day of this 8–12-week journey. The ships held 300–600 human cargo and typically lost 50%, a higher death rate than human freight shipped by the English. If we take the baseline death rate of one per day and then make allowances for the many diseases due to crowding and disorders due to diet, as described by Gottlieb, his assertion that 200 were typically lost on each ship is not unreasonable.

The conditions on board were exacerbated by black, putrid water; rotten, maggot-filled biscuits; and old salted meat—the typical diet of the sailor. The passengers had it better than African and British slaves on one single count: they were allowed, periodically, on deck for air and were also allowed to congregate for the daily funeral. Mittelberger conducted services as a kind of deacon and personally committed 32 children under age 7 to the deep.

The list of afflictions includes but is not limited to: sea-sickness, dysentery, headache, constipation, boils, scurvy, mouth rot:

> ...all of which come from the old
> and sharply salted food and meat, also
> from very bad and foul water... thick full of

worms... so that many die miserably... I myself had to pass through a severe illness... these poor people often long for consolation, and I often entertained and comforted them with singing, praying and exhorting; and whenever it was possible and the winds and waves permitted it, I kept daily prayer meetings with them on deck. Besides I baptized five children in distress... also held divine service every Sunday by reading sermons to the people; and when the dead were sunk in the water, I commended them and our souls to the mercy of God."

Due to the fact that sharks swarmed about the ship, it greatly pained these Christian landsmen that their departed relatives—for few of the Germans came alone, but as families—were being devoured by sea monsters and had no resting place. Resurrection doctrines of the age were focused on an earthly grave, not being consumed by some alien creature.

In 1752, one ship arrived in Philadelphia with its German cargo. Of the 340 persons shipped, only 21 survived. In 1754, on St. James's Day, a ship went down with all 300 souls on board. Another ship had only 63 survivors of 360. The reader should not forget that the sailors shared all of these hardships and more, and that, as wretched as the sailor's life was, dozens of escaped servant advertisements from Philadelphia claim that the runaways were attempting to get work on sailing ships as a means of escape. How bad must servitude have been if folk who had survived this horrific Middle Passage were willing to make it their life in order to get away from their good Quaker masters?

It has long been assumed by myself and other investigators into the trafficking of Europeans to America that the 1600s were more lethal for the human cargo and that the 1700s more benign. Mittelberger's account brings this into question. The voyages to Roanoke, Jamestown and Plymouth Rock, conducted in 1587, 1607 and 1621, respectively, were each undertaken with deaths among the passengers at under 5%, whereas Mittelberger states that roughly 50% of Germans could be expected to perish. There are three differences that may account for this:

1. The earliest shipments had higher percentages of free people, reflecting attempts to ship entire seed communities, in contrast to later voyages which primarily replaced the lower class, who had been worked to death, had escaped, or had worked themselves free, this final outcome being by far the least likely before roughly 1700;

2. The earlier expeditions were intended to establish a viable population, whereas later shipments of slaves were simple chattel shipping ventures;

3. The British slaves were shipped by British companies and sailors, while the German slaves were Christians being shipped by Dutch Jews, with slim expectation of empathy [as neither ethnicity nor faith provided a common bond] on the part of the controlling party.

'All Creep from Below'

The Shipboard Sale of Germans below Philadelphia by Gottlieb Mittelberger

> Before I describe how this traffic in human flesh is conducted, I must mention how much the journey to Philadelphia Pennsylvania costs.
>
> A person over 10 years pays for the passage from Rotterdam to Philadelphia 10 pounds... Children from 5 to 10 years pay half price, 5 pounds...

Mittelberger goes on to explain that the passage from Germany to Holland costs just as much. German agents and Dutch slavers have thus each extracted a significant payment from some of the very slaves destined for market. By maintaining a highly lethal passage, casualties among families ensure more human sales for longer terms. Those Germans who could not afford their passage expected to be sold. But the death tally tax has not been explained. Most the cargo will make the port below Philadelphia in debt to the captain.

The sale of human beings in the market on board the ship is carried on thus: Every day Englishmen, Dutchmen and High-German people come... on board the newly arrived ship... and select among the healthy persons such as they deem suitable for their business, and bargain with them how long they will serve for their passage money...

...adult persons bind themselves in writing to serve 3, 4, 5 or 6 years... according to their age and strength. But very young people, from 10 to 15 years, must serve until they are 21 years old.

Mittelberger goes on to explain that parents are encouraged to sell their children so that they may go free, and that it is common for such parents to never see their children again. *[My comments are in brackets and italics.]*

When people arrive who cannot make themselves free *[were not valuated by potential masters as worth the price their incurred in their passage]*, but have children under 5 years, the parents cannot free themselves by them; for such children must be given to somebody without compensation to be brought up, and they must serve for their bringing up till they are 21 years old. *[Do note that in the 18th*

> *century, children became productive economic*
> *units at age 5.]* Children from 5 to 10 years,
> who pay half price...must likewise serve for
> it till they are 21 years of age...
>
> ...children above 10 years can take
> part of their parents' debt upon
> themselves.

Mittelberger explains that a wife of a sick husband must serve her term and his term and so he hers if she is sick. If they are both sick, they are sent to the sick house until well enough to be purchased.

> It often happens that whole
> families, husband, wife, and children, are
> separated by being sold to different
> purchasers...
>
> When a husband or wife has died at
> sea, when the ship has made more than
> half of her trip *[the vast majority of deaths*
> *were in the second half of the passage]* the
> survivor must pay or serve not only for
> himself or herself, but also for the
> deceased.

Of course, when both parents die at sea, the children were sold off till age 21 to pay for their parent's loss as cargo, thus serving as insurance. What Mittelberger witnessed firsthand was a racket that preyed upon the family as a mutually insuring unit of human cattle. As for the psychological shock, compare these realities with the promises offered by the newlander recruiters.

> The sick always fare the worst, for the healthy are naturally preferred and purchased first; and so the sick and wretched must often remain on board in front of the city for 2 or 3 weeks, and frequently die...

A spouse or child of such a sick person would have already been purchased to cover his passage, so his only mercies possible are death or enslavement. Mittelberger demonstrates elsewhere in his book that only upper-class Germans were rescued by other Germans from such straights.

His summary reads:

> How miserably and wretchedly so many thousand German families have fared, 1) since they lost all their cash means in consequence of the long and tedious journey; 2) because many of them died miserably and were thrown into the water; 3) because, on account of their great poverty, most of these families after reaching the land are separated from each other and sold far away from each other, the young and the old. And the saddest of all this is that parents must generally give away their minor children without receiving a compensation for them; inasmuch as such children never see or meet their fathers, mothers,

brothers or sisters again, and as many of them are not raised in any Christian faith by the people to whom they are given.

We should note that Mittelberger, as was the norm for Christian Europeans of the 18th century, viewed children as cattle and had no moral qualms about people selling their own children, as most parents did. The economy demanded that most parents sell their children. What Mittelberger was outraged about was the unfair dealing of the merchants and the continued attempt of the system to separate parents, free and unfree, from their children and then traffic the children. I found an ad for a runaway German girl of 13 in a Pennsylvania gazette as late as 1801.

Mittelberger wrote an addendum on pages 44–5 declaring that all males of 15 and up were taken from the ship to Philadelphia and made to give an oath of Allegiance. He finished with a statement that such is a good deal for fugitives who "left both his ears in Europe... For gallows' birds and wheel candidates, Pennsylvania is, therefore, a desirable land."

'Daser of Nagold'

The Fate of a German Slaveholder in the Slave Province of Pennsylvania by Gottlieb Mittelberger

In the autumn of 1853, Daser of Nagold, a Würtemberger, arrived below Philadelphia with his wife, eight children and "chattels,"—the latter being human slaves—having been robbed at sea by the English Captain. To get himself and his family off ship, he had to sell all of his goods and slaves. He then brought a lawsuit against the captain and lost, which required him to go into debt to pay the legal costs. As everything he owned was then sold at public auction, Daser became distressed.

But a creditor came to the rescue, promising to lend Daser enough money to purchase a plantation and that the money need not be returned for two years. The contract was written in English, which Daser, being German, did not understand, and the creditor placed next to the number "2" the English word for days rather than years. The creditor never even gave the money over but let the two days expire and brought Daser up on the capital charge of debt. Thus, Daser was in hock. Everything Daser still owned was taken from him, including clothes and items "from his body," and he would have been imprisoned and had his family sold if not for Captain Von Damier coming to his rescue and providing for his housing and food, keeping him as a guest.

However, two of Daser's daughters and his eldest son had to sell themselves, as it seems Diemer's hospitality only extended to the parents and minor children. Mittelberger shared a bed with Daser in Von Diemer's house and the author relates with much sadness that the wealthy man, bereft of all goods, slaves, status and three of his children, was quite insane.

Mittelberger also mentions a noble woman who was similarly defrauded by the Dutch, whose daughters had to sell themselves, and whose son was apparently murdered when he returned to Holland to charge the "great merchants" with this crime.

'When a Serf'

The Plight of German Slaves in Pennsylvania, 1750–54 by Gottlieb Mittelberger

It is telling that, although American academics deny that serfdom ever existed in America, Mittelberger described American servitude as identical, only more duplicitous and dehumanizing, to European serfdom.

> When a serf has an opportunity to
> marry in this country, he or she must pay
> for each year which he or she would have
> yet to serve, 5 to 6 pounds.

Note that the masters pay 10 pounds for 3–6 years of service. Even marriage prices were a racket.

> If some one in this country runs
> away from his master, who has treated him
> harshly, he cannot get far.

First, note Mittelberger's slavish German mentality, unable to contemplate seeking freedom unless one has been cruelly treated. The Penn Family maintained good relations with the Delaware and Susquehannock Indians for the return of runaways. Such longstanding alliances of the ruling class and the aboriginal peoples resulted in later generations of poor frontiersmen, descended from such slaves as Mittelberger, harboring savage animosities towards Indians, resulting in such acts as the Paxton Massacre of the last Susquehannocks and the murder of various treaty chiefs. The provisions below ensured high bounty prices, typically of 3–5 pounds, but sometimes higher.

-A 1-day runaway served an extra week.

-A 1-week runaway served an extra month.

-A 1-month runaway served an extra year.

The fall of bounty prices in the early 1800s spelled the end of Caucasian slavery, just as forced slave-catching duty as a public service, provided by non-slave-owning citizens, spelled the end of African slavery 50 years later.

Mittelberger goes on to describe the work as typical lumber-jacking, engaged in by people of all ages, and that beatings were to be expected and endured.

...such people, who are not accustomed to work, are treated to hard blows and cuffs, like cattle... Many a one, on finding himself thus shamefully deceived by the newlanders, has shortened his own life...

Mittelberger relates a story about a bear eating from his Captain Master's orchard and that the servants must go and get the master so he can arrive with his dogs and his three loaded rifles to slay the bear. At the root of the rural American instinct of gun ownership is this, that over 100,000 Caucasian slaves were unarmed and helpless before a mere few thousand masters and Indians, caught between the paramilitary sea captains of the city and the savage warriors of the forest.

There was, however, a merciful provision for he who survived his term on enslavement:

-A new set of clothes.

If a man, the freedman might also receive:

-A horse;

-A cow;

-A woman—that's right, a slave of his very own.

Plantation Pennsylvania was a comprehensive slave matrix, in which every human except the merchant class was a commodity.

Has America really changed that much?

'Binds the Defendant Over'

Becoming a Slave in Quaker Philadelphia from *Journey to Pennsylvania* by Gottlieb Mittelberger

Any person in Plantation Pennsylvania could have another imprisoned for up to three months for simply charging him with a crime or damages.

For bail, if there was no money to be paid by the defendant or by a friend, a friend might bind himself, meaning that if the defendant fled, then the friend would be imprisoned and sold or forced to forfeit the funds put up for security. Cases were decided by three justices and sometimes took numerous seasons, as the court dates would be scheduled quarterly.

For the first case of theft, the thief was publicly whipped until flesh hung from his bones.

For the second conviction of theft, the thief was hanged.

Hangmen were paid 5 pounds, or the worth of a servant's service for 12–18 months, depending on the servant's condition.

Those found guilty of the unpardonable sin of debt were sentenced according to the standard valuation of 12–18 months of service per each 5 pounds of debt.

Note how easily a person in good social standing could simply have a person of lower status imprisoned and enslaved.

As always, in Plantation Pennsylvania, the authorities lusted after children—the younger the better, as their service was longer.

> ...if he wishes to be released and has children, such a one is frequently compelled to sell a child. If such a debtor owes only 5 pounds, or 30 florins, he must serve for it a year or longer, and so in proportion to his debt; but if a child of 8, 10 or 12 years of age is given for it, said child must serve until he or she is 21 years old.

Imagine a poor man who had a pretty 12-year-old daughter. All a rich neighbor would have to do would be accuse the poor man of owing money, have him imprisoned before trial for up to three months and then, once the case was won, the imprisoned father might be forced to give his daughter to such a man. There is absolutely nothing to suggest that this was not a regular and common practice. The Quaker court system was a

James LaFond

police apparatus for terrorizing and enslaving the many for the few. But these are not the only means by which men without social status or wealth might be enslaved or have their children sold.

'These Greedy Informers'

Censorship and Punishment in Quaker Pennsylvania from *Journey to Pennsylvania* by Gottlieb Mittelberger

Those readers who have followed the second-order guilt and political correctness trend in the postmodern U.S. know that this is a return to the original fabric of European-Americans society. Even in Pennsylvania, where one could practice any faith, including heathenism, paganism, Islam, Judaism and all Christian denominations, there was a 5 pound fine for swearing. This fine would be split between the informer and the court!

Know that this was the basis for child trafficking out of England, by which kidnappers, judges and the king split the sale price of any child who fell into their clutches.

According to Mittelberger:

> "...many a one has been induced by this law to turn informer for the purpose of earning money. During

my sojourn in the country one of these greedy informers got something which he had not bargained for. Having from interested motives informed against a very poor man for swearing, the Justice asked above all things[1] whether this swearer[2] was a rich or poor man, and if he had any children.[3] Being told that nothing was to be got out of him, he ordered that instead of being fined 5 pounds or 30 florins, he should receive 50 lashes upon his posterior. But as the informer was entitled to one-half of the fine[4], the Justice asked him if he was willing to forgo his half of the poor man's penalty. He answered in the negative, when the Justice bid him have patience,

---

[1] The Justice was primarily concerned with looting the accused of property and children.

[2] The accused was considered guilty by virtue of being charged.

[3] The Pennsylvania system of governance seems to have been geared, primarily, towards acquiring children. Hoffman, in They Were White and They Were Slaves, provides examples of Pennsylvania servants having their children taken by Quaker masters.

[4] An informer's fee of one half was more than twice that of the King's fifth enjoyed by the British Monarch for acting as an accessory to child slave trafficking and absolutely ensured a high incidence of false accusations in a system that assumed guilt. Plantation Pennsylvania was a "Gulag Archipelago" prototype.

assuring him that he would duly receive his half. He then ordered that... 25 lashes, well laid on[5], were administered to the greedy informer, who was not a little surprised at this turn of things.

[5] Essentially equivalent to being beaten by a professional fighter.

'To Raise Young Blackamoors'

Race and Servitude in Quaker Pennsylvania, 1750–54 from *Journey to Pennsylvania* by Gottlieb Mittelberger

The addled American mind is constantly barraged with the falsehood that only Southern states, and before them, Southern colonies, permitted the ownership of slaves, when in fact, in 1860, slaves of all races [by this time, overwhelmingly of African and mixed-race origin] were being held and captured in every state and territory of the United States of America. Only the sale of slaves was illegal in certain states and their importation was illegal in all states. As an illustration of how falsely American History has been handled by our academics and media, I quote a man who was there:

> In Pennsylvania and other English colonies there are innumerable negroes, or blacks, who have to serve all their lives

as slaves. From 200 to 300 florins[1] are paid for a strong and industrious half-grown[2] negro. Many are given in marriage by their masters in order to raise young blackamoors by them, who are sold in their turn. These blacks are likewise married in the English fashion.

According to their color the inhabitants of Pennsylvania may be divided into 4 classes. There are, 1. Whites, *i.e.* Europeans who have immigrated, and natives[3] begotten by European fathers and mothers; 2. Negroes, *i.e.* blacks brought over as slaves from Africa;[4] 3. Mulaters or

---

[1] 6.5–10 pounds; this price would leap 10-fold in 50 years as the price of Caucasians dropped by 2- or 3-fold.

[2] Once again, the buyer wants a child between the ages of 7–12 years, or half-grown. Ultimately, English-style plantation slavery was focused on trafficking children due to the extra years of service implicit in their condition. Booker T. Washington was doing what would in postmodern America be considered hard labor at the age of six. It would do at this juncture to remind the reader that the reputation of the American negro as being a poor worker is entirely a modern phenomenon, and that all records indicate that slaves of African origin were every bit the equal of Caucasian slaves.

[3] Native was a term used to describe people of European stock born in America and was not co-opted as a term for Amerindians until the 1900s.

[4] From his wordage, it seems that most breeding of Africans in Pennsylvania was interracial. There is no mention of pure African births and his discussion of mulattoes is so extensive as to suggest that, as children of Caucasian parentage were eagerly sought as chattel

Malaters [mulattoes], *i.e.* such as are begotten by a white father and a black mother, or by a black father and a white mother; these are neither white nor black, but yellowish; 4. Dark-brown, these are the savages or Indians, the old inhabitants of the country... The form of their bodies does not differ from ours, except that they look dark yellow, which, however, is not their natural color, for they besmear and stain themselves thus; but at their birth they are born as white as we are.[5]

---

and parents were so inured to selling their children, mixed-race marriages conceived to breed slaves were common.

[5] Numerous documents from Plantation Virginia indicate that Indians there were also "white", as does the majority of period artwork, 19th century anthropological texts, etc. Such will be the subject of the *Paleface*, the 11th volume in this 13-volume series. The texts after the ellipse comes from another section (page 83) in his book where Mittelberger deals specifically with the Indians.

'A Purchased Woman Servant'

The Fate of an Impregnated German Woman in Quaker Philadelphia from *Journey to Pennsylvania* by Gottlieb Mittelberger

A purchased woman servant in an English house became pregnant by her master's purchased man servant.

The master was a Justice. When the woman came to him about her condition, he advised her against suing the man servant as that fellow had many years to serve and would never amount to anything. The master advised her also to find another Justice and to accuse another man of being the father. The servant instead accused her master. He was arrested, subjected to a hearing and imprisoned, from where he promised to pay for her freedom or marry her, and did the latter.

There was another paternity suit noted in which the defendant pretended to be deaf. Then, when it was yelled in his ear that he would go to prison, he announced that he had raped the woman in the house where she lived and that her screaming had deafened him, to which she rose to the bat and said, "Oh, you godless rogue, how can you say that? I did not speak a word at the time."

Thereby gaining her confession to consent, the man walked free.

Unmarried men and single women were discouraged from participation in society, each being assigned a tax of 2–5 times the ground rent paid by the largest estate owners. Mittelberger also relates tales of polygamy, one in which a dying woman insists that her husband marry their servant girl, who was the nurse of the children, and then after this was done, the wife recovered and the man insisted upon his right to also wife the servant. In another instance, the law against having two wives was easily got around in typical American legalistic fashion by marrying a third.

'This Great Privilege'

Female Status in Pennsylvania, 1750–54 from
Journey to Pennsylvania by Gottlieb Mittelberger

Mittelberger was scandalized throughout his account of life in Pennsylvania that Quaker women conducted and judged religious debates and that English women seemed to be creatures apart, possessed of a preternatural privilege his German mind could simply not grasp. Mittelberger might be accused of overstating the case. But before we consider his opinion, keep in mind that servant women were routinely purchased out of bondage by husbands. This extended to white men in Maryland in the 1800s buying black slave women and then freeing and marrying them. Women had it so much better in Plantation America than men that, of the 933 runaways listed in Maryland advertisements between 1728 and 1775, only 38 were female!

Mittelberger claimed:

> ... it occurs oftener that the bride leaves her bridegroom together with the wedding guests in the church, which causes a cruel laughter...

> ... when a woman will not renounce her lover, they ride off and away together on one horse. And because women have greater privileges than men, the man must sit on the horse behind his beloved."

Mittelberger goes on to explain that any woman that accused her husband of striking her would be hounded by a mob of men.[1]

> I would rather beat three men in England than box a woman's ear but slightly; and if such a thing is done by her own husband and she complains to her neighbors, his life is not safe.

Also, he noted that English women in Pennsylvania were very haughty, would not do any

---

[1] These female-fueled social behaviors and those below, as well as the constant use of the term bitch to describe a woman, were typical Anglo-Irish and Anglo-American behaviors that have been kept alive by the African-American population, as their identity has remained fixated on the slave experience due to the national narrative that objectifies their race as victims without agency, reflected in women being the power brokers of the African-American demographic to this day.

work and demanded to be provided for in style[2]; that English women were smarter and better looking than other women because they were pampered and nurtured in childhood rather than worked; and that they never were exposed to the sun. Additionally, a husband was not allowed to object to his wife throwing extravagant parties.

Finally:

> In court the evidence of one woman is worth as much as that of three male witnesses. It is said they received this great privilege from Queen Elizabeth.
>
> Such whips the women take with them when they ride into the country, into the city, or to church; they keep them in their hands even in church...[3] An English servant woman, especially in Philadelphia, is as elegantly dressed as an aristocratic lady in Germany."

---

[2] Ostentatious dress and flamboyant entertainment were among the most certain inheritances bequeathed the African-American by the Anglo-American slave-owning elite.

[3] Slave mistresses were universally regarded as the cruelest people by all slave narratives I have examined—Caucasian or African. Again, the national narrative of matriarchal martyrdom and absent black male agency has kept slave master brutality alive in the black American population. Currently, black American women are the most likely Americans to beat children and also to use weapons with which to club or whip children or husbands.

Yellow Negroes

The Curious Case of Enslaved Asians in Plantation America

People of mixed race have often been described as "yellow" in Plantation America, particularly in Virginia, with a racial caste known as "high yellow." But I have also found evidence that numerous people of the Indian subcontinent and some other Asiatics had been trafficked into Maryland and Virginia as early as 1676, the year of Bacon's Rebellion, when numerous sea captains helped put the rebellion down.

Ned and Frank

Two Yellow Negroes of Virginia

Although advertisements for the more valuable escaped blacks do not appear as early as those for whites, this researcher finds it desirable to include listings of negro runaways for context and contrast. Below you will see blatant labeling of Asians, possibly Chinese, as well as mixed-race people as negro. The problems with runaway blacks were never, per bondmen, as high as those for whites nor were they as successful. One of the means by which whites found freedom was to enter a rural community of whites—a practice so hated by the elite that their descendants in Hollywood, Manhattan and Washington, D.C. continue to label rural whites as enemies of the State. If white slaves were to be replaced with negroes, then broadening the definition of negro would hopefully prevent a mixed-race block forming as it would in French San Domingo, providing a political safe haven for the largely mongrelized second and third generation African slaves.

Note, below, the case of Henry Cooke, who had to sell himself in order to afford medical treatment. In this way, a plantation economy so retards economic development that a ready source of unfree labor will always be available, as the impoverished wage laborer finds himself unable to compete with the slave owners and sells himself for varying periods. Also, with the criminalization of debt, poverty and homelessness, any economic downturn could fill the local gaols with debtors for sale.

The following advertisements have been compiled by Tom Costa, see Bibliography, bold emphasis and foot notes added.

Virginia Gazette (Purdie & Dixon), Williamsburg, April 19, 1770

£20 Reward. RUN away from the subscriber, on Monday night the 9th instant, three Negro men, two of them slaves,[1] viz.

NED, about 5 feet 8 inches high, 21 years of age, of a **yellow complexion**,[2] a likely well made fellow, his usual clothing an osnabrug shirt, dark gray fearnought waistcoat,[3] cotton breeches, coarse

---

[1] Note that negro and slave are not necessarily synonymous.
[2] Ned is a mixed-race person, not a negro, being yellow, he may well be Asian.
[3] Fearnought was made of a heavy, mixed wool fabric and would be serviceable for some naval duties.

yarn stockings, bad shoes, and a felt hat. He also took other clothes, but what not yet known.

FRANK, a foreign Negro, a very good cook, says he was born in the Spanish West Indies, speaks bad English, as also French, Spanish, and some Dutch, near the same height of Ned, about 30 years of age, of a **yellow complexion, with little or no beard**,[4] and has several remarkable wounds on his body,[5] and a large one near his throat, he is clothed in blue plains, osnabrug shirt, and felt hat, as also a pair of red flannel muffs, and a red cap.

HENRY COOKE, a free Negro, born in Gloucester county, but indented himself for five years for the cure of a pox, about 5 feet 10 or 11 inches high, about 24 years of age, lusty and very well made, of a good black complexion, and thick lips; his clothing mean, being an old brown cloth waistcoat and breeches much patched with green cloth, osnabrug shirt, yarn stockings, very bad shoes, though he took leather with him ready cut out for another pair. He understands a little of the carpenter business, and has likewise followed the water.

---

[4] Frank is also not a negro but a mixed-race person, either a mulatto, quadroon, octoroon or possibly Chinese, as numerous Chinamen were trafficked to Maryland and Virginia and the West Indies throughout the 1700s. Some enslaved Chinese in Maryland won their freedom in court.

[5] These remarkable injuries, to merit this term, must have been deforming or grossly obvious.

It is thought they took with them a Negro fellow belonging to the estate of the late Major William Tate, middle aged, about 5 feet 6 inches high, well set, bow legged, of a **dark copper complexion**,[6] an old offender in this way, and a few years past advertised in the Maryland and Pennsylvania Gazettes by William Tate, deceased, by virtue of which he was taken up near the head of the bay, within a few miles of the Pennsylvania government.

They took with them a yawl[7] of about 18 feet keel, London clinch work painted white to her gunwales, two good sails, rudder, and two new pine oars. The 20£ reward,[8] or 5£ for each, will be paid if taken in any other colony,[9] but if taken in Virginia only 12£ or 3£ for each. WILLIAM FLOOD. WESTMORELAND, April 12, 1770.

---

[6] This negro fellow is also not a negro but a mixed-race person, probably mulatto or half-breed Indian.

[7] A yawl is a speedy, shallow-draft boat with a lot of canvas, well-suited for cruising shallow waterways such as the Chesapeake Bay.

[8] Note that the price is considerably higher for these negroes than for Irish, as three of them are owned outright. They have already left Virginia by boat, so the higher price will be due to their catcher. Note that Tate is the property of a dead man's estate, probably being held for auction.

[9] Note that the term *colony* is used in Virginia, as it is in New England, where in Pennsylvania and Maryland it was more common to see the term *province* used to indicate the imperial administrative unit.

'East Indy Indians'

Strange Records Documenting the Enslavement of Oriental Men, Women and Children in 17th and 18th Century Plantation America

A reading of the property inventories below suggests that English-American ethics fairly smiled on the ownership of any person, whether East Indian, negro, mulatto or white. Around this period, in a census of 1740, it was noted that 40% of all Marylanders were negro slaves. Runaway advertisements and inventories from the same period suggest that the total number of other unfree persons in Maryland equaled or exceeded that of negroes, which would place the free population of Maryland at 20% of the total, or less.

Whites are listed as property alongside chattel of other races. The only difference was that a time limit was placed on white servitude. Once released, penniless, ill-clothed and with no tools, such people were, according to statute, legally subject to abduction and sale as "vagrants." The only real purpose of the release of an indentured servant was to free the owner from being required to feed and shelter the servant. If they stayed in the vicinity and attempted to practice whatever trade they had been used for as servants, they would have to compete with large-scale free labor, so they were generally left with no recourse but crime or reselling themselves.

Overall, one gets the sense after reading the documents below that, according to the law, Asians were regarded as falling somewhere between whites and negroes, and that the societies of Plantation Maryland, Virginia and Carolina were hopelessly corrupted by the central social institution, which was the buying, working, selling and disposing of unfree human cattle.

If a person is referred to as merely a servant, then they are white—not Indian, East Indian, mulatto or negro. The records below were compiled by Paul Heinegg.

Maryland Prerogative Court (Inventories) Microfilm Roll 63, CD 1, ac 1238, Liber 2, 1676 pp.177-178 (CD pp.208–9)

Inventory of Capt Edward Roe 3rd day of July 1676

1 boy servant named John Thorn at 5 years to serve - 2000 pounds tobacco

1 East India servant boy - 2500 pounds tobacco (Talbot County)

Maryland Prerogative Court (Inventories)

Maryland Prerogative Court (Inventories) 1718–1720, SR 4328, filmed by Maryland State Archives pp. 464–469, Inventory of Samuel Chew late of Anne Arundel County this 6 January 1718:

53 Negro men & woman at 30 pounds each 1590 pounds

29 children 580 pounds

2 East India Indians 30 pounds

1 Woman Servant 10 pounds

SR 4333, 1729–1730, Volume 14 p. 251, Inventory of Elizabeth Duhadway late of Ann Arundel County, 1 June 1729

To one East India Indian named Aron Johnson having two years and a half to serve 7 pounds, 10 shillings

1732–1734, Volume 18 p. 310, Mr John Stokes of Baltimore Co, 22 January 1732

1 Negro named Tom aged about 45 years 30 pounds

1 white servant about 14 mos to serve 6 pounds

1 East India Indian about 16 mos to serve 2 pounds

MARYLAND GAZETTE

Continued from Heinegg

Windley, Runaway Slave Advertisements II: p.36–7, Annapolis Maryland Gazette, July 17, 1760

Upper Marlborough, July 15, 1760

Ran away from Mr. Hepburn's Plantation, near Rock-Creek Bridge in Frederick County, on Saturday the 12ᵗʰ Instant, a Negro Man named Will, a little more than 5 feet high; he is of a yellow Complexion, being of a mix'd Breed, between an East-Indian and a Negro, has a large full Eyes, long Wool on his Head, and Lips.

J. Hepburn.

p. 111, May 25, 1775

...living in Prince George's County, near Upper Marlborough, on Sunday the 26 the [sic] of March, a negro man, named Sam, but generally called and known by the name of Sam Locker; between thirty and forty years of age, has rather long hair, being of the East-Indian breed; he formerly belonged to Mr. Isaac Simmons near Pig Point, in Anne Arundel County; the said Simmons now lives near Calvert County court house, and I suppose the fellow may endeavor to get down to his old master's house.

VIRGINIA

Continued from Heinegg

ACCOMACK COUNTY

Orders 1697–1703, p. 251, March 1699/1700, Henry Trent brings his servant Nick an East Indian adjudged 11 years old.

CAROLINE COUNTY

William Matthews, an East Indian,[1] produced a warrant in Caroline County court on 13 February 1752 for taking up a runaway servant woman [Orders 1746–54, 296].

---

[1] An East Indian man is a person from the Subcontinent of India, Southeast Asia, and possibly a person of Malaysian ancestry from Madagascar, generally anyone got from the Indian Ocean region who was not a Negro. Note that this East Indian, who may have been a mixed-race Malay, an Indian or even Chinese, had the authority, through his master, to petition for the recovery of a white person who had escaped. When race is omitted and the term servant is used, that person is white.

LANCASTER COUNTY

Richard Weaver, born say 1675, was called an East Indian by the Lancaster County court on 11 April 1711 when it granted him judgment against the estate of Andrew Jackson for 400 pounds of tobacco due by bill [Orders 1702–13, 262].

William Weaver, born say 1686, and Jack Weaver, "East Indy Indians," sued Thomas Pinkard for their freedom in Lancaster County court on 13 August 1707. The court allowed them five days time to produce evidence relating to their freedom but ordered them not to depart the county to some remote county without giving security to return to their master within the time allowed. Neither party appeared for the trial on 10 March 1707/8 [Orders 1702–13, 183, 176, 185].

RICHMOND COUNTY

Orders 1704–8,

p. 111, 6 February 1705/6, Petition of Sembo, an East India Indian Servant to Jno. Lloyd, Esq., for his freedom.

p. 156–9, Petition of Moota, an East India Indian, servant to Capt. Thomas Beale, surviving executor of Mr. William Colston, deced., for his freedom...ordered and judged that said Moota be free...ordered and adjudged that said Sembo be free.

Orders 1711–16,

p. 479, 2 May 1716, Anthony an Indian v. Long, The Order made last March Court for the Sheriff to summon Henry Long to answer what should be offered against him by Anthony, an East India Indian, is hereby discontinued.

SPOTSYLVANIA COUNTY

Orders 1735–38

p. 440, Zachary Lewis, Churchwarden of St. George Parish, presents Ann Jones, a servant belonging to John West, who declared that Pompey an East Indian (slave) belonging to William Woodford, Gent., was the father of sd child which was adjudged of by the Court that she was not under the law having a Mullato child, that only relates to Negroes and Mullatoes and being Silent as to Indians, carry sd. Ann Jones to the whipping post.[2]

---

[2] Such children of unwed mothers, in Virginia and Maryland were assigned as servants for a term of 31 years to an owner selected by a churchwarden. A child of Negro parentage would be owned at birth by the owner of the mother. I once informed a professional historian of the 18th century Virginia statutes that permitted the Church Wardens to take the children of free white women who had been impregnated out of wedlock and sell them to a master for a term of 31 years. He laughed and said that surely such a law was never enforced. In Ann's case, we have an example of a white servant woman being punished with a whipping according to a related statute, which indicates that if her bastard had been fathered by a negro or mulatto, the child would have been confiscated.

STAFFORD COUNTY

Martha Gamby, born say 1675, was an (East) Indian woman living in England on 5 January 1701/2 when Henry Conyers made an agreement with her that she would serve him in Virginia on condition that he would pay her passage back to England if she wished to return within the following four years. The agreement was recorded in Stafford County court about 1704 [WB, Liber Z:194].

WESTMORELAND COUNTY

Orders 1705–21,

p. 59a, 25 June 1707, Ordered Mr. Daniel Neale bee summoned to bee appear at the next Court held for the County aforesaid to answer the suit of William an East India Indian servant to the sd Neale relateing (sic) to his freedom.

p. 83, 30 March 1708, Will an East India Indian late a supposed slave to Mr. Danll Neale by his Petition to this Court setting forth that some tyme in yeare 1689 being fraudulently trappand out of his Native Country in the East Indies and thence transported to England and soon after brought into this Country and sold as a slave to Mr. Christopher Neale deceased father of his sd present Master And that hee had ever since faithfully served the sd Christopher and Daniel Notwithstanding which the sd Daniel though often demanded denied him his freedome And the sd Daniel being summoned to answer the sd complaint appeared and both parties Submitted the whole matter of the complaint to the Court All which being maturely & fully heard It is considered by the Court that the sd Will ought not to have been sold as a slave and that he is a freeman And doe therefore discharge him from all service due to the sd Christopher or Danll Neale.

YORK COUNTY

Orders, Wills, Etc. no 14, 1709–1716

p. 288, 16 November 1713, Joseph Walker, Gent., in open Court acknowledged his release & acquittance to Moll an East India Indian.

p. 291, whereas an East India Indian woman named Moll (imported into this Colony by Joseph Walker, Gent., ye year 1700 & by him sold to Jno. Tullett, being desirous of freedom...acquit Moll from being a Slave. J. Walker

Orders, Wills, Etc. 15, 1716–20

p. 82, 18 February 1716/7, Petition of Eliza Ives for service from her East Indian woman servt. for the trouble of her house in the time of her lying in is rejected.

Bruton Parish Church, York and James City County:

p. 115, 12 August 1738, burial of ____ny a East Indian belonging to Honble William Gooch, Esq.

VIRGINIA GAZETTE

Continued from Heinegg

15 April to 27 April 1737

Ran away from Col. John Lewis's in Gloucester ... Mulatto Fellow named George ... Ran away in Company with the above-mentioned was an East Indian, belonging to Mr. Heylin, Merchant, in Gloucester. John Lewis and John Heylyn.

4 August 1768. (Rind) Richmond County. Run away the 20th of May last, and East-India Indian, named Thomas Greenwich. William Colston.

7 March 1771. Run away from the sloop Betsy, Edward Massey commander, belonging to Mr. Thomas Hodge, out of Corotoman river, in Lancaster county, three servant men, viz., one named Samuel Tailer, and Englishman ... One Virginia born Negro, named Alexander Richardson about 21 years old ... The other an East Indian, upwards of 5 feet and a half high, about 22 years old, of a very dark complexion.

John Newton, sevt, c. 20, an Asiatic Indian by birth [or mulatto according to another edition of the gazette] has been in Va. about 2 mos. but claims to have lived in England 10 years in the service of Sir Charles Whitworth; ran away from William Brown of Prince William County *Virginia Gazette* 13 July 1776 Purdie edition 19 July 1776, p. 249 Headley

NORTH CAROLINA

Continued from Heinegg

Craven County

Minutes 1772–1778, 12 September 1777, p. 58c–d Peter Charles vs John Egge Tomlinson This Case being Ruled for Trial this Day the Court provided to hear the Parties upon the Examination of Witnesses The court was Unanimous of the opinion that the said Peter Charles is an East India Indian and justly Intitled to his Freedom. Therefore Ordered that he be Immediately Discharged and Set Free and the Defendant John Edge Tomlinson pay all costs.

Mary Dove, born say 1710, was a "Negro woman" slave listed in the Anne Arundel County, Maryland inventory of the estate of Eleazer Birkhead on 28 April 1744 [Prerogative Court (inventories) 1744-5, 43]. Birkhead's widow married Leonard Thomas, and Mary Dove sued him in Anne Arundel County court for her freedom in June 1746 [Judgment Record 1746-8, 118]. The outcome of the suit is not recorded, apparently because Thomas took her with him when he moved to Craven County, North Carolina. In September 1749 the Dove family was living in Craven County when William Smith complained to the court on their behalf that Leonard Thomas was detaining them as slaves:

Moll, Nell, Sue, Sall, & Will, Negroes Detained as Slaves by Leonard Thomas That they are free born Persons in the Province of Maryland and brought to this Province by the said Leonard Thomas

William Smith travelled to Maryland to prove their claim, and they were free by November 1756 when James Dove, a "Negro Servant," complained to the Craven County court that Smith was mistreating him, Nelly, Sue, Sarah, Moll, and William Dove [Haun, Craven County Court Minutes, IV:11–12, 366].

A grandson of Mary Dove named William Dowry was still held in slavery in Anne Arundel County in 1791 when he sued for his freedom in the General Court of Maryland. In October 1791 a fifty-seven or fifty-eight-year-old woman named Ann Ridgely (born about 1734), who was the daughter-in-law of Leonard Thomas, testified in Anne Arundel County that Mary Dove was a tall, spare woman of brown complexion and was the granddaughter of a woman imported into the country by the deponent's great grandfather. The deponent always understood that the grandmother of Mary Dove was a "Yellow Woman," had long black hair, was reputed to be an East Indian or a Madagascarian, and was called "Malaga Moll."[1]

Ridgely testified that Mary Dove had a daughter named Fanny who was the mother of William Dowry who petitioned for his freedom in the General Court of Maryland in 1791. She also testified that Mary Dove sued Leonard Thomas for freedom in Maryland, but before the suit was decided he moved with his family about twenty miles from Newbern, North Carolina, and took with him Mary, her three children, and her grandchildren Will and Sal. A certain Alexander Sands, commonly called Indian Sawony, was a witness for Mary Dove in her suit in Craven County, North Carolina, in 1749 and testified that her grandmother was an East Indian woman [Craven County Miscellaneous Records, C.R. 28.928.10].

---

[1] Madagascar was settled by Malaysians as early as 500 A.D. These people are believed to be responsible for introducing iron-working and the yam to Sub-Saharan Africans, a development that resulted in a massive displacement and killing of the San, Hottentot and related Capoid tribes.

'Keeper at the Gate'

The Question of Hu by Jonathan D. Spence, 1988, Knopf, NY, 187 pages

In the year 1721, Hu, the Keeper at the Gate at the Sacred Congregation for the Propagation of the Faith, was recruited by French Jesuit scholar and rogue theologian Father Jean-Francois Foucquet to assist him in transporting and translating the library of Chinese books being taken back to France for enhancing a study of Chinese religion so that the Catholic faith might be better presented to potential Chinese converts. For instance, Foucquet was convinced that Chinese works such as *The Book of Changes* are remnants of an ancient Chinese Christianity.

Blocked by rival Jesuits in his attempt to hire suitable Chinese scholars to accompany him home and work for a period in France, the rogue priest made a deal with Hu, who, though a passable scribe, could not speak or understand spoken French, which would cause him much heartache and misunderstanding.

After surviving a horrific year-long voyage around the world, led to believe that he would be able to meet the Pope, see the Vatican and preach the faith—and get paid in the bargain—Hu was disappointed on all counts. He was repeatedly berated, beaten, confined, horsewhipped, leashed to a carriage and made to run along behind it like a horse and eventually committed to an asylum, largely because he insisted on speaking with common people and speaking out against [using gestures, a homemade flag and a small drum he fabricated] mixing genders [nuns and priests] in houses of worship. In China, to get converts, the Jesuits permitted the Chinese to continue gender segregation in religious observation, and when faced with this practice in France and the obvious dalliances between nuns and priests, Hu was outraged.

At one point, when a beggar asked for assistance on the wintry road, Hu gave the wretch his own jacket, only to have his French hosts fly into a rage and beat the beggar until he gave the jacket back, which Hu refused to accept. Hu's story was told primarily by his Jesuit hosts, some of whom were outraged at his treatment and arranged for his passage back to China. Two of his letters are extant and reveal a man of average intelligence but deep moral convictions and boundless curiosity who was not afraid to fight, even enthusiastically grabbing a cutlass and standing ready to repel pirates off the coast of Brazil.

Below are some points which bear on the question and conditions of white and Chinese slavery in 18th century North America:

-Hu was treated well by some clergy and poorly by others, well by some elite and poorly by others.

-Hu was treated well by the various police, by all of the poor folk and criminals.

-Hu was treated savagely by the slaves of his guests, the bully servants who accompanied their masters everywhere.

-As a Chinese Christian, Hu's good treatment was a priority for the Church, the officers of which rescued Hu from his abusers and jailers.

-Hu was not paid for any portion of his contract by his employer, Foucquet.

-Police paramilitary forces, archers, horsemen and port police routinely scoured the streets and docks for any able-bodied man who was not enslaved, in the military, part of the church or of the moneyed classes and had them shipped off in chains for sail in Louisiana and other French colonies in the West Indies and North America, as well as to serve in the hellish galleys of the French fleet.

-Organized armed gangs contested control of city streets, including one gang armed with steel knob-topped canes known to kill with blows to the head.

As to the question of Chinese being shipped directly to the New World, Hu's story presents four occasions in which he was almost consigned to plantation slavery:

The ship carrying Hu was blown off course while low on supplies, ending up on the wrong side of the Atlantic. In such circumstances, the ship's offices, invested in their various cargos—including servants such as Hu—might have no choice but to starve or sell off their cargo in the New World.

Hu's ship was mistaken for a pirate and almost taken by a Portuguese warship. Whether taken by pirates—and this was the age of piracy—or by a warship, captured passengers and slaves would be sold under certain conditions.

When Hu ran away from confinement or just went wandering about like a tourist, he was in danger of being swept up by a pressgang and forced to row on a galley, work on a sailing ship or be sold off as a transport to the plantations. Make no mistake, if Hu had been arrested for vagrancy he would have been a felon, and at least under the English system, he would have been liable to serve a double term of 14 years as a convict laborer.

Hu's contract was violated by his master and he was only saved by his master' superiors. Had Hu contracted with an independent, secular master, he may well have been resold as a laborer once he proved difficult to communicate with. Since not honoring contracts entered into with people selling themselves as slave laborers and teachers seems to have been the usual, if not standard, practice once the servant was in the master's power, it is a fair guess that the handful of Chinese and East Indian slaves found in Maryland and Virginia had been duplicitously acquired by plantation slavers from brokers in England, who had access to educated Chinese servants who had contracted to serve in London, and, either after being defrauded by their masters or having served their time, were then vulnerable to kidnappers—no longer being a member of an affluent household but fending for themselves on the streets of a strange and barbarous city.

Jonathan D. Spence, in his biography of Hu, preserved a great deal of period nuance and detail and told an ultimately uplifting story of a stranger in a strange land maintaining his identity and convictions in the face of a cruel world order to triumph in a small way.

Plantation America

Essays and Articles on the American Slave Economy

The White Slavery Trajectory

Seeking an Accurate Perspective

You reminded me—Hoffman just published a piece on Unz.com. Hoffman makes a distinction between white slavery in the 17th and 18th centuries, becoming more indentured servitude into the early 19th century. I don't think you make that distinction, being as you could be flogged to death in your seven-year term—a distinction without a difference. Maybe he means that slavery became more benign over time?

-JR

The Problem with Our National Static Perspective

Herein, I address the general question you posed and will leave a discussion of Hoffman's piece (and recorded interview) and the colony-by-colony and race-by-race trajectories for the final volume in this series, *Plantation America: A History Denied.*

JR, first off, Hoffman and I have just skimmed the surface of this vast well of information concerning our secret history. As recently as last month I had to change my perspective on slave revolts after doing a first of its kind chronology, which ran 85 pages!

Second, not only do we have multiple time periods which do not fit cleanly into our idea of 100-year periods, we also try to answer the question of white servitude according to our present national consciousness, when it was a plantation-by-plantation, colony-by-colony or state-by-state trajectory in the period under discussion.

In my 12th and final book in the Plantation America series, I will present a colony-by-colony trajectory for slavery of all races. It simply was not a racial institution. But the movement of various races of people in and out of servitude offers a true perspective of the bestial economy that terminally infected these shores between 1585 and 1623. Ironically, by claiming that American slavery was purely an issue of white-on-black race hatred, the establishment historians have made this nation, in its gestation, birth and infancy, seem much less cruel, dehumanizing and soul devouring than it was. For most slaves of all races, slavery was worse than depicted in the most accurate [but still flawed] slavery movies, which are *Unconquered, Cool Hand Luke, Mandingo* and *12 Years a Slave.* Note the two earlier movies treat white slavery and the two latter movies treat black slavery.

One should recall the term "soul driver" from black slavery narratives and understand that that was an English term first used by whites to describe their masters and inherited by their black co-chattel.

As far as the "indentured servitude" issue, that was more of a mid-18th century phenomenon and was rare in the 17th and 19th centuries. Most 19th century white slaves who escaped were not described in the wanted ads as indentures. Various types of slaves or servants [two interchangeable terms] crossed all race lines and included but were not limited to:

Term slave of 3–31 years

Headright

Redemptioner

Girl

Boy

Maid

Captive husband [no shit, I'll cover this in Paleface]

Bondman

Bondwoman

Transport

Hoe wife

Wife

Sailor

Soldier

Indented

Apprentice

Slave for life.

Towards the middle of the 19th century, in Maryland, for instance, you had very few slaves for life, regardless of race, though David Holliday was a white man who did serve 37 years as a slave. My best guess is he was a bastard child of a servant woman who would have been surrendered by the mother for a 31-year term upon his birth in 1800, according to the Maryland and Virginia statutes of the period [at which point she would receive 30 lashes at the whipping post], and that he somehow accrued penalties that extended his term.

American slavery over all was unbelievably cruel through its entirety. The cruelest periods were the first half of the 17th century and the mid-19th century, both periods on the eves of massive civil wars. During the latter period, people who held whites in permanent slavery did it according to subterfuge, by tanning them or smoking them in tobacco sheds and claiming they were "colored," while blacks were exclusively brutalized in the exact same way as whites had been in the first half of the 17th century, that earlier period being a time when blacks were ALWAYS better treated than whites.

Indeed, Samuel Wiseman's book of record from 1777 indicates that the Governor of Virginia employed "the Negro" [a singular man] as a supervisor of his lowly white servants, such as the coachman and the hangman.

So, in the 1820s, 30s, 40s and 50s, white slaves lost value below the point where slave catchers did not bother nabbing them and were consequently better treated, with some runaways in the 1800s bringing only sixpence reward, at the same time that blacks were being sold for $1,000 and were being more cruelly treated when they attempted to break free. There have been isolation studies done showing that these expensive black slaves were better fed and housed than poor whites, and they were, if their master had the means. But small slaveholders, like Solomon Northup's master, were being pinched by economies of scale, which made their slaves so valuable that to lose them was to go broke. To be the highly valued slave of a poor, cruel or stupid man generally brings the same hellish conditions.

So, the irony was that generally speaking, across time and space, the less valuable your slaves were, the more poorly they were fed and housed and the more frequent were the beatings intended to inspire productivity.

However, when slaves were highly valued and expensive, such as in 1680 or 1850 Virginia, 1670s New England or South Carolina in the mid-

1700s, the more brutal were the repercussions suffered by slaves trying to break free. There were actually negro runaways being burned alive in Virginia around 1850! That same treatment had been meted out to whites in various colonies in the 1600s, when whites as a group had immense labor value, even though individually they sold for far less than blacks due to the more expensive African supply chain. By the 1840s, black slaves were being burned to death and mutilated in the same fashion that white slaves had been treated exactly 200 years before, when the tiny number of black slaves had been trusted house servants who sometimes commanded white servants and even purchased whites for their own use when free.

The never-ending politics of pitting one race against the other by the class hierarchy resulted in very different patterns in the evolution of the bondage system from colony to colony and state to state.

Generally speaking we have the following bondage trajectories listed in roughly chronological order:

By Plantation, Colony or State
-1 Virginia & Maryland
-2 New York
-3 New England
-4 Pennsylvania

-5 Carolinas

-6 Georgia

-7 Florida

-8 Kentucky & Tennessee

-9 Free Soil [Ohio, Indiana, Illinois, Michigan]

-10 Deep South [Alabama, Mississippi, Louisiana]

-11 West [Arkansas, Missouri, Indian Territory, Texas]

By Race

-1 Irish

-2 British [English, Cornish, Scottish, Welsh]

-3 Indian

-4 African

-5 Asian [Yes, there were Chinese held in Maryland and Virginia as early as the 1690s!]

JR, slavery in Plantation America was so immensely vast, deep and multifaceted that it is beyond the comprehension of almost all American academics, let alone media bots, and its study is a cursed plunge into infamy for anyone who publicly seeks the truth, which makes it clear that America remains a slave nation. Few slaves were ever shackled or locked behind bars but rather lived as free-range livestock, kept close by the master through the naked threat of force, just as the modern taxpayer is kept producing for his masters out of fear. In both eras, only the tiny minority were shackled or locked away at night. Even delving into this issue has now made it impossible for me to live a comfortable life. My end will be the very feared eventuality that keeps taxpayers toiling and groveling—to die broken and poor—which was the same price the so-called indentured servant paid if he or she failed to be repurchased. Only I am a man with a half-century of history here, with enough friends and family to make it certain that I will only die homeless if that is my wish, whereas the millions[1] of poor souls of European descent who died in or out of bondage after being trafficked to their master's promised land were unlikely to have anyone to take them in should they break free of or be discarded by the system.

---

[1] I have the preliminary demographics necessary to arrive at the numbers of European slaves shipped to and born in English North America, and will present that information in Plantation America, after I have had a person with some mathematic credentials check the numbers. It is a certainty that more Europeans were shipped to English North America in bondage than were Africans.

'Boy & Girls'

A Suppositional Anatomy of the Slave Mind

One of the greatest imbalances in our national perception of the United States of America is the idea that all oppression, all forced servitude, was experienced by 10% of our base population [being African-Americans] and that all of this occurred in 25% of our current territory, the Old South. This is the fundamental lie of our national mythos, which has generated a skewed perception of our past, most notably concerning the former servile population of Plantation America, most of whom simply disappeared from the record, literally vanishing into the ground.

Those that survived slavery vanished through the Cumberland Gap, down the Ohio River, across the Great Lakes and the Alabama Plain—white men and women escaping white slave masters as fast as they could, unwittingly blazing the trail for more finesse-oriented slave masters to come.

Much of the Postmodern American angst is harbored in the bitterness of blacks and the cultivated guilt of whites over the belief that this phony history of racial oppression—rather than economic oppression in a capitalist society—is central to their current condition. Central to this, in everyday life, is the connotation of the term *boy*.

The term *boy* came into wide usage in the British Isles as a term for slave before any blacks were held in bondage by British masters. *Lad* was the term one used to describe a youth according to his age. *Lass* was the term for female children, whereas *girl* was a term used to describe a female servant, with maid specifically referring to a female servant who attended a lady.[1] Thus, the term *slave girl* is both redundant and instructive.

So, in the 1600s, when this land was being "planted" with people, to speak of English slaves of

---

[1] The definitions below describe the evolution often the term girl from slave to wage employee to workplace associate in reverse.

Girl, gərl/

noun: girl; plural noun: girls; a young woman of a specified kind or having a specified job.

informal: women who mix socially or belong to a particular group, team, or profession.

dated: a female servant.

Origin: Middle English (denoting a child or young person of either sex): perhaps related to Low German gör 'child.'

both sexes was to speak of boys and girls. Why is it that *girl* is currently used as an endearing term for women of both of the previous enslaved races, *white* and *black*, although they were not regarded as *whites* and *blacks* in 16th and 17th century America?

Also, why is it that white men will often use the term boy in an endearing way, describing a fraternity of men, for instance, or even the entire Major League Baseball organization as "the boys of summer," while black males from two to a hundred seem to resent the term *boy*?

The answer is simple from my perspective.

As most women have no agency and, deep down, wish to belong to someone, to a be a man's or a substitute's [dyke or church or state] property, being named as someone's girl never held as restraining a stigma as the term *boy* did for men. For instance, an English girl could find her fortune in America by being bought as a wife and then possibly rise to the management of a substantial household. Likewise, African-American slave girls achieved power over the men of their own race— and have renewed this hold through the gynocentric welfare system—by gaining direct access to the favor of the majority Caucasian patriarchy via household positions [which they dominated] over field positions [where the vast majority of men were consigned].

The question of *boys*, however, is tougher than that of *girls*.

I saw a news reel of FDR having a picnic dinner with a number of New Deal grunts, whom he referred to as *boys*, with no insult taken or perceived. Many an officer referred to his men as *boys* in wars between the 1600s and today. Even popular songs, such as *The Boys Are Back in Town* by Thin Lizzy, carry no class stigma but evoke a sense of fraternity, of shared experience, among many American men of European origin, particularly working men.

However, the term is taken quite harshly by blacks, who suppose that the term *boy* was invented to describe the condition of their enslaved ancestors, having no idea it was inherited from whites who escaped, worked their way free and revolted to gain their freedom and then moved ever westward to escape the slave economy. Having read hundreds of escaped slave advertisements and over a hundred reports of slave revolts, it is obvious to this researcher that the English-American slave master class learned well the lessons known for centuries by the ancient Romans but which were lost in regards to running chattel slavery plantations.

Plantation America of the 1600s was almost exclusively a white-on-white slave system.

The 1700s was a very mixed-race slave system, roughly 60% white, 30% black and 10% Indian or mixed race, in terms of total bondage ratios across the original 13 states.

The 1800s saw a shift to predominantly African-American servitude.

The stigma of slavery stings harder the man than the woman. This is natural and still apparent today as men continue to break more violently under our system of proxy slavery and to commit many more acts of violence in the workplace, in stark contrast to the home, the long-standing place of the woman's suppression, where the American woman commits twice the level of violence as the man. So, as men feel the yoke of slavery more heavily in conditions of public servitude and women seem to revolt more under conditions of household servitude, it becomes obvious why men of European descent managed to run, work and fight their way out of slavery and made bonds on this basis as they "won the west." Yet, black men, hampered by their women being as likely to align themselves with the white father of their mixed-race children as with the black father of their African children, and being subject to a system that has adapted to prevent a repetition of white slave revolts among blacks—part of this being the separation of the genders of the enslaved people— the American black man must remain bitter in having never had an ancestor to point to as having won his people's freedom. There is no black George Washington.

Although there have been many recent propaganda efforts to convince us that black men that escaped chattel slavery joined the Union Army ranks and won the freedom of their people through numerous heroic battles, the fact is, as at Fort Pillow and Cold Harbor, Union Troops lost most of their battles against Confederate formations and black Union Troops [hastily raised and poorly led] lost almost all the time.

So, as a word meant to consign generations of Englishmen to bondage and eventually inherited by blacks, who by 1860 were virtually the only folk held in bondage in this nation, the term BOY rankles most harshly in the ear of men who know that their ancestors did not win free but were set free. This, in and of itself, is a great weapon against the men of a people, to rescue them from bondage a mere generation before they would have won it themselves by sheer inertia, forever depriving them of the one thing that men of all races crave—real, unimpeachable heroes, heroes who won by their own means.[2]

---

[2] Chattel slavery was a dead letter across the Western hemisphere by 1890.

Cracker-Boy—Slave Boy

Up from the Depths of the Warped American Consciousness

A *cracker* was originally a *cracker* based on the sound of the whip which drove him to his task and then later, for the few who made it to overseer, the sound the whip they wielded made as they drove their master's chattel to their task. The sound is the primary source of the term, with cattlemen in Florida earning it by the crack of their whips, a baseball team by the crack of their bats.

In later times, as the master class cultivated a hatred for those poor members of their own race who fled to the wilderness margins, ran to the hills and held out in the mountains, the term *cracker* became associated with the deficient diet based on cracked corn and the refuge of such souls in strong, homemade sour mash spirits and the story telling that went on as men drank their whiskey, which was likewise associated with the cracked corn, becoming the cracked joke.

In the minds of the black slaves who suffered under the whips of black slaves and white overseers, the low-down portion of the white race became despised as creatures who were both less well-off and freer, which is a sure recipe for hatred. The term *cracker* derives from an old Gaelic term that antedates white over black slavery in America and is associated with the term "get cracking." [See Wikipedia entry for "Cracker (pejorative)."]

'How Could Parents Sell Their Children?'

A Man Question from Megan

I realize that the entire white slavery argument hinges on the willingness of parents to part with their children. Kidnapping was rampant from 1618 to the 1750s but never filled more than half the ships' holds that deposited the youth of the British Isles on these shores to toil, die and be willfully forgotten. However, a multitude of Anglo-Saxons, Welsh, Irish and Scottish willingly sold their children.

Most moderns say that this is inhuman, that they would never do it. But they are wrong, as they have imbibed the lying waters until they float on into delirium.

We inherited the debt-based social model.

Where the early American was inclined to sell his son or daughter for a fixed term of usually seven years, the modern American voter sells his children for life, every time he votes for a politician that borrows money and further inflates the national debt.

The early Americans were—not living a lie like us but facing the ugly truth—superior to us in one specific way: they regarded taxation of wages as immoral. Even to a people who habitually bought and sold others, there was something obscene about the idea that a legal fiction might own a portion of a man's physical effort, forever, for a man who worked for a wage was—and still is—by definition poor.

What You Bought Your Boys With

18th Century Currency & Coinage and Unfree Labor Costs

-Pence [English, penny] 12 pence = 1 shilling

-Shilling [English] = 1 day's wage

-Dollar [Spanish, silver peso "piece of eight"] = 4 shillings & 6 pence

-Pistole [Spanish, gold dubloon] = 18 shillings

-Pound [English] = 20 shillings

-Guinea [English, coin] = 21 shillings

The pound was a unit of measurement and was not represented by a minted coin, making the pistole the de facto capital coin; the guinea was used as a pound coin, though it was rare in the colonies.

The colonial administrations of the plantation provinces were not permitted to coin their own currency.

The pistole was the primary medium of exchange in Virginia from 1700 to 1750. Usually a century-old Spanish coin, but sometimes a French gold Louis d'or, minted in the late 17th century, it was highly sought.

The term "shill," as in a paid advocate, comes ultimately from the shilling.

Three shillings were sometimes termed a "bob."

Servant Cost

-A shilling was the basic value of a laborer's day wage at the beginning of the period in the 1600s.

-The purchase price of a servant was a median of 15 pounds, or 300 shillings.

-The reward price of a runaway servant ranged from 20 to 200 shillings [up to 5 pounds]

-A servant served for 7 years, for just over 300 days per year, including Sabbaths and holidays, bringing 3,500 days of labor to his owner.

-A man who buys a servant to ditch for 7 years would typically pay 300 shillings.

-A man who paid a ditcher by the day would expend 3,500 shillings over the same period.

-If a free man hired a ditcher and competed with a servant speculator for a ditch-digging contract, his single day laborer would cost him more than a servant speculator's crew of 10!

-Peter Williamson was sold for 16 pounds.

-African slaves sold for 25–100 pounds, with a median that seemed to be about 50 pounds, or 2,000 shillings, meaning a slave owner would have a hard time competing with a servant speculator but would still have much cheaper labor than a contractor paying a free wage laborer.

-The problem with servant speculation was runaways, expressed in reward costs and newspaper subscriptions, if the servant was recovered, which was paid for by the servant, who had time added to his term to compensate.

-Ultimately, the prime factors that turned the elite from servant speculation to slave owning were: homebred slaves cost nothing, then lived at the place of their birth, making them less likely to flee than the kidnapped, convicted and indebted servants who had preceded them.

Food is not calculated in these labor comparisons. However, servants and slaves usually ate nothing but water and corn and were therefore more cheaply fed than cattle.

Why Lie About White Slavery?

Bridgette Takes the Author to Task over His "Conspiracy Theory" Allegations about American History

Okay, I understand that some white people may have conspired to keep the black people down and that some black people surely conspired to rise up. So, in that sense, sure, there is such a thing as conspiracies. But to think that rich, poor, black and white all agreed, 'Let's hide this thing,' that's what I have a problem with. -Bridgette

Bridgette, that is not what I am suggesting. Was there a conspiracy to silence the story of white slavery in America? Yes, there was, but only by affluent, white academics from 1865 through today, and more recently, since 1968, among affluent, black academics.

Overall, what occurred on the ground at the very time each individual in each group addressed the issue of servile identity is similar to the one drop rule in America, a rule which was instituted by white slave masters to keep people of African descent with mixed parentage enslaved, and is now, tragically, wholeheartedly embraced by nearly all American blacks. I recently watched a PBS documentary on slavery in which all of the academics appeared to me to be white folk. However, my friend, a black academic, who knew who these people were, kept pointing to them and saying, "No, she's black too." She even pointed to a redheaded woman with pinkish white skin and blue eyes and said that she too was black. There is no more blatant lie than to look at a person of mixed race and say that they are all of one race, that the African blood is better, superior, stronger, and the white blood is weak, inferior, instantly abolished by a superior genetic strain, when you can mate a dark black man with a ghostly white Irish girl and get a child that is exactly halfway between in skin tone and hair texture—for I know such people.

Yet, blacks and whites overwhelming agree that there should be no mixed-race category, that one drop black makes you all black. Why is this? Did all the blacks and whites get together and decide this by vote?

No, the key is that the one drop rule serves everybody except the child, and the child has never had a high standing in European or African culture, so why should we expect our mongrel society to place the child's sense of continuity before our own grand and mean delusions?

The only societies I have studied that truly valued their children were the Amerindian peoples, whom the whites and blacks together displaced from their lands. It seems that raising quality children is a poor group survival strategy compared to breeding as many as possible. Generally speaking, an Indian warrior was worth two whites or blacks on the battlefield. But Indian cultures limited their breeding to maintaining their numbers, not increasing them, so being outnumbered 30–1 by lower-quality men spelled their doom. Ironically, most Indians regarded whites and blacks as members of the same crazy race, as they held to the same greedy values and continually beat their children.

As for the one drop rule, it serves all. Blacks have always been a small minority and wish to increase their numbers so that they have a greater say in politics. Whites, on the other hand, see themselves as the privileged, elite caste in our society, thinking themselves superior to blacks— especially liberals have this opinion and is why they are so palsied with guilt over the black condition in America.

Let us apply this logic to white slavery, which consumed more souls in this land than did black slavery. See *So His Master May Have Him Again* for the numbers.

As first white, class-based servitude ended, soon followed [within a single generation] by black, race-based servitude, who among the following factions would wish to keep alive the story of white slavery?

-Emancipated blacks have gained greatly in moral standing, have indeed become the martyr minority of America, due to their claim of having been the only people ever on this continent to be unjustly held in bondage.

-The white elite, who sat atop fortunes built on the backs of whites and blacks in conditions of horrid servitude, decided to play the lowly whites and blacks off against each other by only recognizing the black condition and hence letting the poor descendants of white slaves take the majority of the blame for black slavery! Now that was some diabolic white deviltry there.

-To cinch the triple-delusion, the poor whites, whose parents or ancestors were servants, let that memory be forgotten as they wished nothing more than to have full rights in a class-based society and had no desire to have marriage options and business partnerships withheld due to their lowly origins. To a large degree, this was pre-ordained, as the jealous slave mentality has persisted in American culture in the cults of greed and celebrity which produced our latest president. There is also the influence of literature. Since literature was produced by and/or for the elite class, when literacy came to the underclass, they identified with those stories that more often than not featured a prince or princess who did not know they were royalty until a transformative moment in the storyline.

There you go, Bridgette, it wasn't a conspiracy, it was a very predictable, tacit agreement between rich whites, poor whites and blacks to forget the millions of worked-to-death white lives interred in unmarked graves. This is reflected in the politics of the Olde Flushing Towne Burial Ground in Queens, New York, where, according to the history inscribed on the memorial marker, large numbers of poor whites were interred over an old Indian burial ground for more than 100 years, with, at the end of its use, black servants and slaves interred there also for a couple decades. Any logical deduction—particularly accounting for the massive known migrations of Irish into New York during the period when it was exclusively a white mass grave site—would conclude that this was a potters' field, desecrating an extinct native burial ground, and was, towards the end of its grisly history, somewhat elevated in stature as a place fitting for beloved black servants of the rich whites to be interred with head stones, where there had been no headstones for the victims of the Irish Holocaust, whose bones moldered beneath the relatively small number of black graves.

Bridgette, we live in an evil society based on greed, force and popularity. In such a pit of vipers, the Truth has no place, and so it must lie defiled beneath the bright, shining lies that bind us, speaking of which, there is a fourth force at work here, the greatest force, the Government, the State, which directs education and walks and lies hand-in-hand with the media and the wealthy elite. The State, as such, is tolerated by people because we believe that it functions justly and for our own good. If it came to be known that slavery was a state policy, that the colonial governments worked hand-in-hand with the plantation owners to enslave white, red and black equally, then we might get the silly notion in our head that the Government is Bad. So, even though all of those in power were white elites at the time the memory of white slavery was dutifully erased from history, it was better to blame it on old and outdated notions of racial prejudice held by their ancestors than to blame it on the very machine that served them so well—then, now and in their ancestral Eden of Plantation America.

If you think the case for government involvement in slavery is overblown, then you have been hoodwinked. Here is one tidbit: the Father of our Country, George Washington, our first president, who turned down the title of king and voluntarily stepped down, had decided that his black slaves would be freed upon his death and replaced by cheaper German servants who could be held in the nation's capital, Philadelphia, 10 times as long as blacks! His evil, bitch wife, Martha, objected to this and the Government sided with her and his slaves remained in bondage.

And we aren't silly, are we, Bridgette?

Father of Our Plantation

Shitlord Boss Big George Washington Directs White and Black Slaves

Look at this painting of Washington and his slaves. The man bending over with the sickle is not a black man. The white man he is talking to must be an overseer surely? But why is he holding a saddle and a farming implement? Maybe he is a stout Rhinelander.

Ol' George has his baton in the ready...

Correction: on a closer look, the saddle is on the horse by the tree, not his shoulder. He is not even allowed to touch that! -Mescaline Franklin

James Describes the Painting, *Washington as Farmer at Mount Vernon*, 1851, Junius Brutus Stearns, located at the Virginia Museum of Fine Arts

From right to left:
1. A white servant, probably German, holding a rake. No overseer holds

anything other than a weapon of discipline.

2. Big Daddy George Washington, negro teeth lining his mouth, stands with the baton of keeping your ass at it, instructing the servant on ground work.

3. A white man bends his back to the grain with his sickle, wearing the standard white servant hat initially used in 1620s Virginia.

4. A negro, sickle in hand, resting while the white man works, drinks water.

5. A negress with a pitch fork, resting by the water bucket.

6. A comely quadroon wench, serving water in fine clothing. One might well assume that she serves her master at night in a like posture, though more lightly attired.

7. A cherubic pair of white baby-youths, the girl having her hair dressed with flowers by the boy of privilege.

8. A negro forks hay up to the hay wagon being loaded by the negress on its back. Even the horses toil in white and brown, the draft team pulling the wagon as salt and pepper as the crew.

9. In the background a negress or mulattress stands drawing cord as the white man—so indicated by his distinctive hat as much as his lighter skin tone—on his Aryan knees,

gathers the hay that will be bound in the cord.

Of the 12 figures, we have:

-Three elites

-Three white servants

-Six black slaves

The 2–1 ratio of black to white unfree labor is in keeping with late 18th century demographics. Consider that of roughly 3 million slaves, only about 17 percent of the colonial population was black, but between 50 percent and 83 percent were unfree whites [mostly in the north], and the 2–1 Virginia ratio seems realistic.

Big Daddy Washington, First Shitlord of these Slave States, does get points for doing his own discipline, which is in keeping with his miserly, alpha male persona.

'The Marks of Severe Whipping'

The Plight of the Native Sons of Plantation Maryland

...people already in the colony were often sold into servitude for various terms because they could not pay their fines and the costs of their prosecutions after they had been convicted of crimes or if they could not pay the costs of the proceedings against them whether they were guilty or not.

—*C. Ashley Ellefson*, The Private Punishment of Servants and Slaves in Eighteenth-Century Maryland

The following chapter is based on a reading of C. Ellefson's *Private Punishments and Seven Hangmen*, and *Seven Hangmen of Colonial Maryland.*

Ultimately, the living conditions and laws of servitude that governed Plantation Maryland derived from the many acts to limit freedom and punish masterless men, such as the Act for the Punishment of Vagabonds enacted by the English

Parliament in 1547, which "any runagate servant, or any other which liveth idly and loiteringly, by the space of three days [homeless, penniless or jobless person]... adjudge him to be slave to the same person that brought or presented him...for two years after... and if such slave absent himself... by the space of fourteen days... further shall be adjudged to be slave to his said master for ever..., and if the said slave shall run away the second time, he shall be adjudged a felon [executed]." The Parliament did distinguish between a servant and a slave.

In Maryland, from 1704, servants had to reimburse the owner in labor for the cost of catching them.

Notable Servant Whippings from the Maryland Archives (Ellefson):

-May of 1746: Benjamin Tasker's runaway convict servant Henry Kirk had been "lately Whipt for his Roguery, and the Stripes remain fresh on his Back."

-June 1746: runaway servant Charles Smith had "the Scars of Whipping on his Back."

-May of 1753: runaway servant William Beall had "several Marks of Correction upon his Back" for running away twice before.

-August 1753: runaway servant Darby Mahoney had "several Scars on his Back, occasioned by whipping," and had "always been a notorious Rogue and Thief."

-September of 1758: an advertisement pointed out that John Syms was an old offender, as could "be seen by the Marks on his Back."

-October of 1768: John Hoget, a runaway in Alexandria, "bore the marks of a recent whipping."

-March of 1747: runaway servant John Hyde had already "lost a Piece of one of his Ears," was "as great a Villain as . . . [the] Age . . . [could] produce" and had recently been severely whipped.

-April 1758: runaway convict servant Sarah Davis had "many Scars on her Back occasioned by severe Whippings from her former Master."[1]

-November 1767: runaway convict servant Joseph Haines' body was "much scarified."

-August 1769: runaway convict servant Thomas Moore had been "severely whipt, which appears on his Back now in Scars."

-December 1770: runaway convict servant Thomas Burn was "remarkably cut on the Buttocks by a Flogging he received from a former Master."

-July, 1771: runaway convict servant William Springate wore "the Marks of a severe whipping given him lately for breaking into a house."[2]

---

[1] It was common for a servant to be owned by two or more masters at varying times, not always consecutively, as a landless person could fall into servitude and be sold for debts, poverty, homelessness or any number of minor crimes.

[2] Breaking into a house was a capital crime and he could have been executed, so the boy got off lucky.

'Such Servant so Wrong'd'

Lash Laws in Plantation Maryland

...many people were transported to America for seven or fourteen years or for life after they were convicted of crimes in England or if, like destitute children, beggars, vagabonds, and political and religious non-conformists, they were considered undesirables for some other reasons.

-*C. Ashley Ellefson*, The Private Punishment of Servants and Slaves in Eighteenth-Century Maryland

Continued from Ellefson:

Penalties for Excessively[1] Beating Servants

Until 1715:

1st Offense: fine, in tobacco, not to exceed 1,000 pounds

---

[1] This was undefined, but by 1700, all were in agreement in the plantations of America that burning was needlessly cruel.

2nd Offense: the same fine

3rd Offense: the servant may be freed[2]

-The Council of Trade and Plantations demanded action from the Governor and/or Maryland Assembly in 1691, 1692, 1693, 1698, 1699, 1703, 1704, 1713 and 1714, with the colonial officials resisting legislation against brutality towards servants until 1715. Those colonial attitudes extended throughout the 18th century, and in this researcher's opinion, were often motivating factors [slavery being another] in the revolution of 1776. Indeed, Father Joseph Mosely, writing in 1772, declared the masters' treatment of servants in Maryland to be "...cruel, barbarous and unmerciful."

Lash Laws from 1715

-A master could whip any servant with 10 lashes or fewer.

-If he thought that the servant deserved more than 10 lashes, he had to take his complaint before a magistrate.

-The magistrate could order the servant whipped with no more than 39 lashes.

---

[2] All offenses accumulated only against the same servant. Masters got around this by beating servants in rotation, by restricting servant access to the courts and by keeping private burial plots for slain servants.

-The new law said nothing about limiting the master's punishment of his own slave, only his servants.

-The fire director of Annapolis could order any servant who refused to obey orders in fighting a fire whipped up to 39 lashes.

". . . if any Master or Mistress of any Servant whatsoever or overseer by order or consent of any such Master or Mistress shall deny and not provide Sufficient Meat drink lodging and Clothing or shall unreasonably burthen them beyond their strength with labour or debarr them of their necessary rest and sleep or excessively beat and abuse them [**] the same being sufficiently proved before the Justices of the County Courts the said Justices have hereby full power and Authority for the first and second offence to levy such ffine upon such Offender as to them shall seem meet not exceeding one thousand pounds of Tobacco to the use of her Majesty her heires and Successors for the Support of Government and for their third Offence to sett such Servant so wrong'd at liberty and free from Servitude."

-1704, c. 23, Md. Arch., XXVI, 259.

Despite the above law, servants such as Elizabeth Sprig and James Revel [he being held in Virginia] were explicit in their complaints that they ate nothing but corn and slept on the barn floor.

'From Their Said Masters'

Decisions of the General Court of Virginia, 1640

The Court ruling below is used by modern academics as a false explanation for white slavery being "replaced by the racially [meaning white over black] based slave system," which it was not.

Quoted from the General Court of Colonial Virginia:

July 22nd, 1640. Whereas complaint has been made to this Board by Capt. William Pierce, Esqr., that six of his servants[1] and a negro of Mr. Reginald's has plotted to runaway unto the Dutch plantation[2] from their said masters, and did assay to put the same in Execution upon Saturday night, being the 8th day July, 1640, as appeared to the Board by the Examinations of Andrew Noxe,

---

[1] Captain Pierce might have had as many as 100 servants. Twenty servants would barely be enough to work a modest plantation.
[2] The Dutch plantations were in New Jersey

Richard Hill, Richard Cookeson and John Williams, and likewise by the confession of Christopher Miller, Peter Milcocke and Emanuel, the foresaid Negro, who had, at the foresaid time, taken the skiff of the said Capt. William Pierce, their master, and corn, powder and shot and guns to accomplish their said purposes, which said persons sailed down in the said skiff to Elizabeth river, where they were taken and brought back again, the court taking the same into consideration as a dangerous precedent for the future time (if left unpunished), did order that:

-Christopher Miller, a dutchman (a prime agent in the business), should receive the punishment of whipping, and to have thirty stripes and so be burnt in the cheek with the letter R[3] and to work with a shackle on his legg for one whole year and longer if said master shall see cause, and after his full time of service is Expired with his said master to serve the colony for seven whole years,

-and the said Peter Milcocke to receive thirty stripes and to be Burnt in the cheek with the letter R, and after his term of service is Expired with his said master to serve the colony for three years,

---

[3] The R was burned with gunpowder, not with a branding iron. Two years later, those in Virginia branded with the R would serve for life, regardless of race.

-and the said Richard Cockson, after his full time Expired with his master, to serve the colony for two years and a half,

-and the said Richard Hill to remain upon his good behavior until the next offence,

-and the said Andrew Noxe to receive thirty stripes,

-and the said John Williams, a dutchman and a chirurgeon [surgeon] after his full time of service is Expired with his master, to serve the colony for seven years,

-and Emanuel, the Negro, to receive thirty stripes and to be burnt in the cheek with the letter R and to work in shackles one year or more as his master shall see cause.

Analysis

Despite this document being cited by revisionist historians as proof that the punishment of Emanuel the Negro represented the turning away from an economy based on universal enslavement to one based on racial enslavement, the evidence proves otherwise at 6 white to 1 black. Thirty-six years later, the ratio would be roughly 10 white to 1 black.

Unlike 18th century notices in Virginia, Emanuel is not referred to as a slave but as a negro. It is assumed that he is a servant. In this period, it was also assumed that all whites were servants, unless listed as masters. The different distinction here is that Emanuel is of a class that received no surname, therefore deriving his identity from his master, not from his heritage, which had been stolen. The chief difference between whites and blacks of this period was a lack of recognized heritage for the blacks. This fact is what made them increasingly valuable as slaves, being less willing to run than whites, as they were socially identified with their master. Note that two, possibly three, of these slaves had been Dutchmen and that they sought to flee to the Dutch colony in New Jersey. This heritage issue, of Dutch, Scotch, Irish, English, Welsh and Indian fleeing to live in free communities of their ethnicity, caused a continual bleeding off of labor into the hinterlands and back to the Old Country. This eventually justified the triple or quadruple cost of a negro, and this additional expense also encouraged the idea of a single, lifetime term of service rather than the cyclical re-enslavement of less cooperative whites. High negro cost also encouraged their breeding, which was already in effect for white servant girls as a gambit to retain them as free servants through their child's term of 31 years of servitude.

Severity of Punishment

The list below details the severity of punishment meted out in 1640, from most to least severe, with notes on ethnicity.

1. Christopher Miller, Dutch

2. Peter Milcocke, Orphan [European, ethnicity unknown]

3. John Williams, Dutch

4. Emanuel, negro

5. Richard Cockson, English

6. Andrew Noxe, English

7. Richard Hill, English

Based on the above ranking of punishment severity, the administrators of this English colony were most severe to the Dutch, least severe to the English, and the negro Emanuel seemed to fall somewhere in between. Note that Peter, either English or Dutch by his name, was brutally treated, second only to the ring leader, reflecting the strong animus English plantation owners directed against orphans.

Do note that Emanuel was obviously used by the Dutch ring leaders to get their hands on his master's boat. In this light, his easier sentence than the Dutch is understandable, as is his more severe sentence than the English, who come off as lackeys. Note that John Williams is an educated professional and the orphan, Peter, was probably a key pawn of the two adult Dutchmen, as boys tended to have more access to the houses of their master and neighboring masters due to their duties as messengers. Emanuel, for his part, seems to have been a trusted man charged with the care of a valuable vessel.

'Under the Statute of Incorrigible Rogues'

Virginia Statute on Runaway Servants, (Hening, Vol. 1, ACTS XX – XXII, pages 252-5). This author has added paragraph breaks to the original text for ease of reference to footnotes.

ACT XX

WHEREAS many great abuses & much detriment have been found to arise both against the law of God and likewise to the service of manye masters of families in the collony occasioned through secret marriages of servants, their masters and mistresses being not any ways made privy thereto, as also by committing of fornication, for preventing the like abuses hereafter, *Be it enacted and confirmed by this Grand Assembly* that what man servant soever hath since January 1640 or hereafter shall secretly marry with any mayd or woman servant without the consent of her master or mistres if she be a widow, he or they so offending shall n the first place serve out his or their tyme or tymes with his or their masters or mistresses, and after shall serve his or their master or mistress one compleat year more for such offence committed, And the mayd or woman servant so marrying without consent as aforesaid shall for such her offence double the tyme of service with her master and mistress, And a ffreeman so offending shall give satisfaction to the master or mistress by doubling the value of the service and pay a ffine of five hundred pounds of tobacco to the parish where such offence shall be comitted,[1]

And it is also further enacted and confirmed by the authority of this Grand Assembly that if any man servant shall comit the act of fornication with any mayd or woman servant, he shall for his offence, besides the punishment by the law appointed in like cases, give satisfaction for the losse of her service, by one whole year's service, when he shall be free from his master according to his indentures, And if it so fall out that a freeman offend, as formerly he shall be compelled to make satisfaction to the master or mistris of the said woman servant by his service for one compleat year, or otherwise give forthwith such valuable consideration as the comissioners in their discretion shall think fitt.

---

[1] This is the strongest evidence that servants had no rights other than to appeal for cruelty. It is clear that the master owned a servant woman's body. The woman in such an illegal relationship is punished roughly seven times more severely than the man.

ACT XXI

WHEREAS complaints are at every quarter court exhibitted against divers persons who entertain and enter into covenants with runaway servants and freemen who have formerly hired themselves to others to the great prejudice if not the vtter vndoing of divers poor men, thereby also encourageing servants to runn from their masters and obscure themselves in some remote plantations, Vpon consideration had for the future preventing of the like injurious and vnjust dealings, Be it enacted and confirmedthat what person or persons soever shall entertain any person as hireling, or sharer or vpon any other conditions for one whole yeare without certificate from the commander or any one commissioner of the place, that he or she is free from any ingagement of service, The person so hireing without such certificate as aforesaid, shall for every night that he or she entertaineth any servant either as hireling or otherwise, fforfeit to the master or mistris of the said servant twenty pounds of tobacco, And for evrie freeman which he or she entertaineth (formerly hired by another) for a year as aforesaid, he or she shall forfeit to the party who had first hired him twenty pounds of tobacco for every night deteyned. And for everie freeman which he or she entertaineth (though he hath not formerly hired himselfe to another) without certificate as aforesaid,

And in all these cases the party hired shall receive such censure and punishment as shall be thought fitt by the Governor and Counsell: Allways provided that if any such runnaway servants or hired freemen shall produce a certificate, wherein it appears that they are freed from their former masters service or from any such ingagement respectively, if afterwards it shall be proved that the said certificates are counterfeit then the retayner not to suffer according to the penalty of this act, But such punishment shall be inflicted vpon the forger and procurer thereof as the Governor and Council shall think fitt.

ACT XXII

WHEREAS there are divers loytering runaways in the collony who very often absent themselves from their masters service, And sometimes in two or three monthes cannot be found, whereby their said masters are at great charge in finding them, And many times even tot he losse of their year's labour before they be had, Be it therefore enacted and confirmed that all runnaways that shall absent themselves from their said masters service shall be lyable to make satisfaction by service at the end of their tymes by indenture (vizt.) double the tyme of service soe neglected, And in some cases more if the comissioners for the place appointed shall find it requisite and convenient. [2]

And if such runnaways shall be found to transgrese the second time or oftener (if it shall be duely proved against hem) that then they shall be branded in the cheek with the letter R. and passe vnder the statute of incorrigible rogues. [3]

Provided notwithstanding that where any servants shall have just cause of complaint against their masters or mistrises by harsh or vnchristianlike vsage or otherways for want of diet, or convenient necessaryes that then it shall be lawfull for any such servant or servants to repaire to the next comissioner to make his or their complaint, And if the said commissioner shall find by good and sufficient proofes, that the said servant's cause of complaint is just, The said comissioner is hereby required to give order for the warning of any such master or mistris before the comissioners in theire seuerall county courts, where the matter in difference shall be decided as they in their discretions shall think fitt, And that care be had that no such servant or servants be misvsed by

---

[2] These were standard penalties, except for the next clause, which is extreme and resulted in a legislatively recognized class of "Christian servants for life."

[3] They might be branded with a brand. However, the common method, which could be done on the trail by the slave catcher, was to form a letter *R* on the cheek with gunpowder and then light it.

their masters or mistrises, where they shall find the cause of complaint to be just.[4]

Be it further also enacted that if any servant running away as aforesaid shall carrie either peice, powder and shott, And leave either all or any of them with the Indians, And being thereof lawfully convicted shall suffer death as in case of ffelony.[5]

---

[4] There is scant evidence that such laws were enforced and there was resistance to colonial statutes by owners and local assemblies that made such rulings, usually under pressure from the home country, and thus had little desire to enforce them.

[5] This is clear evidence that, in Virginia, individual fugitives were seeking homes among the Indians. This would be addressed by the governor, who later armed the tribe based at Richmond Falls against "the giddy multitude," as he called the entire unfree underclass, which numbered over 90% of the population.

'Bee it Enacted'

Old Dominion Servant Laws: Virginia Statutes 1658–61

March 1658

Hening, Vol. 1, page 445, ACT XXVI

Against Tradeing with Servants.

WHEREAS divers ill disposed persons do secretly and covertly trade and truck with other mens' servants and apprentices which tendeth to the great injurie of masters of ffamilies their servants being thereby induced and invited to purloine and imbezill the goods of their said masters, Bee it therefore enacted for redresse of the like disorders and abuses hereafter that what person or persons shall buy, sell, trade or truck with any servant, for any comoditie whatsoever without lycence or consent of the master of any such servant hee or they so offending against the premises shall suffer one monthes imprisonment without bail or mainprize and also shall forfeite and restore to the master of the said servant fower times the value of the things so bought, sold, trucked or traded for.

1659

The special Act concerning enslavement of Irish, requiring servitude of six years was onerous and discouraging the importation of Irish slaves, hence all servants, "of what Christian nation soever" were put on equal footing (Hening, Vol. 1, page 538, ACT XIV), with a confirmation that political dissidents (Hening, Vol. 1, page 531-2, ACT IV) could be trafficked along with the poor and debtor class. This decision will inform the next 16 years of Virginia history by placing politically astute, active and literate persons in bondage, essentially gifting the white slaves of Virginia with a leadership cadre.

March 1661 (Hening, Vol. 2, page 26, ACT XXII)

BEE itt enacted That in case any English servant shall run away in company with any negroes who are incapable of makeing satisfaction by addition of time,[1] *Bee itt enacted* that the English so running away in company with them shall serve for the time of the said negroes absence as they are to do for their owne by a former act.

---

[1] Indicates that some, not all, negroes were serving for life. It was not until such time as it was normal for a negro to serve for life that the term slave and negro became synonymous. At the time of writing of this statute, Virginia was still a generation away from comprehensive enslavement of blacks on a racial basis.

March 1661 (Hening, Vol. 2, page 117, ACT CII)

WHEREAS the barbarous usuage of some servants by cruell masters bring soe much scandall and infamy to the country in generall, that people who would willingly adventure themselves hither, are through feare thereof diverted, and by that meanes the supplies of particuler men[2] and the well seating his majesties country very much obstructed, *Be it therefore enacted* that every master shall provide for his servants component dyett, clothing and lodging, and that he shall not exceed the bounds of moderation in correcting them beyond the meritt of their offences; and that it shalbe lawfull for any servant giving notice to their masters (haveing just cause of complaint against them) for harsh and bad usage, or else for want of dyett or convenient necessaries to repaire to the next commissioner to make his or their complaint, and if the said commissioner shall find by just proofes that the said servants cause of complaint is just the said commissioner is hereby required to give order for the warning of such master to the next county court

---

[2] The King of England was scandalized to discover that two of every three soldiers in New England were white slaves. Also, 1660 saw Virginia Planters so short on servants, from working them to death, that they began buying free whites from Indians in large quantities.

Yes, read that last sentence again.

where the matter in difference shalbe determined,
and the servant have remedy for his grievances.

'To Be Admitted to the Sacrament'

1662–67: The Years During Which Blacks Became Slaves by Birth in English Virginia

The author's comments are in italics.

December 1662 (Hening, Vol. 2, page 170, ACT XII)

WHEREAS some doubts have arrisen whether children got by any Englishman upon a negro woman should be slave or ffree, *Be it therefore enacted and declared by this present grand assembly,* that all children borne in this country shalbe held bond or free only according to the condition of the mother, *And* that if any christian shall committ ffornication with a negro man or woman, hee or shee soe offending shall pay double the ffines imposed by the former act.

This was a false ruling, a lie at its legislative birth, as white women bred by their masters with negro men had their children taken as slaves for life by law, from this point on.

September 1667 (Hening, Vol. 2, page 260, ACT III)

WHEREAS some doubts have risen whether children that are slaves by birth, and by the charity and piety of their owners made pertakers of the blessed sacrament of baptisme, should by vertue of their baptisme be made ffree; It is enacted and declared by this grand assembly, and the authority thereof, that the conferring of baptisme doth not alter the condition of the person as to his bondage or ffreedome; that diverse masters, ffreed from this doubt, may more carefully endeavour the propagation of christianity by permitting children, though slaves, or those of greater growth if capable to be admitted to that sacrament.

The docile nature of negro slaves compared to white slaves is indicated, in part, by the near universal adoption of Christianity by black American slaves, including their hunger for scriptural enlightenment even against the desire of their masters, where, by contrast, escaped white slaves often renounced their English heritage and Christian faith in favor of native adoption.

'By Hue and Crye'

1670–72 The Years in which Blacks and Indians Were Barred from Their Previous Privilege of Owning and Trafficking Englishmen

The author's comments are in italics.

October 1670 (Hening, Vol. 2, page 280-1, ACT V)

WHEREAS it hath beene questioned whither Indians or negroes manumited, or otherwise free, could be capable of purchasing christian servants, It is enacted that noe negroe or Indian though baptised and enjoyned their owne ffreedome shall be capable of any such purchase of christians, but yet not debarred from buying any of their owne nation.

This law is clear evidence that: 1) Indians and blacks had owned whites up to this point; 2) that they were free citizens often enough to experience success as landowners, necessitating the ownership of people, and current with this statute, enjoyed the ownership of humans of their own race; and that 3) there had hitherto been no limitations on ownership of people based on racial status, indicating that Virginia had been a total slave matrix up to this point.

September 1672 (Hening, Vol. 2, page 299, ACT VIII)

FORASMUCH as it hath beene manifested to this grand assembly that many negroes have lately beene, and now are out in rebellion in sundry parts of this country, and that noe meanes have yet beene found for the apprehension and suppression of them from whome many mischeifes of very dangerous consequence may arise to the country if either other negroes, Indians or servants should happen to fly forth and joyne with them; for the prevention of which, *be it enacted by the governour, councell and burgesses of this grand assembly, and by the authority thereof,* that if any negroe, molatto, Indian slave, or servant for life, runaway and shalbe persued by the warrant or hue and crye, it shall and may be lawfull for any person who shall endeavour to take them, upon the resistance of such negroe, molatto, Indian slave, or servant for life, to kill or wound him or them soe resisting; *Provided alwayes,* and it is the true intent and meaning hereof, that such negroe, molatto, Indian slave, or servant for life, be named and described in the hue and crye which is alsoe to be signed by the master or owner of the said runaway. And if it happen that such negroe, molatto, Indian slave, or servant for life doe dye of any wound in such their resistance received the master or owner of such shall receive satisfaction from the publique for his negroe, molatto, Indian slave, or servant for life, soe killed or dyeing of such wounds; and the person who shall kill or wound by virtue of any such hugh and crye any such soe resisting in manner as aforesaid shall not be questioned for the same, he forthwith giveing notice thereof and returning the hue and crye or warrant to the master or owner of him or them soe killed or wounded or to the next justice of peace....

This evil document was a hunting license to kill escaped slaves of all four races, including the "servant for life" unfree white persons numbering in the thousands in colonial Virginia, who were held in the exact conditions as the sainted negro martyrs of revisionist history, who supposedly suffered this indignity alone. This rebellious situation and its expansion, so dreaded by the drafters of this statute, would continue to worsen and lead to Bacon's Rebellion four years later. The statute also confirms the ruling from 1667 that blacks and mulattoes were considered natural born slaves and that whites and Indians were not regarded as destined for servitude from birth.

'Or Other Slaves'

The 1680 Virginia Law That Said It All

June 1680 (Hening, Vol. 2, page 481-2, ACT X)

WHEREAS the frequent meeting of considerable numbers of negroe slaves under pretence of feasts and burialls in is judged of dangerous consequence[1]; for prevention whereof for the future, *Bee it enacted by the kings most excellent*

---

[1] After Bacon's Rebellion in 1676, and the Tobacco Cutting Riots when Thomas Hellier butchered his owners in 1678, and with shipments of blacks straight from Africa then numbering 5,000 a year [though 10,000 whites were also shipped into the colony that year], the masters were right to fear uprisings as they were flooding the land with unfree people, most of whom would die in bondage, and in 1682 the last joint white-black uprising would occur. Frequent burials should say something about the hellish conditions of plantation.

* In each of these clauses, "or [other] slave" is a clear reference to white slaves, as the Indians were all but gone from settled areas by this point, with Bacon having wiped out the Richmond Falls tribe of slave-catching Indians allied to the Governor in 1676. The fact that the term *slaves* is used rather than simply *negroe* is a direct refutation of the belief that only blacks were enslaved.

majestie by and with the consent of the generall assembly, and it is hereby enacted by the authority aforesaid, that frm and after the publication of this law, it shall not be lawfull for any negroe or other slave* to carry or arme himselfe with any club, staffe, gunn, sword or any other weapon of defence or offence, nor to goe or depart from of his masters[2] ground without a certificate from his master, mistris or overseer, and such permission not to be granted but upon perticuler and necessary occasions; and every negroe or slave* soe offending not haveing a certificate as aforesaid shalbe sent to the next constable, who is hereby enjoyned and required to give the said negroe twenty lashes on his bare back well layd on, and soe sent home to his said master, mistris or overseer. *And it is further enacted by the authority aforesaid* that if any negroe or other slave* shall presume to lift up his hand in opposition against any christian, shall for every such offence, upon due proofe made thereof by the oath of the party before a magistrate, have and receive thirty lashes on his bare back well laid on. *And it is hereby further enacted by the authority* that if any negroe or other slave shall absent himselfe from his masters service and lye hid and lurking in obscure places, comitting injuries to the inhabitants, and shall resist any person or persons that shalby any lawfull authority be imployed to apprehend and take the

---

[2] Slave passes are the source of passports, identification cards and driver's licenses.

said negroe, that then in case of such resistance, it shalbe lawfull for such person or persons to kill the said negroe or slave* soe lying out and resisting, and that this law be once every six months published at the respective county courts and parish churches[3] within this colony.

---

[3] Anglican churches provided churchwardens charged with assigning a master to any white child borne out of wedlock, the price for being born a bastard being 31 years a slave!

'Lie Hid and Lurk in Obscure Places'

April 1691 (Hening, Vol. 3, page 86, ACT XVI)

WHEREAS many times negroes, mulattoes, and other slaves[1] unlawfully absent themselves from their masters and mistresses service, and lie hid and lurk in obscure places killing hoggs and committing other injuries[2] to the inhabitants of this dominion, for remedy whereof for the future, *Be it enacted by their majesties lieutenant governour, councell and burgesses of this present generall assembly, and the authoritie thereof, and it is hereby enacted,* that in all such cases upon intelligence of any such negroes, mulattoes, or other slaves[1] lying out, two of their majesties justices of the peace of that county, whereof one to be of the quorum, where such negroes, mulattoes or other slave[1] shall be, shall be

---

[1] White slaves are still being named and are not distinguished from Indian slaves, although they are considered a different, joint category than the half-white mulatto.

[2] The worst offense was killing hogs, the lesser injuries would be theft of crops and tools, injuries in this context indicating financial loss to the legislative class.

impowered and commanded, and are hereby
impowered and commanded to issue out their
warrants directed to the sherrife of the same county
to apprehend such negroes, mulattoes, and other
slaves,[1] which said sherriffe is likewise required
upon all such occasions to raise such and soe many
forces[3] from time to time as he shall think
convenient and necessary for the effectual
apprehending such negroes, mulattoes and other
slaves,[1] and in case any negroes, mulattoes or other
slave[1] or slaves lying out as aforesaid shall resist,
runaway, or refuse to deliver and surrender him or
themselves to any person or persons that shall be by
lawfull authority employed to apprehend and take
such negroes, mulattoes or other slaves[1] that in such
cases it shall and may be lawfull for such person and
persons to kill and distroy such negroes, mulattoes,

---

[3] To raise forces meant conscription, or forced service
as a slave catcher, which would continue to be the
greatest question—though never discussed by
backward-looking modern historians—concerning
black chattel slavery, that poor whites must take time
away from their labors to round up the escaped slave
labor of the planter class. This law would be identical to
Walmart or other massive retailers sponsoring
legislation assigning the duty of rounding up their
shopping carts to nearby small businesses. We moderns
think that slavery was a purely moral issue, when in fact
it was predominantly an economic issue, with the
keystone being the insistence of the slave-owning class
that non-slave owners of far lesser means be charged
with maintenance of the police state and service in its
ranks.

and other slave[1] or slaves by gunn or any otherwaise whatsoever.

Provided that where any negroe or mulattoe slave or slaves shall be killed in pursuance of this act, the owner or owners of such negro or mulatto slave shall be paid for such negro or mulatto slave four thousand pounds of tobacco by the publique.[4]

---

[4] When the rich man's slave has escaped, and the poor man has been forced to recover him, if that slave is killed, the taxpaying collective shall compensate the rich man for his loss! There is a curious absence of the white slave in the last clause. In each of the eight clauses, the white and/or Indian slave [legally the same category] is scrupulously designated. But, when it comes to compensating the slave owner for the killing of his runaway, the collective will not be held accountable for killing a white or Indian runaway. Does this represent the high cost of blacks, which at this stage Maryland planters still complained they could not afford, or does this represent state pressure on slave owners to traffic ever more in blacks and ever less in whites? Keeping in the spirit of these laws, this author suspects that legislating compensation for whites was discouraged to benefit the wealthiest planters, who could better afford the more expensive African servants, at the expense of smaller planters, not of the legislative class, who would be more dependent on cheap white labor.

'That Abominable Mixture and Spurious Issue'

April 1691, Virginia Race-Mixing Statute (Hening, Vol. 3, page 86-8, ACT XVI)

...And for prevention of that abominable mixture and spurious issue which hereafter may encrease in this dominion as well by negroes, mulattoes, and Indians intermarrying with English, or other white women,[1] as by their unlawfull accompanying with one another, *Be it enacted by the authoritie aforesaid, and it is hereby enacted,* That for the time to come, whatsoever English or other white man or woman being free shall intermarry with a negroe, mulatto, or Indian man or woman bond or free[2] shall within three months after such

---

[1] Other white women would have included Irish, Scottish, Welsh, German Catholics from the Rhineland.
[2] Resistance to the planter class was now predominantly in the hands of mixed-race groups of runaways and displaced Indian tribes who had adopted runaways and captives heavily to replace losses from disease. Banishment rather than service was an extreme leap under Virginia law, indicating that substantial

marriage be banished and removed from this dominion forever,[3] and that the justices of each respective countie within this dominion make it their perticular care, that this act be put in effectuall execution, *And be it further enacted by the authoritie aforesaid, and it is hereby enacted,* That if any English woman being free shall have a bastard child by any negro or mulatto, she pay the sume of fifteen pounds sterling, within one moneth after such bastard child shall be born, to the Church wardens of the parish where she shall be delivered of such child, and in default of such payment she shall be taken into the possession of the Church wardens and disposed of for five yeares, and the said fine of fifteen pounds, or whatever the woman shall be disposed of for, shall be paid, one third part to their majesties for and towards the support of the government and the contingent charges thereof, and one other third part to the use of the parish where the offence is committed, and the other third part to the informer,[4] and that such bastard child be bound out as a servant[5] by the said Church wardens untill he or she shall attaine the age of thirty yeares, and in case such English woman that shall have such

---

populations of runaways and mixed-race Indians lived in the hinterlands.

[3] "This dominion" indicates Virginia.

[4] Informers were just as important in plantation America as they were in any 20th century communist regime.

[5] To be "bound out" is to be sold into slavery.

bastard child be a servant, she shall be sold by the said church wardens, (after her time is expired that she ought by law to serve her master) for five yeares, and the money she shall be sold for divided as is before appointed, and the child to serve as aforesaid.

And forasmuch as great inconveniences may happen to this country by the setting of negroes and mulattoes free, by their either entertaining negro slaves from their masters service, or receiveing stolen goods, or being grown old bringing a charge upon the country[6]; for prevention thereof, *Be it enacted by the authority aforesaid, and it is hereby enacted,* That no negro or mulatto be after the end of this present session of assembly set free by any person or persons whatsoever, unless such person or persons, their heires, executors or administrators pay for the transportation of such negro or negroes

---

[6] Slave masters generally had no desire to support worn out old slaves and would typically cast them out, sometimes building an unheated death shack in the winter woods where the person would expire out of sight. Such persons able to make their way to a church might then become "a charge upon the county" as churches were supposed to provide for the destitute. Despite the Anglican Church's deep involvement with human trafficking, its clergy and wardens did abide by a moral code that planters generally spurned, with this legislation being part of the evidence that the church took seriously its role in alleviating the suffering of the destitute, which was an ancient tradition reaffirmed in numerous English "poor laws" since the signing of the Magna Carta in 1215.

out of the countrey within six moneth after such setting them free[7], upon penalty of paying of tenn pounds sterling to the Church wardens of the parish where such person shall dwell with, which money, or so much thereof as shall be necessary, the said Church wardens are to cause the said negro or mulatto to be transported out of the countrey, and the remainder of the said money to imploy to the use of the poor of the parish.

---

[7] Such laws mark a realization that free blacks would, as would whites, assist members of their race to freedom. The absence of communities of free blacks was one of the reasons they were imported at such high expense— that they would have no place to flee. However, as of 1676, maroon communities were living in tribal seclusion in wilderness holdouts [mostly in wetlands, not the mountains where the whites typically fled] and provided a support base for runaways. Thus were enacted laws that would even prevent the first president of the United States from freeing his slaves.

'And other Slaves'

A 1664 Maryland Act of Assembly (Maryland State Archives, Vol. 1, page 533-4, Assembly Proceedings, September 1664)

Bee itt Enacted by the Right Honble the Lord Proprietary by the advice and Consent of the upper and lower house of this present Generall Assembly That all Negroes or other slaves already within the Province And all Negroes and other slaves to bee hereafter imported into the Province shall serve Durante Vita [for life] And all Children born of any Negro or other slave shall be Slaves as their ffathers were for the terme of their lives...

Although the act above clearly denies that negroes were the only people held in slavery, and historians admit that whites were held in slavery under special conditions and that there is zero evidence that Indians were held as slaves in Maryland, and notwithstanding the fact that only the very richest Marylanders could afford to imports blacks until the 1700s, they insist on assuming that 17th century legislators defined slavery as an exclusively negro condition, despite the clear evidence in the statute that this was explicitly not the case.

However, such sources as Wikipedia (article titled *History of Slavery in Maryland*] should be mined, not abandoned, as their footnotes may be traced and the delusional prejudice of modern academics is made clear.

This entry also states the following:

The first documented Africans were brought to Maryland in 1642, as 13 slaves at St. Mary's City, the first English settlement in the Province.

This tiny number of unfree blacks was dwarfed by the average of 10,000 whites brought into English North America every year, with 1623 seeing the sale of 30,000 Irish in Virginia alone. In the 1640s, 300,000 Irish were sold into slavery by the British. Total African imports to English North America did not reach 5,000 per year until the 1680s.

Jubilee

Another Look at Leviticus 25 (New International Version) and its Early American Interpretation

Below, I have arranged the pertinent verses out of order to more clearly define the ethnic basis for chattel bondage from the Old Testament, which in Plantation America, provided justification for the enslavement of Anglicans by Congregationalists, Catholics by Quakers, and heathens by anyone.

44 "'Your male and female slaves are to come from the nations around you[1]; from them you may buy slaves. 45 You may also buy some of the temporary residents living among you and members of their clans born in your country, and they will become your property. 46 You can bequeath them to your children as inherited

---

[1] Temporary residents and people of other nations who were enslaved were not Israelites and therefore did not fit the modern definition of an inhabitant, who in liberal societies are often construed as having rights.

property and can make them slaves for life, but you must not rule over your fellow Israelites ruthlessly.[2]

39 "'If any of your fellow Israelites become poor and sell themselves to you, do not make them work as slaves. 40 They are to be treated as hired workers or temporary residents among you; they are to work for you until the Year of Jubilee. 41 Then they and their children are to be released, and they will go back to their own clans and to the property of their ancestors. 42 Because the Israelites are my servants, whom I brought out of Egypt, they must not be sold as slaves. 43 Do not rule over them ruthlessly[2], but fear your God.

The Year of Jubilee

8 "'Count off seven sabbath years—seven times seven years—so that the seven sabbath years amount to a period of forty-nine years. 9 Then have the trumpet sounded everywhere on the tenth day of the seventh month; on the Day of Atonement sound the trumpet throughout your land. 10 Consecrate the fiftieth year and proclaim liberty throughout the land to all its inhabitants.[1]

54 "'Even if someone is not redeemed in any of these ways, they and their children are to be released in the Year of Jubilee, 55 for the Israelites belong to me as servants.[2] They are my servants,

---

[2] Of those people in bondage, it is clear that only the Israelites are to be spared ruthless treatment, for they are God's servants.

whom I brought out of Egypt. I am the LORD your God.

In summation, these certain passages of Leviticus stood as a clear justification for the holding of people of other nations as chattel—with the idea of Jubilee becoming intertwined in the minds of Christian slaves with the Second Coming. The stumbling block for Christians was the extra-ethnic nature of their faith, igniting debates for centuries over the question of holding any Christian in bondage for life. This drove the trade in Irish Catholics and heathens of various races in the 1600s and 1700s and culminated in the ridiculous excusing of holding negroes in bondage for life based on the biblical claim that the descendants of Noah's disrespectful son, Ham, migrated to Africa and therefore possessed a 5,000-year-old inherited guilt, for which they might be justly punished.

'Three Green Hills'

Cornwall Iron Furnace, Cornwall, Lebanon, County Pennsylvania

Nero the Pict took me as his guest to the only surviving intact charcoal cold blast furnace in the Western Hemisphere. This was a self-contained iron plantation, founded in 1742 by Peter Grubb, purchased by Robert Coleman in 1798 and operated by his descendants through 1883.

Numerous advertisements for runaway slaves, both black and white, were featured in the second half of the 1700s in local and Philadelphia gazettes.

Originally, most of the 23 workers were unfree servants. But by the 1800s, only colliers and woodcutters were unfree men, living in the woods year-round, tending charcoal hearths as they turned the primeval forest into a moonscape like Saruman's orks. By the mid-1800s, there were 150 company houses, a company store and paid child labor, with boys of eight used to haul slag, wives of employees engaged in domestic work and servants relegated to the family mansion, the charcoal hearths and receding forest. The three iron-rich hills were green no more. This iron plantation was the prototype of the self-contained company mining town of Appalachia that kept its employees impoverished like industrial sharecroppers as a more sophisticated system of debt-servitude was brought into being, featuring the hostage family of a man who typically died from his labors by age 40.

Temperatures in the various rooms of the forge where servants toiled ranged from 115-156 degrees. The attendants worked in gangs of 15 for 12 hours, keeping the furnace stoked for 11 months and rebricking it for one month during winter, when the water of the stream that provided its power iced up. Most lumbering was done during the winter, a very dangerous business with nothing but axes. A typical worker cut two cords of wood per day. The men who hauled the ore and charcoal in one-man buggies, which must have weighed at least 200 pounds empty, were operating under extreme labor conditions which would require power lifters and weight lifters of today's men.

There was only one negro slave woman employed at the forge, along with records of four white women.

The Cornwall Iron Furnace fits neatly into the very limited picture of African-American servitude in the State of Pennsylvania:

1681: The foundation of the Province of Pennsylvania employed white slaves and barred the trade in black slaves.

1727: The African slave trade was sanctioned in Pennsylvania.

1769: The first African slaves were worked at the forge, though they never accounted for half or more of the slaves.

1790: The number of African slaves at the furnace dwindled.

1796: On 17 April, 1796, "Governor Dick," a famously productive woodchopping African, with scarified face and a cleaved toe, made his escape and had still not been recovered by July 8, when an advertisement for his capture was posted.

1798: Slaves of African descent were no longer employed on the plantation.

1800s: Though some number of white slaves were employed as domestics in the main house and woodcutters and colliers in the woods, their numbers dwindled as the staff of the Cornwall Iron Plantation evolved into an integrated, mixed-race workforce of men who depended on the company for housing for their families and lived from hand-to-mouth, with barely enough income to survive on goods purchased at the company store, but they received a Christmas turkey and were seemingly free of the brutal beatings meted out to sailors, workhouse inmates and agricultural slaves.

One must remember that virtually all the forests of Pennsylvania were clear cut, and most of those in our age are young, allowed to grow after food production moved to the Ohio Valley and later the Great Plains in the second half of the 19th century.

Whipt and Branded

An Example of What Men Risked When They Went to Sea in the Age of Sail (French)

To George Washington from Robert French, 24 April 1789

From Robert French

St Croix 24t Apl 1789

Heads of a Petition from Rt French, Mariner of Philadelphia Confin'd in the Fort, Island St Croix

To his Excellency the President and To The Right Honourable the senate and Congress of the United States the humble petition of Rt French respectfully Sheweth, that Your humble petitioner has a truly distress'd Family of a Wife and two Children in Philadelphia, that he has been a true and faithful Subject of the United States since the Year 1778 the period when he arriv'd there, from which period 'till his present Misfortune he has supported an irreproachable Character in every Capacity that a Mariner can serve on board, a Merchantman, and in all according to the Laws of Commerce—your humble petitioner, hopes from a consideration of those Facts, and the following, that Your honours will cause him to be demanded from the Danish Government, to be sent for to Philadelphia there to be tried by the Laws of his Country.

The Cause of Your humble petitioners request is as follows—In the Month June Last 88 I commanded a Sloop of Mr Jno. Wilcocks to this Island (Your humble Petitioner Previous to this Command had been involv'd in Debt by the failure of a Mr Geo. Henry a Ship of whose he Commanded) in the Latter of sd Month being ready for Sea, I receiv'd from Mr Wilcocks the Sum of 96 half Joannes's to be delivered here to Messrs Wm & Saml Newton Unexpected Demands coming on me the very Day I sail'd from Philadelphia I Made Use of part of this Money, being well Assured I had Venture on board more than sufficient to reimburse the Money. I Navigated the Vessel & took Care of her & Cargo to the best of my Knowledge, And arriv'd safe in this port, both Vessel and Cargo in good order, Notwithstanding the very severe Gales Wind we had and the Quantity of Water the Vessel made, which I think wou'd have Justified me in putting in to any other port, where, had my intentions been to Defraud, I might have left the Vessel, immediately on my Arrival here I acquainted the Mr Newtons with the Sum I had received Delivered their Letters with Bill of Lading inclos'd; I us'd every Effort to dispose of my

Venture in order to make up the Money but it all prov'd ineffectual, three Days after my Arrival here I went to St Thomas a Danish Island 8 Leagues Dist. from St Croix in order to dispose of a few Articles which I compleated & was on the point of my return the Afternoon of the same Day I left this Island, when a Kings Sloop arriv'd with Orders from his Exellency the General of those Islands to apprehend me, in Vain did I beg to be sent over to this Island to deliver up the Effects I had for the Benefit of Mr Wilcocks. I was carried to the Fort and close Confin'd in a most miserable Room the description of which wou'd strike terror into the breast of any Human being. I was continued there for 10 Days then brought over here and lodg'd in close Confinement no person being Admitted to See me. I was carried after some time under a Strong Guard to Court, where I acknowledg'd the receipt of the Money Told the Necessities that Urdg'd me to lay it out, & the Means I had of reimbursing it, inform'd the Court that I appeal'd to the laws of my Country for there, and against them I had transgress'd and that not intentionally, after the expiration of 3 Months Judgment came out of the lower Court wherein it was declar'd that nothing Criminal was in my Case, and that it did not come Under the Danish Law. his Excellency the General at whose option it lies whether to Ratify a Judgment or not, and at the Same time was my prosecutor, appeal'd it to the upper Court here, after the expiration of three Months without ever been call'd to Court, to Defend myself, there was a most Dreadful Sentance read off to me.

It is that I am to pay the Sum in the Bill Lading Viz. 96 Joes Double that to the King as fine, to be Whipt and Branded under the Gallows all my Effects to be forfeited to the King, then put in Irons & there to remain during Life.[1]

Oh Merciful God to thee & the Laws of my Country I appeal for Mercy.

I have appeal'd to the Supreme Court in Copenhagen in order to gain time to lay my dreadful Situation before Your honours & most Humbly begs & prays for your humane interpositions, as I have never in the smallest matter Transgress'd Against the Laws of Denmark. I will chearfully Submit to the Laws of my Country, and with a Christian like resignation receive the Judgt

---

[1] A sea captain with no criminal history, a free man, is to be whipped and branded, his freedom taken for life and the evidence for this exists in our National Archives, yet, most historians take great pains to declare that slaves were not beaten and branded, and that no white man would ever be held in bondage for life. Right Wing historians, such as Jared Taylor, descendent of prominent slave owners, will deny that black slaves were cruelly treated as a matter of course. Likewise, Leftist historians, such as Breen, will deny that white slaves were beaten and branded in the same manner as blacks were. Neither face of the forever bartered coin of our great lie tells the truth but merely offers an alternative to it.

my unhappy Case may be deem'd deserving of[.] I Humbly beg & pray that your Honours will be pleas'd to take my Case into Consideration, that I may have the Benefit of those Laws, that I have Fought for & Bled to Support And in Duty I shall for Ever pray

Rt French

'My Enemy Passing By'

The Sand-Hills' Crest by Robert E. Howard,
Reading from *A Word from the Outer Dark*, pages 22–
4

Although a racialist who appears to have
believed in blood memory, among Howard's
strongest recurring themes is what I have labeled
Trails, the idea that the man takes on some of the
character of and is literally sculpted—mentally,
spiritually and physically—by his habitat, by his
man-forging path through the crucible of life.

The Sand-Hill's Crest is a tale of bitter failure,
poverty, proud heritage, emasculation, traitor-
dealing, moon-shining and fatalistic retribution.

A son of Tennessee and the Confederacy has
fallen by stages from the social and material
standards of his ancestors and now suffers as a
bondman, a self-sold slave in the post oak region of
East Texas, where his only freedom is distilling corn
liquor in secret. He has been discovered and turned
in by a neighbor and aims to set things right,

harboring no illusions that he will get away with the crime of True Justice.

The nine verses range from four to 16 lines and are densely set in westward ethnic pride:

(When my grandfather was a lad,

A hundred slaves his father had;

He clothed them better than I am clad.

They were sleek and fat and prime,

I've been hungry many a time.

They fed full, child man and wife;

I've been hungry most of my life.)

"I found a man to go my bond—he knows that I won't run..."

In modern times, we see bonding as insurance that a housekeeper or security guard will not steal our things and if they do, we are compensated by the third-party insurer. But as recently as the 1920s, Americans understood that to be bonded is to be owned and that running away is a theft of your master's property—which is the very person of the bondman. This is still accurately reflected in the trade of the bail bondsman, who enslaves people as a mercenary overseer of the current police state and is often regarded as a hero, lionized in film and reality TV.

To get a better picture of our American past, understand that to owe even a dollar was a crime and that losing your freedom was a direct result of the debt, not of a failure to pay off the debt according to some schedule. Where we are now owned surreptitiously by a free-range corporate debt slavery system, our ancestors were owned as cattle for falling even a day's wage into debt. One ruse that was used to enslave Scottish boys in the 1700s was the gift of a hat, a jacket or a meal by a friendly adult. Then, once the boy had donned his cap or eaten his meal, he was owned and sold for periods ranging from 7 to 31 years.

Slavery and Survival

Would You Submit to Slavery? Getting into the Mental Space of Plantation America

If you lived in Plantation America, would you submit to slavery?

We would all like to think not.

So, what questions can we honestly ask ourselves about life today that might give us a slave's-eye view of life when most men were owned like cattle?

If a tactical squad kicked in your front door while you were eating breakfast, would you fight to the death with a kitchen knife, put up a token struggle or go easily?

You might say that you are not a criminal and would never face such a situation. However, every day in Baltimore, an innocent person is arrested by armed goons in blue.

Do you die, do you take a face-saving beating and then do deep time or do you go easily, hoping to talk or work yourself free?

If you chose the last two, you, like most people, are more willing to wear another man's chains than to die fighting as a free man.

If You Were Born a Slave, Would You Run Away?

This is easy, would you quit school or your job, steal the principal's or boss's car, flee across state lines and try to assume a new identity?

That is the postmodern equivalent to running away from your master in early modern times.

You must keep in mind that a slave was essentially a large piece of equipment, which would be equal in value to a motorcycle or automobile. You would not be running away from injustice as we see it but stealing, travelling without permission, crossing state lines without permission and committing fraud. These were all capital crimes. Honestly, the only type of people who ran away in Plantation America were the type of folks inclined to committing felonies, for running away even one time was the commission of at least three felonies by today's standards:

1. Theft of self

2. Theft of clothes

3. Travelling without a permit [driver's license]

4. Travelling without authorizing documents [passport]

5. Assuming a false identity, entailing forgery and giving false testimony

6. Sometimes theft of a horse or boat

About Slavery

Baruch and James on First-Person Servitude

I spent eight years in the military, which is basically indentured servitude.

One of the funniest things you hear from civilians is, "I couldn't do the military—I don't like taking orders."

It's funny because they are so far removed mentally from the reality of being a soldier that they might as well be imagining life as an astronaut: "Ah, man, I couldn't deal with all those aliens popping out of people's chests!"

I would have no problem with a term of slavery if the owner played it straight. If it was one of those deals where the guy tries to kill you though overwork and hunger or to add to your time, I'd take my chances with the law and Indians...

-Baruch

Baruch's perspective has been echoed by other "servicemen" I have known, who make no bones about the fact that they were "owned" or "the property of" their branch of the armed forces of their nation.

At this point, as we delve into the psychology of a Plantation world, of a matrix in which being the property of a person who had more rights to your body than you did, was the norm in society, we should make two things clear:

1. As Baruch said, "if the owner played it straight," meaning, as was intended, a probable seven-year term of servitude [a third of the expected productive life of a man] is not unreasonable in light of the fact that government employees in our time are mentally owned for the same ratio of their productive life. The abuses—gross abuses—that emerged in this system from the outset were not an aim and could fall under the rubric of unintentional, if predictable, consequences of such a system. Mind you that the English Plantation system was based on family values—the beating of children being a core Anglo-Saxon family value—and that it was inspired, justified and regulated by Scripture and Gospel, the very books which had given hope to the poor for a millennium, and was in no ways intended to be cruel.

2. Going back to our government employee analogy. An employee is one "to be used," to "be employed," with this term coming from the French for tool and having the same social roots as *boy* [English male slave], *servant, serf, servile, service*, all coming down through the Latin from human property, *thrall*, the Norse term for human

property, *slave*, the Arabic term for Slavic sexual property, flowing to us on the many-branched and crooked trail of human ownership down to our present deluded day. Believe me, the modern government employee, and by extension the American citizen in general—for the government employee is the house slave to the American Citizen's field slave—the modern American Civil Servant [that word meant slave through all of history, until now] is every bit as owned in his mind, opinion and feelings as the orphan boys of Jamestown and Plymouth Colony were in body.

On their death beds, the Duty Boys, who were bought, owned and worked to death by Puritanical slave master William Bradford, refused to convert to his religion even as he offered salvation [and presumably better medical care] as they lay dying. These illiterate slaves of the sainted founders of our sick nation remained who they were to the grave—emaciated little heroes in the face of Death, turning their backs on the mind games of their cruel earthly master. Yet, the modern person, whose body is sacrosanct— worshipped in its ideal forms in the media, tended to by our largest institutions [hospitals] and assigned natural rights in the temples [courts] of this temporal cult—may not utter an opinion considered cross by his mind masters, may not sign his name to a dissenting view of society without the very real and proximate fear of ostracism [the eldest of human penalties] and oral exile, may not disagree with his master without being labeled "monster," "Nazi," "coon" or "white devil."

Have we really left slavery behind?

Is it a coincidence that public and academic discourse on the matter has assigned the terms of *master* and *slave* exclusively to the ownership of the body and excluding the concept of ownership of the mind?

The following series of analogies will seek to establish a common link with us and our more grossly brutalized ancestors, beginning with what was well-intentioned and morally high-minded about the establishment of white slavery in Plantation America, then documenting how this social framework twisted into something monstrous.

In the end though, we should not forget that the evidence points to roughly as many slave masters "playing it straight" as took the monstrous road. In actuality, many more slave masters than not were well-intentioned people who "played it straight." The problem was, the ones who played it crooked went through many more slaves and hence became bitterness engines that fueled hate and retribution as most slaves were funneled through their cruel clutches, as the decent owners of human beings had a much higher employee retention level back when labor retention literally meant keeping your boys and girls alive.

Richard Spencer Can't Read or Write?

Signatories and Objectors to the Declaration of Independence in Harford County Maryland, from Geneology Trails, with footnotes by the author and additional comments in *italics*.

The names of the men who signed and declined to sign this document will be compared with the runaway servant advertisements from the period to determine if runaways and their descendants were more or less likely to side with the crown or the provincial landowners. Thanks to Mescaline Franklin for this find.

Association of Freemen of Maryland

There were in Harford County by the census of 1840 ten persons drawing pensions as soldiers of the Revolutionary War. They were Andrew McAdow, Jarret Tracey, Thomas Schivington, William Sloan, Henry Long, John Heaps and Archibald Heaps.

The following named persons were designated by the Harford Committee to solicit subscriptions to the Association of the Freemen of Maryland, viz:

Deer Creek Upper—John Donohoo, Wm. Fisher, Jr., and Alex. Rigdon.

Deer Creek Lower—John Winston Dallam.

Bush Upper—William McComas, Jr., John Kean and Robert Harris.

Spesutie Upper—James Moores, (tanner), Bennet Mathews, James Clendenin and David Clark.

Spesutie Lower—Edward Hall, Jacob Forwood, Francis Holland.

Susquehanna—James Horner, John Rodgers, John Rumsey, Samuel Howell and Samuel Bayless.

Gunpowder Lower—Henry Wetherall, John Day, Jr., John Durham, Alex. Cowan, Benjamin Rumsey.

Bush Lower—John Taylor, Gabriel Vanhorn, William Bond, Henry Wilson, Jr.

(From a detached paper from the clerk's office, 1776:)

Note that all the signatories are given according to what river or creek they lived on, as these were the highways and power sources of the age.

A List Of Non-Associators

Benj. Herbert, Jr., refuses to sign through religious principles.

Richard Hargrove refuses to sign through religious principles.

William Wilson, son of John, refuses to sign through religious principles.

Benj. Harboard refuses to sign through religious principles.[1]

Michael Bocer don't sign by reason he signed before.

Thomas Gilbert don't sign by reason he don't choose it.

Thos. West don't sign by reason it is a mystery to him.

Philip Cummins don't sign by reason he don't understand the matter.

John Ward don't sign by reason the Congress don't sign and by reason he thinks that if the English gain the day then the Congress and the great people will turn the scale and say the commonality of people force them to stand in opposition to the English.[2]

---

[1] In Maryland more likely because they were Anglicans [members of the Church of England] than that they were pacifists Congregationalists.
[2] This demonstrates a deeper distrust of colonial politicians than royal officials, suggesting he may have been a slave.

John Clark don't sign by no reason he can give.

Ephraim Arnold don't sign for fear it would fetch him into a scrape.

Isaac Penrose don't sign for reason he don't choose to fight for liberty and never will.[3]

Benjamin Fleetwood refuses to sign. He says he will go in a vessel, but will not fight by land.

Samuel Gallion says if he should sign he may fetch on himself that he cannot go through.

Richard Spencer says he cannot write nor read, and shall not sign any paper.

—History of Harford County, Maryland: From 1608 (the Year of Smith's Expedition) to the Close of the War of 1812, Walter Wilkes Preston, 1901 sd

The signers outnumbered those who abstained 29 to 14, roughly 2–1, if we take Michael Bocer at his word.

Thanks to the publishers of the Geneology Trails website for the preservation and use of this historical document. Please patronize their site (see bibliography entry: (Trails)).

---

[3] This was understood to be liberty from England for the landed class, not liberty of common men from servitude under the landed class. Indeed, the Articles of Confederation and eventually the Constitution would strengthen and affirm the power of landowners over the lower class.

'Manly Opposition to Uncontroulable Tyranny'

Declaration of the Association of the Freemen of Maryland, July 26, 1775 (Archives of Maryland, Vol. 78, page 17)

The long premeditated, and now avowed design of the British government, to raise a revenue from the property of the colonists, without their consent, on the gift, grant, and disposition of the commons of Great Britain; and the arbitrary and vindictive statutes passed under colour of punishing a riot, to subdue by military force, and by famine, the Massachusetts bay; the unlimited power assumed by parliament to alter the charter of that province, and the constitutions of all the colonies, thereby destroying the essential securities of the lives, liberties, and properties of the colonists; the commencement of hostilities by the ministerial forces, and the cruel prosecution of the war against the people of the Massachusetts bay, followed by general Gage's proclamation, declaring almost the whole of the inhabitants of the united colonies, by name or description, rebels and traitors; are sufficient causes to arm a free people in defence of their liberty, and justify resistance, no longer dictated by prudence merely, but by necessity, and leave no other alternative but base submission, or manly opposition, to uncontrollable tyranny. The congress chose the latter, and for the express purpose of securing and defending the united colonies, and preserving them in safety against all attempts to carry the above mentioned acts into execution by force of arms, Resolved, That the said colonies be immediately put into a state of defence, and now supports, at the joint expense, an army to restrain the further violence, and repel the future attacks, of a disappointed and exasperated enemy.

We, therefore, inhabitants of the province of Maryland, firmly persuaded that it is necessary and justifiable to repel force by force, do approve of the opposition by arms, to the British troops employ to enforce obedience to the late acts and statutes of the British parliament, for raising a revenue in America, and altering and changing the charter and constitution of the Massachusetts bay, and for destroying the essential securities for the lives, liberties, and properties of the subjects in the united colonies. And we do unite and associate as one band, and firmly and solemnly engage and pledge ourselves to each other, and to America, that we will, to the utmost of our power, promote and support the present opposition, carrying on, as well by arms, as by the continental association, restraining our commerce.

And as in these, limes of public danger, and until a reconciliation with Great Britain, on constitutional principles, is effected, (an event we most ardently wish may soon take place) the energy of government may be greatly impaired, so that even zeal unrestrained may bo productive of anarchy and confusion; we do, in like manner unite, associate and solemnly engage, in maintenance of good order and the public peace, to support the civil power in the due execution of the laws, so far as may be consistent with the present plan of opposition, and to defend, with our utmost power, all persons from every species of outrage to themselves or their property[1], and to prevent any punishment from being inflicted on any offenders, other than such as shall be adjudged by the civil magistrate, the continental congress, our convention, council of safety, or committees of observation.

Signatories

The signatories below will be compared with escaped servants in the Maryland Appendices to determine the ratio of escaped servants that made it into the propertied class.

---

[1] Two-thirds of humans in Maryland were listed as property, not as citizens.

Mat.
Tilghman
John Reeder
Junr
Richd
Barnes
Jereh Jordan
Jn. A.
Thomas
W.
Smallwoo
d
Danl Jenifer
R. Hooe
J. H. Stone
Will.
Harrison
S. Hanson of
Sam.
Jno. Dent
Edwd Gantt
Samuel
Chew
Edwd
Reynolds
Benj.
Mackall
4th
Josia Beall
Robt. Tyler
Rhos Contee
Joseph Sim
Turbutt
Wright
Jas.
Tilghman

of
Annapolis
Th. Wright
Jas Hollyday
Rd Earle
Soln Wright
Jas Loyd
Chamb-
erlaine
Nic.
Thomas
Edwd Lloyd
Peregrine
Tilghman
Wm
Hindman
R. Tilghman
Jun.
Rams
Benson
F. Baker
Benn Hall
John Contee
W. Bowie
O. Sprigg
Jos. Beall
Thos Gantt
Junior
Walter
Bowie
David
Crauford
Stephen
West
Tho. Sim
Lee

J. Rogers
Samuel
Chase
Th. Johnson
Junr
Brice B.
Worth-
ington
Rezin
Hammon
d
J. Hall
William
Paca
Matthias
Hammon
d
Chas.
Carroll
Chas.
Carroll of
Carrollto
n
Ephraim
Howard
of Hy
Thomas
Dorsey
Robert
Golds-
borough
Henry
Hooper
James
Murray

Thos
   Ennalls
Nath. Potter
Will,
   Richardso
   n
Richd
   Mason
Joshua Clark
Peter Adams
John
   Stevens
Wm Hopper
Henry
   Dickinson
Wm Waters
Wm
   Rolleston
George
   Dashiell
John Waters
Gustavus
   Scott
H. Griffith
Th. Sprigg
   Wootton
Richd.
   Brooke
John
   Hanson Jr
Joseph
   Chapline

Thos.
   Cramphi
   n Jr
Upton
   Sheredine
Benj.
   Nicholso
   n
Wm.
   Buchanan
J. Toy Chase
John
   Cradock
Thomas
   Harrison
Darby Lux
John Moale
Robt
   Alexande
   r
Chas
   Ridgely
   son of
   Wm
Saml.
   Handy
Sadok
   Purnell
Wm. Morris
Thos Stone
Benect
   Edwd
   Hall

Ths Bond
Richd
   Dallam
Ignatius
   Wheeler
   Jr.
Wm. Webb
John Veazey
   Junr
Jno. D.
   Thompso
   n
John Cox
Peter
   Lawson
Nat. Ramsey
William
   Currer
Chas
   Rumsey
W. Ringgold
   Junr
Thos Smyth
Joshh Earle
Th. B.
   Hands
Thos
   Ringgold
J. Nicholson
   Jr.

The 110 signatories, based on the surviving record from Harford County, would represents roughly two-thirds of what would be 160–170 leading men, or freemen, people regarded as sufficiently propertied or of high enough social standing not to be subject to forced labor.

The signatories represent almost exactly 10% of the free population of Maryland, which was 17,100 men and women who owned households and were responsible for dependent children and bound people. Assuming three children per household and rounding up, we arrive at 70,000 free Marylanders.

The population of Maryland (Springston) is said to have stood as high as 300,000, but the 1770 census, counted 202,599, suggesting that the 1776 population was no more than 250,000 and probably far less. For this analysis, I will estimate a population of 210,000, as a minimum, with the maximum free Marylanders at 70,000 making the most optimistic ratio of free to unfree Marylanders at 1 in 3.

By 1755, 40% of Marylanders were "black," though white slaves for life were counted as black as well as Asians and mixed-race people by this method. To declare any more than 35% of Marylanders black at this period is a gross exaggeration. Working with such politicized numbers, the best conclusion for the period between the French and Indian and Revolutionary Wars for Maryland is that Maryland was split into three roughly equal demographics, free whites, unfree whites and unfree blacks, with small numbers of free blacks.

The Wikipedia page "History of Slavery in Maryland" is patently false in some regards, suggesting that conditions for whites in Europe improved in the 1640s and African imports were used to fill the gap. This is a criminal abolition of facts:

My Slave Name

Genetic Testing Supports Family Tradition

My Grandmother LaFond always told us that she was descended from British orphans who had been sold to French Canadians. She was named Alberta Roy by her parents. I always found it interesting—and cute—that my grandfather, who passed when I was six and who in retrospect seems to have been something of a Hobbit, used to call her Roy, reminding her of her maiden name, indicating his relatively affluent French lineage.

My youngest son recently had one of these commercial genetic tests done, indicating that he inherited a relatively high proportion of Neanderthal genes among other things. He was skeptical of the test to begin with and chose one that confirms various attributes he could check.

Virtually all of his ancestry is English and Irish, with there being a distinction between the two according to this scheme. [I suppose all of that English-master rape of Irish-slaves muddied the genome quite a bit.] The fascinating finding is that my son has no trace of French ancestry—so Grandma was right: she and her husband were both English after all.

Another slave trace in his test is the finding that on his mother's side, there was, in the 1700s, a Jewish father. This makes good sense in that, according to the genealogy that his mother's uncle did, their family is descended from Cornish slaves who escaped from their slave masters in New York, where the slave trade was dominated by Dutch Jews—no slave name, but some slave rape, on that side. It seems that my Irish slave ancestors, shipped to Maryland in the 1630s were not the only pale chattel in our family heritage.

To me, though, the most important thing is that some of our Neanderthal ancestors raped some modern human bitches while their homeland was being overrun.

'Gallantry'

On Confederate Hill with Nero the Pict, Tuesday, May 8, 2018

My good friend Nero the Pict and I had three hours to find Confederate Hill in Loudon Park, between Wilkens and Frederick Avenues in West Baltimore, before meeting Erique for training.

At the front gate of the park are buried about a regiment's worth of Maryland Union soldiery, right on the main drag, where the descendants of those they fought to free sell dope and murder at cut-rate prices.

Further back in the cemetery, beneath centuries old oaks, which the grounds keepers are letting fall prey to parasitic vines, are buried a battalion-strength of Maryland Confederates, 650 in number.

Five large monuments grace the hill overlooking an abandoned, bronze-doored church, buried in the opposite hillside, a elegantly haunted hilltop, tastefully away from the Yankee road and so much more appropriate to the Lost Cause these men fought for.

A relation of John Wilkes Booth's lies there under sunny turf.

A number of unknown soldiers lie their somewhat accounted for among the ranks of others, from Alabama, to Georgia to Maryland, mostly men who died of starvation and illness at Point Lookout between October 1864 and February 1865.

Among them was a member of a Maryland Artillery unit who won the Confederacy's highest honor and survived the war into honored old age.

A man who commanded cavalry in a Maryland raid has a monument dedicated to his gallantry in the soft shade of the massive oak.

Next to him, beneath the monument to an unnamed Confederate Army general reminiscent of Robert E. Lee, the wife of this grey rider has her own better preserved and touchingly inscribed monument, proclaiming her a woman of grace.

Among them is a monument to a youth who was slaughtered by federal troops in the paleface Baltimore Riot.

Most striking to me was that this hill for the remembrance of those we hate, because they were better than we, has retained the solitude of a time earlier than theirs, under the shade of a tree that three men could barely join hands around, a tree such as their slave ancestors felled by the millions to make this land ripe for the twin tyrannies that would deprive them of prosperity, march them off to war, kill them and then replace them.

The irony is that they fought to preserve their own poverty at the hands of a slave race, and their masters and those who defeated them ultimately fought to ensure that their descendants would be driven from their hometown by the savage scions of those they freed.

Seeing the many battle flags and remembrance cards left by an organization dedicated to preserving their memory and measuring the grace of their shaded place next to the ranked white rows of Union boys whose headstones face one of the most blighted boulevards of their ravaged hometown, one wonders if it's better to fight for the cause bought and lost or the one won and sold?

Perhaps it is only of importance that these men remind us that there was once a time when men were credited for loyalty and courage rather than having the luck of being owned by the winning machine.

1865 marked the end of the gross, government-mandated ownership of humans and the advent of its refined evolution, a world where one is reduced to a debt cipher and must either be alternately lied to that his people where either the only slaves or never slaves, so that the debtor might not be haunted by the fact that he lives under the same exact threats as his shackled and branded ancestor, most likely a doomed youth who was put to murdering the world's largest living things so that his grandchildren might be replaced by a people better designed to thrive in a barren world bereft of their shade.

At least the bones of these 650 men and a few of their women lie beneath a shaded patch of our stone memories, lingering still and stoic in a world dedicated to the collective pursuit of social amnesia.

Runaway Advertisements

A Sample of Annotated Newspaper Subscriptions for the Return of Escaped Bondmen and Bondwomen

Cornwall Furnace: A Photo Study

The photos of runaway ads were taken at Cornwall Furnace in the Autumn of 2017.

The conditions at Grubb's forger were horrendous, with the men performing extremely hard labor in temperatures around 120 degrees Fahrenheit. The wood-cutting job to generate fuel for the furnace was more dangerous than most jobs in Plantation America but was a dream job for the poor men forced to labor for an iron works. In the litany of Maryland runaways at the end of this book will be found numerous crews from at least three Maryland furnaces that ran away as a team, some wearing shackles. Imagine working in 120-degree heat wearing iron and steel collars and leg irons.

London Journal, February 1ⁱ, 1770.

WAS taken up the [...] [...]nt, in this town, on
suspicion of bei[...] [...]y, a man who calls himself Henry Smith, or otherwi[...] [...]ry Easton, a middle-sized
well-set fellow; had on, whe[...] taken up, a grey nap double
breasted jacket, and white swanskin under ditto, a pair of leather breeches, almost new, a pair of brown ribbed worsted
stockings, a pair of shoes, with pewter buckles, a check shirt,
and felt hat; all which clothes are yet pretty good, has brown
hair, and grey eyes; says he worked as a collier, at Mr. Grubb's
Iron-works, last Christmas. Any person, or persons whatsoever,
claiming the said man, as being his or their servant, may come,
pay his charges, and take him away, in three weeks after the
[...] hereof, otherwise he will be sold out for the same, by
                                    GEORGE EASLEY, Gaoler.

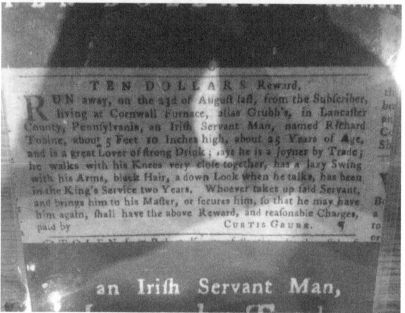

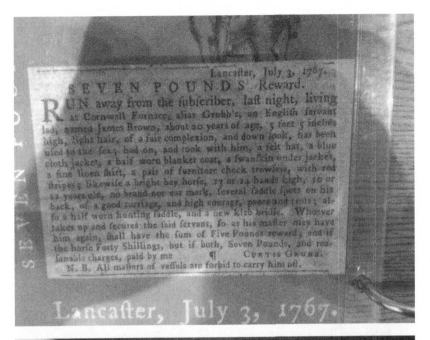

SEVEN POUNDS Reward.

Lancaster, July 3, 1767.

RUN away from the subscriber, last night, living at Cornwall Furnace, alias Grubb's, an English servant lad, named James Brown, about 20 years of age, 5 feet 5 inches high, light hair, of a fair complexion, and down look, has been used to the sea; had on, and took with him, a felt hat, a blue cloth jacket, a half worn blanket coat, a swanskin under jacket, a fine linen shirt, a pair of furniture check trowsers, with red stripes; likewise a bright bay horse, 13 or 14 hands high, 10 or 11 years old, no brand nor ear mark, several saddle spots on his back, of a good carriage, and high courage, paces and trots; also a half worn hunting saddle, and a new kirb bridle. Whoever takes up and secures the said servant, so as his master may have him again, shall have the sum of Five Pounds reward; and if the horse Forty Shillings, but if both, Seven Pounds, and reasonable charges, paid by me ¶ CURTIS GRUBB.

N. B. All masters of vessels are forbid to carry him off.

Lancaster, July 3, 1767.

EIGHT DOLLARS Reward.

RAN AWAY last night from Cornwall Furnace, Lancaster county, an Irish Servant, named ROBERT EARLEY, about 23 or 24 years of age, 5 feet 9 or 10 inches high, round shouldered, much pitted with the small-pox, grey eyes and black hair. Had on and took with him, a coarse grey upper jacket, under ditto, a new pair tow linen trowsers, one pair ditto, partly wore, an old felt hat, and old shoes. It is supposed he will forge a pass, and pretend to be a schoolmaster. Whoever takes up said servant and secures him in any goal, so that his master may get him again, shall receive the above reward, and reasonable charges, if brought home, paid by ¶ CURTIS GRUBB.

May 30, 1785.

an Irish Servant,

named ROBERT EARLEY

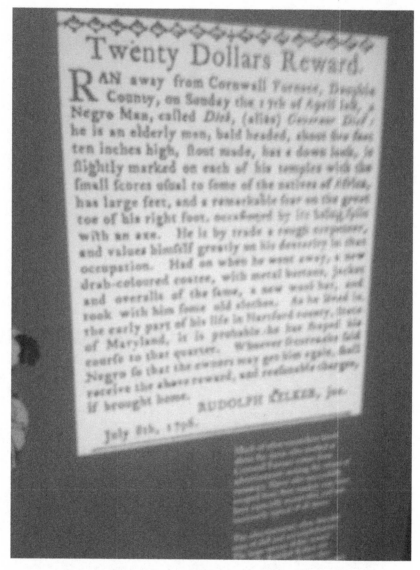

Negro Dick, whose escape notice is reproduced above, was a famous woodcutter who is the subject of the runaway display at the museum, even though he and his African brethren were in the minority among Grubb's slaves. He was apparently the most productive woodcutter in the history of the furnace and brought a great reward.

Runaways by Date -- 'Before the Lord Mayor'

IRELAND OLD NEWS

This is a massive resource which I have used to examine the character of Pennsylvania Dutch Slavery. Along with the accounts of Peter Williamson and Benjamin Franklin, Irish Old News paints a brutal picture of soul-devouring toil under the Christian whip of the profit-centric Protestant Congregationalist pyramid scheme known as Penn's Woods—a forested slave plantation ordained by greed, policed by savage, heathen Indians, blessed by God—a pit into which a million or more souls were fed into the fires of avarice over a century. The sin that was Pennsylvania paved the way for modern corrections systems, municipal licensing, bounty hunting and ultimately the cult of the American frontiersman, as the most able slaves worked, ran or fought their way over the Appalachians, then down the Ohio River and conquered a land dozens of times larger than the slave islands out of which they had been shipped (Flood):

> Passing over twenty years, during which there was a constant stream of emigration from Ireland to America, I find another interesting document chronicled under date of May, 1751:
> "One hundred and fifty Passengers, including 50 Irish Servants (many of them Catholics who were bound as Servants before the Lord Mayor of Dublin) sailed for Philadelphia, on board the Homer, Captain John Slade, Commander." The list of names is not complete, owing to damp, but I have made out the following as among those who sailed on the Homer from Dublin, in May, 1751: John O'Toole, Thomas Cassidy, James Fennell, James O'Neill, James Hickey, Edward Doran, John Callaghan, Catherine Cullen, Eleanor Cody, John Connery, Catherine Lawler, William Coffey, John Slattery, Philip MacNeill, Giles Power, Anne Connolly.

Benjamin Franklin's biographer, Thomas Day, estimated that at the time of the American Revolution, roughly one half of Pennsylvania's labor force was legally unfree—bound to someone else as property, for many years or for a lifetime.

Such second- and third-hand sources are available in the Ireland Old News online archive, along with numerous transcribed slave catcher ads from the 1700s.

'An Irish Papist'

John Lee is Worth an Astonishing 20-Pounds
Reward, Virginia Gazette (Parks) Williamsburg,
March 4 to March 11, 1736 [1737] (Carter)

RAN away from the Subscriber's House in
King George County, the latter End of April last, a
white Irish Servant Man named John Lee, he is by
Trade a Joyner, a short thick well-set Fellow, fresh
Colour'd, pitted with the Small Pox, with a Scar in
his Forehead,[1] speaks through the Nose, and has the
Brogue in his Speech, and stoops forward as he
walks:

He was pursued to Susquehannah Ferry,
where he pawn'd his Rule for his Passage;[2]

The Horse he took with him, was seiz'd near
the Ferry; it is suppos'd he was harbour'd by some

---

[1] Such scars were typically caused by a master or
overseer striking downward with the butt of a whip. A
facial scar is evidence of a confrontational personality in
the person of the slave or servant.
[2] Lee fled through Maryland to the river that must be
crossed to enter Eastern Pennsylvania. He sold the
measuring tool used in his trade.

of the Irish Inhabitants in these Parts[3], and is since gone to New-York, or to Mr. Skeler's Works; he chang'd his Name to George Falmouth.

Any Person that will apprehend the said Servant, and convey him to my house in King George County, in the Colony of Virginia, shall be paid by me the Subscriber, upon the Delivery of him, Twenty Pounds Current Money, or if they will apprehend and secure him in some Public Goal, and give me immediate Notice, they shall have Ten Pounds Current Money of Virginia Reward:

He is an Irish Papist.[4]

Also a Mulatto Fellow, named Watt, ran away some Time before Christmas last; he is middle-siz'd, with some dark Spots in his Face; he was taken in Execution[5] by Mr. Henry Power, as part of the Estate of Matthew Anderson, of Hanover County, and bought on Account of the Subscriber, by Mr. Augustine Graham:

He is conceal'd by his late sister[6], or some other ill designing Person in the said County.

---

[3] Pennsylvania held as many Irish slaves as the entire southland, with the number of Irish slaves in Pennsylvania at the drafting of the U.S. Constitution in 1787 being over 200,000. By contrast, all of the negroes in America numbered only 600,000, free and owned.
[4] A Catholic.
[5] Like a piece of furniture
[6] This is chilling, that a man's blood kin are no longer considered his kin after they are parted by the condition of slavery. From the very beginning of the

I do hereby declare, if any Person entertains the said Slave, that I will prosecute them with the utmost Severity, unless they immediately deliver him up, to be sent from Constable to Constable, to me.

And whereas, some Time before Christmas, I wrote a Letter by my Servant, that I sent in Pursuit of the said Slave, to Matthew Anderson, wherein I did engage to pay Ten Pounds for a white Servant Man, to be bought[7] by the said Matthew Anderson, on my proper Account, and for the Use of the said Matthew Anderson, during the Time he continued to deserve the Favour at my Hands, provided he delivered up the said Slave Watt, to my Servant, which he refused to do, pretending that he knew nothing of him. I therefore give public Notice, that I will not pay the above said Sum, on the said Matthew Anderson's Account. Charles Carter.

---

colonial era, one notices the increased brutality of Virginia masters over their northern counterparts. As Watt is a mulatto, it is possible that his sister is white. One suspects she is close to Matthew Anderson, perhaps his wife.

[7] The anonymous white man was to be bought like a horse or a dog and treated less well, for the men of Virginia were renowned for brutal treatment of their human property.

'Witness our Hands'

Three Runaway Gaels in Plantation America, Virginia Gazette (Parks), Williamsburg, From August 7 to August 14, 1746. (Mitchell, Lynn and Dick)

RAN away from the Subscribers on the 31st of July last, Three Servants, viz. Daniel M'Craw, a Scots-Highlander,[1] of a short Stature, speaks broken English, about 5 Feet 2 Inches high, of a swarthy Complexion, with short curl'd Hair:

Had on when he went away, a coarse Bear-skin Coat, with Brass Buttons, a Pair of brown Linen Trowsers and Shirt.

He belonged to Mr. Charles Dick, in Fredericksburg.

John Ross, a Scots-Highland Boy, about 16 Years of age, of a ruddy Complexion, full-fac'd, speaks broken English, and has his Hair cut: He

---

[1] This man was one of the many prisoners of war sold into slavery after the Scottish Jacobite uprising of 1745–6, probably captured after the Battle of Culloden, 16 April 1746.

carried with him an Oznabrig Shirt, a Pair of Oznabrig Trowsers and Breeches, a Tartan Waistcoat without Sleeves, lin'd with green Shalloon, a brown Holland and a white Linen ditto, a Silk Handkerchief, a Felt Hat, and a Leather hunting Cap. He belonged to Mr. John Mitchell, in Fredericksburg.

Thomas Haily, an Irishman, about 36 Years of Age, of a fair Complexion, about 5 Feet 8 Inches high; had on when he went away, a dark colour'd Broad-Coath Coat, double-breasted with Metal Buttons, a Pair of Trowsers, an Oznabrig Shirt, a white Linen ditto, and a fine Beaver Hat. He belonged to Doctor William Lynn, in Fredericksburg.

Whoever apprehends the said Servants and brings them to their Masters aforesaid, shall receive a Pistole[2] Reward for each, besides what the Law allows.

Witness our Hands[3] this 21st Day of July, 1746. Charles Dick. William Lynn. John Mitchell.

---

[2] A Spanish gold dubloon was worth 18 shillings to the 20-shilling pound. These servants were not stated to be indentured and were described as property. This is a low reward, perhaps resulting from the glut of POWs sold in the Plantations over the course of the summer.
[3] The joining together in a runaway complaint to save expenses indicates that these owners were not wealthy.

The joining together in a runaway complaint to save expenses indicates that these owners were not wealthy.

'Late from Ireland'

James Garlen Has Run Away in the Province [not colony] of Pennsylvania (Penn.)

September 15, 1763, The Pennsylvania Gazette

FIVE POUNDS Reward.

RUN away from the Subscriber, living in Sadsbury Township, in the County of Lancaster, and Province of Pennsylvania, a Servant Man, named James Garlen, late from Ireland, about 5 Feet 6 Inches high, of a dark Complexion, round faced;

had on, when he went away, a blue Coat, Jacket and Breeches of the same, a new Felt Hat, a brown Wig, light blue rib Stockings, square Buckles in his Shoes, one of them Brass, the other Whitemetal; he is about 25 Year of Age, speaks pretty much in the Irish Dialect.

Whoever takes up said Servant, and secures him in any of his Majesty Goals in this Province, shall have the above Reward, and reasonable Charges, paid by HUGH RUSSELL.

'Pretends to Know'

Another Self-Made Fiction Absconds with Itself (Penn.)

Plantation America was utterly as materialistic in its worldview as our more rarified form of social degeneracy and this poor bastard had the gall to slip through its grasping talons.

August 16, 1764, The Pennsylvania Gazette

RUN away the 10th of this instant August, from the Subscriber, in Upper Makefield, Bucks County, an Irish Servant Man, named Connor Gleson, about 5 Feet 5 or 6 Inches high, of fair Complexion, and has short curled Hair:

Had on, when he went away, a new Felt Hat, Linen Shirt, Tow Trowsers, half worn Shoes, with Brass Buckles, and drab coloured Broadcloth Jacket, with Cuffs;

he is very talkative, speaks much with the Brogue, and pretends to know great Part of Ireland. Whoever takes up and secures said Servant, so that his Master may have him again, shall have Forty Shillings Reward, and reasonable Charges, paid by me JAMES McNAIR.

'At Their Peril'

Two Semi-Literate Thugs Want Their Beasts of Burden Back

September 13, 1764

The Pennsylvania Gazette

RUN away from the Subscribers, living near Witherspoon, in New Castle County, on the Borders the Maryland, two Servant Men,

one named George Rankin, about 35 Years of Age, five Feet seven Inches high, long Visage, dark Complexion, black Hair:

Had on when he went away, an old Felt Hat, Linsey Jacket, trimmed with Brass Buttons, old Cloth Breeches, new blue home made Stockings, and old Shoes; took with him, a Pair of long Ozenbrigs Trowsers, a fine Shirt, and a half worn coarse ditto, is apt to get drunk at every Opportunity, and is very talkative: He came from

Ireland about ten Months ago, and formerly served his Time[1] in this Country.

The other named William Price, about 40 Years of Age:

Had on when he went away an old light coloured Coat, with white Metal Buttons, with a Hole burnt in one of the Sleeves, a Cloth under Jacket, tow[2] home made Shirts, tow Pair of Trowsers, old Shoes tied with Strings, old Cotton Cap, and an old Felt Hat. He is of a sandy Complexion, and is remarkable by having two Thumbs on his Right Hand, and is blind of the Left Eye, is apt to get drunk, and squeaks when he speaks high:

He ran away in the Year 1762, and says he drove a Team at Pott Ironworks,[3] and called himself John Reese.

Whoever secures said Servants in any Goal, so as their Masters may have them again, shall have Five Pounds Reward for both, or Fifty Shillings for

---

[1] Despite the modern fantasy of lucky servant apprentices being saved by kind masters and taught a trade, the poor in the British Isles and America were repeatedly bought and sold across the span of their miserable lives, as likely as not to be forced to do work for which they were untrained.

[2] His fucking master can't fucking spell, so I'm leaving the typos in.

[3] Worked for a wage. If he had been used as a servant this would have been indicated. That he did something on his own without a whip to his back indicates that during the war men could get wage employment.

either, paid by JAMES WILSON, and JOHN DOBBINS.

N.B. All Masters of Vessels are forbid to carry them off at their Peril.

'A Taylor by Trade'

'Whoever takes Up Said Servant Man...'

September 20, 1764, The Pennsylvania Gazette

RUN away from the Subscriber, living in Market street, Philadelphia, an indented Servant Man, named William Long, about 21 Years of Age, 5 Feet 5 Inches high, born in the North of Ireland, a Taylor by Trade, is of a pale Complexion, has brown curled Hair, and a remarkable Lump over his left Eye;[1]

had on, when he went away, a brown Broadcloth Coat, with yellow Metal Buttons, a brown Allopeen Jacket, without Sleeves, full trimmed, with Whitemetal Buttons, both Coat and Jacket lined with white Shaloon, a Pair of blue Broadcloth Breeches, two Pair of Stockings, one Thread, and the other Worsted, two Shirts, the one

---

[1] The most common cause, then and now, for a lump over the left eye is to be stricken by another human from the front with a blunt object, which is, 19 of 20 times, wielded in the right hand.

white, the other Check, two Pair of Pumps, one of which new, the other somewhat worn, large yellow Buckles, and a turned Beaver Hat.

Whoever takes up and secures said Servant, so that his Master may have him again, shall have Four Dollars Reward, paid by JOHN ELLICK.

'On Suspicion of Being Runaways'

The Criminal State in Action: York PA, 1764 (Penn.)

October 11, 1764, The Pennsylvania Gazette

York Prison, September 29, 1764.

WAS committed to the goal of this county, on suspicion of being runaways, the two following persons, viz.

Thomas Lester, born in England, about 40 years of age, of a fresh complexion, about 5 feet 6 inches high, says he always followed the sea, has on a short brown jacket, coarse trowsers, white yarn stockings, old hat, and half worn shoes, and says he came last from Jamaica.

Patrick Troy, born in Ireland, about 16 years old, of a ruddy complexion, has a defect in his right eye; says he came in with Captain Miller last fall, from Derry, and that one William Marbuckle has his indentures; has on an old light coloured coarse jacket, old tow trowsers, old homespun shirt, no shoes nor stockings, and speaks somewhat foolish.

Their masters, if any they have, are desired to come in 30 days, from the date thereof, and take them away, otherwise they will be sold out for their charges, by JACOB GRAYBILL, Goaler.

Though Patrick Troy, apparently retarded, is admittedly justly owned and escaped property, with no right to live as he sees fit, Thomas Lester, after having spent a lifetime at sea, is going to be sold for a seven-year term for the crime of stepping off a ship a free man and neglecting to seek out a local official to draw up freedom papers. A man survives the horrors of the sea in the Age of Sail only to be condemned to toil into what was then old age for the crime of walking the roads of the slave Province of Pennsylvania.

'Their Masters, If Any They Have'

Samuel Raine, Abductor for the Slave Province of Pennsylvania (Penn.)

October 18, 1764, The Pennsylvania Gazette

Chester Goal, October 8, 1764.

NOW in Custody of the Subscriber as Runaways, two Lads, one of the Name of John Kearney, alias Young, the other named John Williams, this Country born, the former born in Ireland, but speaks good English; they both say they came from Lancaster County.

Their Masters, if any they have, are desired to come and take them away. SAMUEL RAINE, Goaler.

It was the most common fate of those born in The Plantations of "this Country" to be enslaved. The Irish kid is obviously a slave. But that the local boy is arrested merely for being free is telling. Perhaps he was free and was helping his Irish friend escape? Was he too an escaped slave? Whatever his previous status was, what will become of him?

Some person might come forward and claim to be his master and then have him for years as a servant. If no such man comes forward, he will be held indefinitely and auctioned off whenever practical to cover gaoling costs.

'Had a Forged Pass'

Breaking Out During the Colonial Crackdown in Plantation America

Beginning in 1764, the first full year without French and Indian hostilities, the slave masters of Plantation America were intent on returning any and all runaways, war veterans, refugees or freemen who had neglected to acquire a Freedom Pass back to work. A man who worked off his apprenticeship, indenture, redemption fee, repayment of a loan or other debt or conviction terms had no proof that he was free, the proof lying on his former master's desk as a pair of matching, signed indented [perforated] forms. A kind master might make out a freedom paper, but kindness was in short supply in the Land of Planted People.

The reaction to the disarmament, disbandment and re-enslavement of soldiers and of the increased shipments of servants seems to have been team efforts at breaking out. More and more listings feature jailbreak crews working as a team have been noted in the record.

The men below make a good case study as to how one gains his freedom in a total slave society. The aspect of total enslavement that the modern person, unaware of his debt slavery and focused on prisons, does not understand is that when over half of a society is enslaved, one can no longer house them profitably. They must be let range about enough to do their work. This reality brings into being a strong police state, in which every man not of the upper class is viewed as a fugitive from the just, holy and glorious state of servitude to which he belongs as a thing owned.

May 2, 1765, The Pennsylvania Gazette (Penn.)

RUN away from on board the Ship Sarah, James Drew, Master, lately arrived from Bristol, two Servant Men, one named Fergus Kagan, born in the County of Kildare, in Ireland, and bred a Coachman,[1] is about 26 Years of Age, 5 Feet 8 Inches high, rather of a slender make, wears black Hair, which curls in Ringlets down his Neck, has a smooth Face, and appears a likely active young Man, he was dressed in a Check Shirt, blue cloth upper Jacket, and under Jacket of blue and white stripe, coarse Kersey Breeches, Yarn Stockings, and had also a

---

[1] The phrase "bred a coachman" indicates that his father was a coachman and that he was expected to serve as his father had. This is a holdover from feudal life when the lord owned all who were part of the land he owned.

coarse Drab coloured Kersey Jacket, the same of his Breeches.

The other named Patrick Lachay, of Tyrone, in Ireland, a Linen Weaver, about 25 Years of Age, about 5 Feet 5 to 7 Inches high, square set, and a little round shoulder, fair Complexion, has dark brown Hair; had on a light grey Cloth Coat, brown Linen Jacket, scarlet Plush Breeches, and Worsted Stockings.

Any Person that delivers the above Servants to the Subscribers in Philadelphia, shall receive Eight Dollars Reward for each of them, with reasonable travelling Charges; but if secured in any of his MajestyGoals at a Distance, so that the Subscribers may have them again, Four Dollars Reward for each, from WILLING and MORRIS.

N.B. It is said these two Servants went off on Sunday Evening last, in Company with William Mallet, an Apprentice to Nathaniel Cope, Blacksmith on Society hill, and that the said Mallet had a forged Pass, for three People.[2]

---

[2] The semantics of the age and our modern slavish devotion to their most benign interpretation shines through in this passage to give a savage glimmer of what America was—a slave plantation.

'A Butcher by Trade'

An Indented Servant Man Has Stolen Himself and His Clothes!

In what kind of society does one keep prisoner butchers, lumber jacks and ditch diggers armed with exceedingly deadly implements?

In a police state, where he knows that the hand of every free man will be against him.

October 18, 1764, The Pennsylvania Gazette (Penn.)

RUN away from the Subscriber, living in Philadelphia, an Indented Servant Man, named Francis Campbell, about 20 Years of Age, 5 Feet 6 Inches high, born in Ireland, is of a dark Complexion, wears black hair, has a Scar on his right cheek, and is a Butcher by Trade;

had on, when he went away, a brown Broadcloth Coat, with fine Whitemetal Buttons, a red Plush Jacket, without Sleeves, and a Pair of Breeches of the same, a Pair of white striped Ditto, a Pair of light blue Worsted Stockings, a Pair or Silver buckles, and a red Flannel Jacket with Sleeves.

Whoever takes up and secures said Servant, so that his Master may have him again, shall have Three Pounds, Reward, paid by LODOWICK SINGIZER.

John Cooper

A Black Man Born in Ireland, Who Soldiered Against the French and Then Was Sold to a Master Who Would Have Him Back Again

This man might have been black, as the term was sometimes used in this era, or he may have been of the "black Irish" a dark-haired and dark-complexioned people. In any case, his race is thought little of in this advertisement, being of less consequence than his national identity.

November 8, 1764, The Pennsylvania Gazette (Penn.)

A Certain John Cooper, born in the North of Ireland, by Trade a Weaver, has been in the Army to the Northward, about 5 Feet 6 or 7 Inches high, a slim, black, thin faced Man, between 30 and 40 Years of Age, much given to gaming and drinking, hired from the Subscriber, living in George Town, Kent County, Maryland,

[stole] a dark coloured Mare, 4 Years old last Spring, between 12 and 13 Hands high, paces and

trots, has a Star in her Forehead, branded on the near Buttock P M D, may not be easily seen on Account of the old Hair, ringed with 3 Rings, the upper Ring broke out of the Flesh, and hangs on one Side;

he had a Bag behind, or under him, with Apron Check, white Linen, and some Clothes, which he may offer for Sale; he has several Changes of Clothes, one light Colour, one blue, and the other a brown, with a black jacket, red Breeches, and new Castor Hat, &c.

Whoever brings the said Cooper and Mare to the Subscriber, shall have Three Pounds Reward, or Thirty Shillings for the Mare, with reasonable Charges, by me PHILIP McDERMOTT.

N.B. An old Saddle and Bridle was hired with the above Mare; and it is supposed he is gone towards Philadelphia or New York.

'Scars on His Head'

The Hunt for Discharged Veterans to Enslave Continues to Heat up in the City of Brotherly Love

Patrick Joyce is not stated to be an 'indented' servant man but just a servant man. Many runaways are not listed as 'indented' or 'on redemption' but simply servants and they are declared as such in a manner that bespeaks an expectation that servitude for them is a lifetime condition. Here is yet another military veteran who is thought to be willing to enlist as a seaman, one of the single most dangerous occupations of the era. What must he be running from?

November 8, 1764, The Pennsylvania Gazette (Penn.)

THREE POUNDS Reward.

RUN away from the Subscriber, on the 29th of October last, a Servant Man, named Patrick Joyce, aged 40 Years, about 5 Feet 3 Inches high, born in Ireland, round faced, of a ruddy Complexion, light brown Hair tied behind; had on, when he went away, a blue Coat, Jacket and Breeches and the Coat bound round the Edges;

has served his Majesty, in Col. Stuart Regiment, in Germany; has a few Scars on his Head and is very apt to get drunk, being a Taylor by Trade.[1]

Whoever takes up said Servant and secures him, or bring him home to my House in Front street, next Door but one to John Wood, Watch maker, shall have the above Reward, and all other Charges, paid by JOHN GRANT.

N.B. All Masters of Vessels are forbid to carry him off at their Peril.[2]

---

[1] Apparently tailoring was a condition that tended to drive its practitioners to drink.

[2] After an earlier war in Maine and Canada, notices forbidding captains from taking on passengers or sailors discharged from military service began [in the 1740s] and the threat, backed by the Admiralty, seems to be coming back into increased use by masters in search of runaway property.

'Excessive Fond of Strong Liquor'

Travelling with and without Papers in Plantation America

January 17, 1765, The Pennsylvania Gazette (Penn.)

RUN away, about the first of November last, from the Subscriber, living near Bladensburgh, in Prince George County, Maryland, a Convict[1] Servant Man, named Patrick Carroll, born in Ireland, by Trade a Butcher; he is a lusty well set Fellow, about 5 Feet 8 Inches high, he has lost the fourth Finger of his left Hand, has remarkable black Hair, which he wears short, and is pitted with the Small Pox, is very talkative, and excessive fond of strong Liquor;

had on, when he went away, a dark Cloth Coat, Check Shirt, and a Pair of Boots, the rest of his Apparel I cannot describe; he carried with him a dark Chestnut sorrel Horse, about 13 Hands high.

---

[1] This typically meant a 14-year term of labor.

He obtained a Pass from a Magistrate of this County, by making him believe he was a Free man.[2]

Whoever takes up the said Servant, and secures him in any Goal, so that I get him again, shall receive Two Pistoles Reward, from NATHANIEL POPE.

January 24, 1765, The Pennsylvania Gazette

Joppa, December 19, 1765.

Committed to this Goal as Runaways, the two following Persons,viz.

a young man, who calls himself John Wilson, born in Ireland, about five Feet nine Inches high, much pitted with the Smallpox, and badly cloathed.

And a Negroe Man, who has been in Goal about two Months, five Feet ten Inches high, has a small round Mark over his left Eye, speaks bad English.

Whoever owns the said Runaways, may have them again by applying to JOHN TAYLOR, Goal keeper.

---

[2] In Plantation America, any poor man without a pass could be captured and sold, as indicated by the advertisement below. The goalor does not know if or from whom these men escaped. If a person does not come forward with proof of ownership they will be sold for fresh terms of servitude, the negro probably for life. In what kind of world is any person not carrying a pass or owning property assumed to be a fugitive?

'A Thick Spoken Fellow'

James Ferguson on the Run from the Man

February 7, 1765

The Pennsylvania Gazette

THREE POUNDS Reward.

RUN away, from the Subscriber, living in Warminster Township, Bucks County, an Irish Servant Man, named James Ferguson, it is thought he will change his Name;

he is about 20 Years of Age, fresh Complexion, a thick spoken Fellow, about 5 Feet 8 Inches high, midling thick set, wears his Hair tied behind, but perhaps he may cut it off;

had on, when he went away, a good Felt Hat, a thin white Shirt, a light blue Cloth Coat, with Metal Buttons, a brown jacket, without Sleeves or Skirts behind, he took with him a brown Worsted Jacket, lined with light red, a white Leather Apron, a good Pair of Buckskin Breeches, with flat Metal

Buttons, grey Yarn Stockings, a Strong Pair of Shoes, with Pinchbeek[1] Buckles in them.

Whoever takes up the said Servant, and secures him, so that his Master may have him again, shall have the above Reward, and reasonable Charges, paid by JONATHAN WALTON.

N.B. He came from Ireland in the Jupiter, Capt. Hawthorn.

---

[1] I have found no definition for a pinchbeek buckle, however, I have located a description of a "pinchbeek metal watch," suggesting that pinchbeeking is a method of crimping light metal.

'Marked with the Small Pox'

Thomas Newlan, Another Irishman on the Run

Below is one of the barest-bones servant advertisements I have found. The price for his recovery is no higher than it would have been two generations earlier. He also had had small pox. We think of small pox as a disease of Amerindian genocide, however, it primarily afflicted poor whites. There was even a small pox outbreak in Philadelphia after the Civil War, which was blamed on buffalo robes shipped east from the Musselshell region, traded from small-pox-suffering Indians. I have not gathered a broad enough base of servant samples to attempt arriving at a ratio of small pox sufferers.

February 14, 1765, The Pennsylvania Gazette (Penn.)

RUN away last Summer, from the Subscriber, in Hanover Township, Lancaster County, a Servant Man, named Thomas Newlan, born in Ireland, speaks with the Brogue, about 5 Feet 5 Inches high, marked with the Small Pox; had on, when he went away, a Provincial Regimental Coat.

Whoever takes up the said Servant, and secures him in any County Goal in this Province, shall have Forty Shillings Reward, and reasonable Charges, paid by TIMOTHY GREEN.

'A Coach and Harness Maker'

James Bell, alias 'Johnson' or 'Thompson'

February 14, 1765, The Pennsylvania Gazette (Penn.)

FORTY SHILLINGS Reward.

RUN away, the 28th of January, a certain James Bell, but may change his Name to Johnson, or Thompson, as he has gone by both,[1] was born in Ireland, 5 Feet 6 or 7 Inches high, thin Visage, brown Hair tied behind;

had on a Felt Hat, and wore the Peak behind, a brown Coat, blue Jacket, Ditto Plush Breeches, Leather Apron, Check Shirt, and Ditto, blue Yarn Stockings, old Shoes, round Steel Buckles,

by Trade a Coach and Harness maker, and took sundry Tools with him, a Handsaw, Chissels, sliding Gunter, and a Common Rule, some Awls, &c. very subject to Drink, and perhaps may pawn or sell them for Liquor.

---

[1] Indicates that James has escaped and been recaptured on at least two other occasions.

Any Person that will apprehend said Fellow, so as his Master may have him again, shall have the above Reward, and reasonable Charges, paid by JOHN WITHY, in Chester, Pennsylvania.

'A Person of Such Vile Principles'

A Case of Misplaced 'Confidence and Compassion'

June 27, 1765, The Pennsylvania Gazette (Penn.)

Trenton, June 24, 1765.

ONE HUNDRED DOLLARS Reward.

MADE his Escape from Samuel Tucker, Esq; of Trenton, Sheriff of the County of Hunterdon, in New Jersey, in April last, one Hugh McCan, but has changed his Name, and now calls himself Hugh Johnson;

he sailed from Philadelphia about the 20th of April last, in the Sloop Adventure, Captain Matthews, for St. Kitts, and returned again in the same Vessel to Philadelphia on Tuesday last;

he was born in Ireland, is near 60 Years of Age, about 5 Feet 7 Inches, has black or hazel Eyes,[1]

---

[1] A description likening hazel eyes to black ones supports the use of "black" to describe Europeans of darker hues rather than Africans, in this case a dark-haired and fair complected man.

large black Eyebrows, wore his Hair when he went away, which is grey, sometimes wears a white Cap, or black or brown cut Wig, takes Plenty of Snuff, fair Complexion, addicted to strong Liquor, and very talkative when intoxicated;

he can scarce write his Name intelligibly, but pretends to be well versed in Trade, which he has followed in the Retail Way, together with the manufacturing of Wheat, at his late Gristmill at Almetunk River; he also had Sawmill and Fulling mill, is a Fuller by Trade, and will brag largely of his Knowledge in dying Cloths of two Colours, the one Side scarlet, the other blue.

Whoever apprehends and secures the said Hugh McCan, alias Johnson, and causes him to be delivered to the Sheriff of Philadelphia, shall receive One Hundred Spanish Dollars, and all reasonable Charges, paid by the Subscriber. It is hoped that all Persons will be diligent to apprehend him, with a View to detect a person of such vile Principles, that deserted the said Sheriff, who placed a Confidence in him out of Compassion, and let him pursue his Business, rather than lock him in Goal, which he was liable to, and justly deserved.

SAMUEL TUCKER, Sheriff.

The reason for the institution of laws against Indians and blacks and non-Christians holding white Christian slaves was that, in this debt-worshipping society, any businessman could fall on hard times or do poorly for himself and then find himself being sold to pay off his debts. And no white man wanted to be sold to a person of another race.

'At the Sign of the Lamb'

Robert Jones Must be Delivered to the Subscriber

June 20, 1765, The Pennsylvania Gazette (Penn.)

RUN away, the 9th of this instant June, a Servant Man, named Robert Jones, born in Ireland, about 5 Feet 3 or 4 Inches high, full Visage, black hair, and much pitted with the Small pox;[1]

had on, when he went away, a half worn Felt Hat, grey Coat, whitish Jacket, with Sleeves, white Tow Trowsers, hemp Shirt, white Stockings, and Shoes tied with Strings.

---

[1] Descriptions of servants are commonly accompanied by notes that they are marked from the small pox, a reminder that European immigrants suffered terribly from disease. Increase Mather's account of the 1676 Indian War mentions much sickness among the colonists. Of course, lacking immunity, Indians suffered more, and with a society organized to maintain a stable population rather than exponential growth, were less able to recover from plagues.

Whoever takes up said Servant, and delivers him to the Subscriber, living in Lebanon Township, Lancaster County; or to Jacob Barge, at the Sign of the Lamb, in Philadelphia; or secures him in any Goal, so that his Master may have him again, shall have THREE POUNDS Reward, and reasonable Charges paid by JOHN SMITH.

'Are Forbid to Carry Him Off'

Irish Servant Lad Archibald Kelly

February 28, 1765, The Pennsylvania Gazette (Penn.)

RUN away from John Pierse, on Sunday the 24th Instant, about Three o'Clock in the Morning, an Irish Servant Lad, named Archibald Kelly, between 16 and 17 Years of Age, about 5 Feet 6 Inches high, of a fair complexion, long Visage, down Look, has dark brown hair, but it is likely he may have it cut off;

had on, when he went away, a blue Surtout Coat, with gilt

Buttons, a blue Cloth Coat, with Brass Buttons, a scarlet

Cloth Jacket, without Sleeves, both Coat and Jacket have been turned, blue Cloth Breeches, with washed Buttons, Worsted Stockings, Check Linen Shirt, and Pinchbeck Shoe Buckles.

He is very much given to lying, and will persist in a Lie a long Time.[1] It is supposed he intended going off in one of the first Vessels to Ireland, or else is gone in the Stage to New York.

Whoever takes up said Servant, and brings him to his Master, shall have Forty Shillings Reward, and reasonable Charges, paid by JOHN PIERSE.

N.B. All Masters of Vessels are forbid to carry him off.

---

[1] In most ads, it seems that it was unusual for an escaped servant to lie, with many admitting that they were fugitives and even from whom they had run. Beginning in the 1750s, according to the samples this reader has examined, charges that servants will lie, have forged documents, and will use disguises and adopt assumed names seem to have increased markedly.

'Pretends to be a Seaman'

John Malone, Another Veteran Willing to Brave the High Seas Rather than Slave in Plantation America

September 26, 1765, The Pennsylvania Gazette (Penn.)

RUN away from the Subscriber, living near George Town, in Kent County, Maryland, a Convict Servant Man, named John Malone, about five Feet seven Inches, about 20 Years of Age, born in Ireland, but speaks good English, has a flat crooked Nose,[1] is much pitted with the Small pox, knock kneed, was in the Transport Service last War, pretends to be a Seaman, and it is thought will endeavour to get on board some Vessel in Philadelphia, as he was near being taken at Chester and Schuylkill, on the 23d and 3d Instant but escaped; the Little Finger on his Left hand grown fast to the next, as far as the Middle Joint. He stole and took with him, a new blue homespun Frock Coat, lined with coarse Sheeting, with long Cuffs to

---

[1] A classic boxing injury.

the Elbow, and white Horn Buttons, a white Shirt, and a Check Ditto, Tow Linen Trowsers, Worsted Stockings, old Shoes, and a Felt Hat, also a Kersey Great Coat, and a Hanger or Cutlas,[2] with a Snakeskin over the Scabbard.

Whoever secures said Servant, in any Goal, so as his Master may have him again, shall have Three Pistoles Reward, paid by JOHN SEWELL.

All Masters of Vessels are forbid to carry him off.[3]

---

[2] A hanger is an infantry cutlass with a bar hand guard rather than a cupped knuckle guard.
[3] Although the owner claims Malone's trade as a sailor is false, he believes that masters of ships might think otherwise, a clear betrayal his own lie in that dispute as to the trade of the man he has publicly judged false.

'By Trade a Plaisterer'

Two Convict Sailors on the Run

August 29, 1765

The Pennsylvania Gazette

EIGHT POUNDS Reward.

RUN away, in the Night of the 21st of August, from the subscriber, living in Cecil County, Maryland, two Convict Servant Men,

one named William Callahan, born in Ireland, by Trade a Plaisterer, about 30 years of Age, about 5 Feet 6 Inches high, wear an old grey cut Wig, a light coloured short kersey Coat, with Metal Buttons, Ozenbrigs Shirt and Trowsers, old Shoes, and Yarn Stockings;

he is of a swarthy Complexion, has grey Eyes, pitted with the Small Pox, very talkative, much given to Drink, has served some Time on board a

Man of War,[1] and came in the Country about 12 Months ago.

The other named Edward Thompson, a Convict, lately imported, an Englishman, a very lusty well looking Man, with black Beard and Eyes:

He had on a light coloured Jockey Coat, blue Serve Vest, with Leather Buttons, Shoes and Stockings, an old fine Hat, with a black Crape Band round it;

he also took with him a light coloured Bearskin Great Coat, a Snuff coloured Thickset Coat, and sundry other Things, likewise a small old sorrel Horse, with a Star in his Forehead, paces slow, and very stiff;

he is a stout resolute Fellow, is apt to drink, and then very insolent;

they are both well acquainted with the Water, and may probably pass for Sailors.

Whoever takes up and secures the said Servants in any Goal, so that their Masters may have them again, shall have Five Pounds Reward for Thompson, and Three Pounds for Callahan, if taken out of this Province, paid by ANDREW PEARCE, HENRY W. PEARCE and JOHN WARD.

---

[1] Serving on board a man-of-war was the worst military job of the age. How bad must servitude have been for these men to seek service at sea? Perhaps it was not the physical hardship as much as the humiliation of being beaten by a farmer or shopkeeper rather than a marine.

'An Old Offender'

Another Sailor on the Run

August 29, 1765, The Pennsylvania Gazette (Penn.)

RUN away, in the Night Time, between the 25th and 26th Day of the 8th Month, 1765, from George Ashbridge, of Goshen, in Chester County, Pennsylvania, a Servant Man, named Cornelius Leeson, but may be likely to change his Name; he came from Ireland, and has been on Shore but about twelve Days;

is about 5 Feet 8 Inches high, [th]in chinned, and a little out mouthed, pretty full breasted, and walks a little stooping, wears brown hair; had on, and took with him two Check Shirts, a Pair of old Velvet Breeches, and Linen Trowsers, one old light grey Nap Jacket, the Nap partly wore off, not made for him and one old dark coloured SailorJacket, a Pair of brown Yarn Stockings, and half worn Shoes;

he has been in this Country a Servant some Years ago, served Part of his time in Bucks County, and ran away from thence, and got to Ireland again, so that it appears he is an old Offender, and acquainted with this Province; it is suspected that he will make for the back Parts of this Province,[1] or Virginia, or to Sea again.[2]

Whoever takes up and secures the said Servant in any Goal, so that his Master may have him again, shall have Forty Shillings Reward, and reasonable Charges, paid by GEORGE ASHBRIDGE.

---

[1] The frontier.

[2] The great number of soldiers and sailors released after the Seven Years' War provided many servants for the plantation provinces as unemployment was a capital crime, and any recently released veteran who did not find himself a master would have one found for him. Pennilessness was also a crime and many sailors were discharged without pay as they had been impressed to begin with. Lastly, homelessness was a capital crime and any man not immediately able to secure lodgings for himself would also have a death sentence or a 14-year stint in the plantations hanging over his head. Cornelius had just freed himself for the third time. Would he escape or be returned to bondage?

'Wears His Hat Soldier Like'

A Classic Character on the Run

November 28, 1765, The Pennsylvania Gazette (Penn.)

Philadelphia, November 25, 1765.

RUN away, on the 16th Instant, from John Faries, a Servant Man, named Edward Carlow, but has changed his Name to Collins, and may go by some other Name;

he is a spry Fellow, and wears his Hat Soldier like, on his Right Eye, has a brown Wig, red Hair, white Eyebrows, Freckles on the Back of his Hands, is about 5 Feet 6 Inches high, wore a brown Coat, blue Velvet Jacket, red or brown Breeches, commonly wore white Thread, or black Silk Stockings, walks fast, when he travels, speaks good English, pretends to have two Uncles in New London, both Ministers, says he has a small Estate in Ireland,[1] and is well beloved amongst the Women.

Whoever secures said Servant in any Goal in this Province, so that his Master may have him again, shall have Three Pounds Reward, and if out of the Province, Five Pounds, paid by me JOHN FARIES.

N.B. All Masters of Vessels, and others, are forbid to harbour or carry him off, as they may expect to be proceeded against as the Law directs.

---

[1] At least one Irish heir was sold into slavery, and his case was in court at the time of this advertisement, so it seems likely that this runaway's claims—very similar to James Annesley's circumstances—were inspired by actual events in Ireland and England, an example that Collins trafficked in much fiction making his way in a slave society.

'Has a Sour Look'

Nicholas Coffey, Age 25, Once a Sailor, Once a Soldier, Twice a Slave

February 20, 1766, The Pennsylvania Gazette (Penn.)

TWO POUNDS Reward.

RUN away, on Sunday Night last, from the Subscriber, living in East Whiteland, Chester County, a Servant Man, named Nicholas Coffey, born in Ireland, about 25 years of Age, tall and slender, long visaged, has a sour Look, of a sandy Complexion, and lisps a little;

had on a Boyfine Hat,[1] half worn, light coloured Fustian Coat, blue Jacket, with Metal Buttons, a brown Camblet under Jacket, the back ripped, old white Shirt, Leather Breeches, white Yarn Stockings, the Top of one of them old, and half worn Shoes and Buckles.

---

[1] A knit cap, commonly called a ski-cap in modern times

He served a Time in Philadelphia, has been since at Sea, likewise campaigning, is acquainted in most Parts of this Province, and may thereby the better pass for a Freeman. He has at Times the Third day Ague,[2] the Fit coming on him in the Evening, and is a remarkable Liar.

Whoever secures the said Servant so as his Master may have him again, shall have the above Reward with reasonable Charges, from RICHARD RICHISON.

---

[2] Malarial fever: Many British troops were lost to malaria and yellow fever during operations in the West Indies immediately after the French and Indian War. (Buchan)

'A Tolerable Good Scholar'

'An Irish Servant Man, Named Henry Crown'

May 22, 1766, The Pennsylvania Gazette (Penn.)

RUN away from the Subscriber, living near New Castle, on Sunday Night last, the 18th of this instant May, an Irish Servant Man, named Henry Cowan, about 24 Years of Age, dark Complexion, about 5 Feet 6 Inches high, pretty fat;

had on when he went away, a light blue Serge Coat, Nankeen Jacket[1] and Breeches, white Linen Shirt, white Thread Stockings, new Pumps, and wears his own black Hair; came from Ireland last Fall, in the Ship Marquis of Granby, Captain Macilvaine, and as he is a tolerable Good Scholar,

---

[1] Nankeen is a yellowish or buff colored cotton cloth that takes its name from the Chinese city of Nanking (Nanjing) where it originated. This goes some way towards explaining the presence of yellow negroes, Chinese and slaves from India in the American Plantations, a dozen ports of call in a global trade network.

may forge a Pass, perhaps; from under the Captain Hand.

Whoever takes up and secures said Servant, so that his Master may have him again, shall have Five Pounds Reward, and reasonable Charges, paid by MATTHEW CANNON.

N.B. All Masters of Vessels are forbid to carry him off at their Peril.

'She Will Be Sold'[1]

Isabel Beard, Slave Girl

April 24, 1766

The Pennsylvania Gazette

Lancaster, April 15, 1766.

WAS committed to my Custody, on the 11th of this Inst. on Suspicion[2] of a Runaway Servant, a Girl, who calls herself Isabel Beard, she was born in Ireland, and came in the Snow Pitt above two Years ago;

she is about 4 Feet 8 Inches high, very thickset;

had on, when committed, a blue Stuff Gown, striped Linsey Petticoat and Bed Gown, old Shoes and Stockings;

she says she belongs[1] to a certain William Grimes, a Jobber, and late of York County, where she says she left him.

Her Master therefore, if any she has, is hereby desired to come, pay her Charges, and take her away, otherwise she will be sold[1] for her Fees,[2] by MATTHIAS BOOGH, Goaler.

[1] Establishment historians would have us believe she was not a slave.
[2] On suspicion of being a runaway, one could be jailed and then sold for the jailing fee, and this was not slavery, not a slave state, but a land of freedom and opportunity?

'ABSCONDED from his Service'

Andrew Haddock, Runaway School Teacher

May 8, 1766, The Pennsylvania Gazette (Penn.)

Albemarle, April 9, 1766.

ABSCONDED from his Service, on Saturday, the Fifth Instant, a Servant Man, belonging to the Subscriber, named Andrew Haddock, a Native of Ireland, about 5 Feet 10 Inches high, well set of a ruddy Complexion, grey Eyes, dark brown Hair, which he commonly wears tied up in a String, has lost one of his upper fore Teeth,

dressed in a Pair of Buckskin Breeches, red Waistcoat, Snuff coloured Cloth Coat, and a blue Cloth or Drab Surtout,[1] the small Cape lined with Velvet of the same Colour, he is Master of a tolerable good Address;[2]

he rode a likely bay Mare, between 13 and 14 Hands high, is fond of strong Drink, writes a good

---

[1] A surtout is a man's overcoat.
[2] He is well spoken.

Hand, is tolerably well acquainted with Figures, and pretends to be so with the Latin Language, and some Branches of the Mathematicks;

his Employment[3] was to keep School.

Whoever takes up and secures the said Runaway, so that he be delivered to me, or shall bring him to me, living in the lower Part of Albermarle County, shall receive, if taken up in this Colony, Five Pounds, besides what the Law allows, or if taken up out of the Colony, Ten Pounds,[4] paid by JOHN LEWIS, junior.

---

[3] Employment comes from the French term "to use," as one would employ a tool, a method or a beast of burden in a task. The modern use of the term employee as a free agent has done much to muddle the semantics of the white slavery question. Consider though, that it is currently the fashion of those employers in the U.S. which pride themselves on developing good work conditions and a loyal staff to call their employees associates, not employees, which is rightly regarded as a demeaning categorization. Also, professionals are rarely categorized as employees but "associates." Even in retail, "sales associate" or "associate" is the preferred designation in staffing situations above the bottom rung of the economy.

[4] This was an outrageously expensive Irishman.

'Cannot Do Any Other Work'

Walter and Winford Pritchet, Enslaved Married Couple Escaped from their Master

July 3, 1766, The Pennsylvania Gazette (Penn.)

FIVE POUNDS Reward.

RUN away from the subscriber, a servant man and woman, named Walter and Winford Pritchet;

the man is a taylor to trade, and cannot do any other work; the woman is a stay maker, and very handy at house work;

they both speak good English, but low, take snuff, and love liquor;

the man is about 5 feet 7 inches high, has black hair, and grey eyes; the woman is but low of stature, pretty likely, has black eyes and black hair;

as they came lately from Ireland, their clothes are but ordinary, and probably have changed them.

Whoever secures them in any goal on this continent, and lets me know in the public paper of this province, shall have the above reward for both, or Fifty Shillings for either. I hear the man is listed, and has taken his wife with him to Fort Pitt. All gentlemen of the army are forbid to list or harbour them, and Captains of vessels to carry them off, at their peril. HENRY NEILL.

'Two Irish Servant Lads'

Moses Irving and George McCullough Want Their White Slave Boys Back

July 31, 1766, The Pennsylvania Gazette (Penn.)

RUN away from the subscribers, living in Drummore township, Lancaster county, on the 24th of this instant July, two Irish servant lads;

the one named John Riley, about 22 years of age, about 5 feet 9 inches high, a broad well set fellow, wears his own brown hair, which curls a little, and speaks with the brogue;

had on, when he went away, a blackish mixed home made cloth coat and jacket, felt hat, coarse shirt and trowsers, white ribbed yarn stockings, and good channel pumps.

The other named Philip Meganaty, about 17 years of age, a slim thin visaged lad, about 5 feet 5 or 6 inches high, wear his own hair, which is brown, straight, and commonly tyed, and speaks a little with the brogue;

had on, when he went away, a drab coloured coat and jacket, bound with worsted tape of the same colour, but not lined, a felt hat, check shirt, blue breeches, white ribbed yarn stockings, good channel pumps, and took with him a pair of check trowsers.

They both came from the north of Ireland this summer.

Whoever takes up and secures said Servants, so as their masters may have them again, shall have Four Pounds reward, or Forty shillings for either, and reasonable charges, paid by MOSES IRVING,[1] or GEORGE McCULLOUGH

---

[1] A peculiar aspect of escaped white slave ads is the fact that a high proportion of their owners seem to have Old Testament names. Since English Protestants in America were so keen on being as Jewish as possible, it is difficult to know whether these were Jewish or gentile slave owners. An adherence to the biblical code of Leviticus, which promotes and sanctifies enslavement for life of people outside of God's Chosen People, was a strong aspect of slave master morality in plantation America, with Methodist and Anglican parishes holding particularly harsh, Old Testament views on chattel. The 49-year Jubilee cycle, while looked upon by American Christian slaves as a possible source of manumission, was not in force, even among ancient Jewry after the separation of the tribes—at which point the Jubilee manumissions were null and void—in ancient times. It should be noted that Quaker and Jewish slave owners were regarded by most runaways as less cruel than most owners.

'He Will Pass for a Reaper'

Another Military Veteran Escapes from His Civilian Master

July 17, 1766, The Pennsylvania Gazette (Penn.)

RUN away from the Subscriber, living in Little Britain Township, Lancaster County, an Province of Pennsylvania, on the 10th inst. July,

an Irish Servant Man, named Patrick Campbell, about 20 Years of Age, 5 Feet 9 Inches high, has a down Look, stoop shouldered, with his Hair tied, some old Scars on his Temple, is a middling good Scholar,[1] speaks with the Brogue,

had on, when he went away, an old Hat, a short blackish Coat, with small Lappels, and no Lining in it, two Shirts, one of which he made use of for a Wallet, long Ozenbrigs Trowsers, Stockings, and Shoes, without Buckles;

---

[1] The educational level of the runaways seems to have increased after the end of the Seven Years War. One dynamic was the ability to forge a slave pass.

he had a Sickle with him, and it is thought he will pass for a Reaper; he informed me he was in the King Service in Ireland and Portugal.[2]

Whoever takes up said Servant, and secures him, so as his Master may have him again, shall have Three Pounds Reward, and reasonable Charges, paid by JAMES JOHNSTON.

---

[2] Throughout the 1600s, 1700s and into the Napoleonic Era, Great Britain and Portugal had a close military alliance, with the Portuguese army being trained and even officered by British soldiers, while at the same time, the perennial British enemy, Spain, employed Irish mercenaries itching to strike a blow at the nation that raped their homeland.

'A Sly Still Fellow'

Renowned Runaway, James Fennel

August 14, 1766, The Pennsylvania Gazette (Penn.)

FIVE POUNDS Reward.

RUN away from the Subscriber, living near Chester, on Delaware, an indented Servant Man, named James Fennell, about five Feet ten Inches high, twenty Years of Age, has a thinish Face, down Looks, brown Hair, lost one of his fore Teeth, walks wide, and has a Kind of rocking in his Gait, like one that is just come from Sea:[1]

took with him, a blue Cloth Coat, the Lining torn, a brown Saggathy Coat, with a Rent in the Back, a figured brown Velvet Jacket, two white Shirts, one Check Ditto, a new Pair of Check Trowsers, three or four Pair of Stockings, and a Pair of Shoes almost new.[2]

---

[1] Perhaps Mister Fennell was a sailor before his enslavement.

[2] According to the wording, Mister Fennell owned no clothes of his own.

It is supposed he will steal a Horse (being an arrant Thief) and make towards the Frontiers, forge a Pass,[3] and change his Clothes; he is a sly still Fellow, looks like country born, tho' he came from the West of Ireland last Fall, where he was advertised, with a large Reward.[4]

Whoever takes up and secures said Fennel, so as he may be had again, shall have the above Reward, and reasonable Charges, paid by JAMES WILLCOX.

---

[3] Literacy among the servile class was becoming a dilemma for slave masters. After the white working class attained literacy, maintaining them in a passport-regulated open chattel system would be all but impossible. No wonder negroes were forbidden to learn to read and write. Also, note the increased willingness of men to head for the frontier since the French and Indian War.

[4] It seems that Fennel was enslaved in Ireland, escaped, was recaptured at great expense and then sold into the Plantations.

'Served His Time'

Another Runaway Tailor

August 7, 1766, The Pennsylvania Gazette (Penn.)

Salem, July 30, 1766.

RUN away, on the Tenth Day of June last, from his Bail, a certain Edward Ashton, born in Ireland, by Trade a Taylor, served his Time[1] in Bristol, Pennsylvania, about 5 Feet 6 Inches high, of a sandy Complexion;

has on a new Fustian Coat,[2] with gilt Buttons, old blue Everlasting Breeches,[3] white thread Stockings, good Shoes, and a Pair of Silver Buckles, marked S. W.

---

[1] This should indicate that the man worked off his sentence, yet he is still wanted and for a substantial sum.
[2] Thick, durable twilled cloth with a short nap, usually dyed in dark colors.
[3] The author could not find a description of everlasting breeches, but the term is found in other runaway slave advertisements.

He was seen at Bristol the 28th Instant, with a blue Coat and Jacket and a Pair of striped Holland Trowsers on.[4]

Whoever takes up and secures said Runaway in any Goal, if in the Province of Pennsylvania, shall receive Eight Dollars Reward; and if in the Province of New Jersey, Ten Dollars, and reasonable Charges, paid by JOHN BREEDING.

---

[4] Woolen dress pants.

'Loves Strong Drink'

An Irish Servant Lad Fleeing is Sober Master

September 11, 1766, The Pennsylvania Gazette (Penn.)

RUN away on the 5th of this instant, September, an Irish servant lad, named William Sheppard, about 18 years old, 5 feet 4 or 5 inches high, has light strait hair, and grey eyes;

had on, a half worn felt hat, a long dark grey Irish frize surtout coat, white homespun linen shirt and trowsers, strong shoes, and brass buckles.

He served his time in Ireland to a weaver, and may have his indentures with him, with a clearance from his master in Ireland.[1]

He can read and write, is very impudent and talkative, much given to cursing and swearing, and

---

[1] Based on his age, William was first sold at age 11–15 and, despite being freed from that master and having a pass, is now twice owned at age 18. This was not uncommon. Benjamin Franklin had been sold by his father twice by the time he was William's age.

loves strong drink, and may have forged a pass to travel with.[2]

He pretended to be lame in his foot, with a sprain, when he went away, and came from Ireland last spring with Captain Mackey.

Whoever takes up said servant and sends him to Philadelphia goal, or secures him in any other goal, and sends him to the Philadelphia goaler, shall have Thirty Shillings Reward, and reasonable charges.

---

[2] Once again, in Plantation America, it was illegal to travel without a pass!

'Pitted with the Small Pox'

John Purday and His Wife Escape

October 30, 1766, The Pennsylvania Gazette (Penn.)

RUN away from the Subscriber in Newport, an Irish Servant Man, named John Purday, and Mary, his Wife,

the said John Purday is about 5 Feet 9 Inches high, and about 27 Years of Age, is pitted with the Small pox, has strait pale Hair commonly tied behind;

had on, when he went away, a light coloured Coat, and Thickset Jacket and Breeches, Worsted Stockings, his Hat sharp cocked, and appears very neat in his Clothes, has been a Soldier in Flanders, speaks very good English, a little inclined to the Scotch Accent.[1]

---

[1] It appears that by 1764, buying, working, selling and recapturing military veterans in the post-war Plantations was a mainstay of the economy.

His Wife is a little short thin woman, dark Complexion, dark frizled hair, speaks broad Scotch.[2]

They are about 6 Weeks in from Ireland, and came in the Ship Marquis of Granby.[3]

Whoever takes up the said John Purday, so as his Master may have him again, shall have Twenty Shillings Reward, and reasonable Charges, paid by me ROBERT ALL, or by applying to Mr. JAMES ALEXANDER, Merchant in Water street, Philadelphia.

ROBERT ALL.

---

[2] This woman, Mary, was sought for capture, although she was not a servant but rather married to one, which implies that she was living in absolute destitution, as servants drew no wages but merely worked off their time.

[3] John may have been sold to satisfy a debt or for committing a crime. He may also have sold himself to get him and his wife across to The Plantations. Consider, though, that The Plantations had an evil reputation among the Irish.

'Has a Dull Look'

Samuel Askin, Lad of Unknown Age, Is at Large

November 6, 1766, The Pennsylvania Gazette (Penn.)

THIRTY SHILLINGS Reward.

RUN away, on the 2d Instant, from the Subscriber, living in Leacock Township, Lancaster County, a Servant Lad, named Samuel Askin, came lately in the Ship Rose from the North of Ireland;

he is a short set Lad, with long black Hair, commonly hanging round his Shoulders, thin Visage, small brown Eyes, and has a dull Look:

Had on, when he went away, a brown Coat, with a small Cape, slash Sleeves, and yellow Buttons, Cloth Jacket and Breeches, something different in Colour from the Coat, and full long for him, with yellow Buttons, Dimity or Linen under Jacket, bluish rubb Stockings,[1] and half worn Shoes.

---

[1] My search for rub stockings turned up pornography suggestions for stocking fetish films.

Whoever takes up and secures said Servant, so as his Master may have him again, shall have the above Reward, by applying to James Stephens, in Philadelphia, or to the Subscriber, MOSES BRINTON.

N.B. It is supposed said Servant is now in Philadelphia.

'The Master of the Servant'

Convict Servant Woman, Alice McCarty, Is No Longer Barefoot

'The Master of the Servant', November 13, 1766 (Penn.)

The Pennsylvania Gazette

RUN away, the 29th of October, from the Subscriber, living at Christine Bridge, Newcastle county, a convict servant woman, named Alice McCarty, alias Eleanor Brown, about 35 years of age, born in Ireland, has brown hair, very lusty and fat;[1]

had on, and took with her, an old brown camblet gown, 2 short gowns, the one white linen, the other dark calicoe, both new, a cream coloured skirt, a red quilt, 2 check aprons, a pair of neat made mens shoes, and a pair of diamond cut silver buckles, marked E. H. a linen handkerchief, spotted

---

[1] The fact that Alice was a convict does not mean she committed a crime as we know it, for being homeless, jobless, penniless or without a travel pass were all crimes punishable by enslavement.

red and white, coarse sheet and blanket, and a pair of womens shoes, all which she stole when she went away;[2]

it is supposed she is in company with a man, his name unknown. Said servant has been several times whipped in the workhouse, in Philadelphia, and whipped for theft at the public post.[3]

N.B. The master of the servant forgot to put his name to his advertisement.

---

[2] Note that every stitch of clothing Alice wore was stolen, meaning she was normally barefoot, presumably dressed only in a shift or slip.

[3] Alice would have her upper body stripped naked as she was publicly whipped.

'Born in Philadelphia'

Young William Hewes Seeks the Sea

February 19, 1767, The Pennsylvania Gazette (Penn.)

RUN away, on the 10th of January, from the Subscriber, living in St. George Hundred, New Castle County, a Servant Man, named William Hewes, born in Philadelphia, about 5 Feet 4 Inches high, fair Complexion, round Face, about 21 Years of Age, has lost a Joint of the fore Finger of his Left Hand:

Had on, when he went away, a knit Cap, with brown, red and white Diamonds, coarse homespun Cloth Jacket, and a brown under Jacket, Buckskin Breeches, blue Yarn Stockings, and good Shoes, with Brass Buckles.

He has been in several parts of Europe,[1] and came last from Ireland, says he served some time

---

[1] These are indications that William was working at sea from a young age.

with James Chattin, Printer. He is supposed to be gone toward Philadelphia.

All Masters of Vessels are desired not to harbour or carry him off.

Whoever takes up said Servant, and secures him, so as his Master may have him again, shall have Thirty Shillings Reward, and reasonable Charges, paid by HENRY WALL.

Running Away from Samuel Finley

Another Taylor Absconds with Himself

March 19, 1767

The Pennsylvania Gazette

Leacock, Lancaster County, March 4, 1767.

TEN POUNDS Reward. MADE his Escape from Samuel Finley, Constable,[1]

Cornelius McMurphy, a Taylor by Trade, born in the County of Antrim in Ireland;

about 25 Years of Age, 5 Feet 10 Inches high, pale Visage, dark Complexion, with black curled hair;

had on when he went away, a blue Serge Coat, Leather Breeches, white Shirt, woollen Stockings, old Shoes, with square Silver Buckles;

he has a Silver Watch with a Steel Chain, supposed to have taken with him a Sky blue coloured Coat, and a Silk Orange coloured Jacket,

---

[1] Cornelius' escape from the constable marks the second stage in his escape from Benjamin Vernor.

with Flounces[2] down the Breasts and Skirts; one Pair of new Pumps, a Beaver Hat, and other Clothes not known;

he has one if his Fingers on this Left Hand a little crooked by a Swelling lately in it;

he worked down by SmithFurnace at this Trade;

when he drinks much his Face gets very red.

Whoever takes up said Fellow, and secures him in any of his MajestyGoals, shall receive the above Reward, paid by SAMUEL FINLEY, or BENJAMIN VERNOR.

N.B. All Person are forewarned not to harbour the above Person, and all Masters of Vessels are forbid to carry him, off, at their Peril.

---

[2] A wide ornamental strip of material gathered and sewn to a piece of fabric, typically on a skirt or dress; a frill; ruffle, ruff.

'He Speaks Erse'

Samuels Smith and Price Have Run Off from New Castle

April 30, 1767, The Pennsylvania Gazette (Penn.)

RUN away from the subscriber, living at the Cross Roads, near New Castle, a servant man, named Samuel Smith, about 34[1] years of age, about 5 feet 7 inches high, pock marked, short black hair, and a Roman nose; he speaks Erse,[2] is much given to drink, swears much when in liquor, and came from Ireland last fall with Capt. McIlvaine;[3]

had on a brown cloth coat and jacket, buckskin breeches, and new shoes.

---

[1] Samuel Smith is quite old to be a servant, if we are to believe the standard historical narrative that claims that all servants were voluntary indentures signing up for what amounted to an apprenticeship at age 18 and then given their freedom to build a farm and log cabin...
[2] The Scottish or Irish Gaelic language.
[3] He was shipped as cargo by said captain, not serving as a sailor. Such ships had tiny crews.

There is supposed to be with him a servant, named Samuel Price, a Woolcomber, and has been long in this country.

Whoever takes up said servants, and secures them, to that their masters may have them again, shall have Four Pounds for both, or Forty Shillings for each, with reasonable charges, paid by ANDI MCBAY, or JOHN SINGLETON.[4]

---

[4] It seems that John Singleton could not afford to take out an ad for his servant. We should remember that many servant owners had purchased a man to double their own one-man work force and would be in sorry straits should their labor investment escape, putting them one step from slavery themselves.

Goy Boy on the Loose

Peter Kline Wants His Irishman Back!

April 23, 1767, The Pennsylvania Gazette (Penn.)

THREE POUNDS Reward.

RUN away from the subscriber, living in Lampeter township, Lancaster county, on the 12th of April inst. a servant man, named James Foral,

by trade a blacksmith, born in Ireland, and came to this country about 10 months ago, he is about 5 feet 9 or 10 inches high, of a fair complexion, pitted with the small pox,[1] has stoop shoulders, and bends out at the knees very much as he walks, and short curled hair;

had on and took with him, when he went away, a blue broadcloth coat, red double breasted

---

[1] In school and in many a book and documentary since, I was taught that small pox afflicted Native Americans, and that the European settlers were "immune" to this pathogen that they carried into Native lands. The evidence from the period, however, is that small pox was a scourge upon all.

jacket, cloth coloured cloth breeches, and striped trowsers.

Whoever takes up and secures said servant, to that his master may have him again, shall have the above reward, and reasonable charges, paid by PETER KLINE.

'Chunkey Made'

John Dawson, Another Soldier Turned Slave, Has Run Away from Master Clench

May 21, 1767, The Pennsylvania Gazette (Penn.)

RUN away from the subscriber, living in Leacock township, Lancaster County, on the 10th of this inst. May, a servant man, named John Dawson, born in Scotland, and came in with one John Donnal, from Belfast, near two years ago, aged about 22 or 23 years, about 5 feet 5 or 6 inches high, chunkey made, of a sickly complexion, and dull look, black hair, commonly tied behind;

wears a good felt hat, with yellow buttons, a blue coat and waistcoat, with horn buttons, a new coarse shirt, old patched buckskin breeches, old white yarn stockings, old shoes and brass buckles.

Whoever secures said servant, so that his master may have him again, shall have thirty

Shillings[1] reward, and reasonable charges, paid by ROBERT CLENCH.

N.B He had been some time a soldier in the Queen regiment in Ireland.

---

[1] A 30-shilling reward is equal to 30 days' pay for a free laborer. John would be required to compensate his master after capture by serving additional time.

'Very Fond of Negroes Company'

Brawling Welch Servant Man and War Veteran William Jones

May 21, 1767, The Pennsylvania Gazette (Penn.)

RUN away, on the 8th of February last, from the Subscriber, living in Blockley Township, Philadelphia County, a Servant Man, named William Jones, but since he left me goes by the Name of William Evans,

by Trade a Tanner, about 25 Years of Age, 5 Feet 9 Inches high, a dark Complexion, a lively light footed[1] Man, has short black Hair, is well set, his two little Fingers are crooked, talks Welch, and is a Welchman, though he says he is an Englishman,

he served 7 Years in the Town of Bristol, in Old England, and can do almost any Sort of Farming Business;[2]

---

[1] Sounds like quite a boxer.
[2] At age 25, he had served in the military for at least two years, served nearly a year on this term, and served out

had on, when he went away, a light coloured Nap Coat, with a bluish home made Worsted Lining, a light coloured cloth jacket, remarkably pieced and short, without Pockets or Sleeves, black buckskin Breeches, black ribbed yarn Stockings, a Pair of half worn Calfskin Pumps, with a Patch on the Toe of one, Buckles not Fellows, an old Check Shirt and a new Wool Hat;

he is a great Liar, and very fond of Negroes Company, drinking and fighting;[1]

came into this Country with Captain Byrn last Fall from Ireland;

he has been in this Country before a Soldier, and has got his Discharge with him.[2]

Whoever takes up said Servant, and secures him, so that his Master may have him again, shall have Three Pounds Reward, and reasonable Charges, paid by ROBERT HOLLAND.

---

7 years in England, which places his slavery as beginning at age 15 at the youngest.

'A Lusty Well Set Fellow'

John Christy, Sold for Polygamy, Has Run Away

July 30, 1767, The Pennsylvania Gazette (Penn.)

THREE POUNDS Reward.

RUN away, the 22d inst. from the Subscriber, in London grove Township, Chester County, a Servant Man, named JOHN CHRISTY, a lusty well set Fellow, about 26 or 27 Years of Age, 5 Feet 10 or 11 Inches high, has strait brown Hair, of a fair Complexion;

he has been lately in Lancaster Goal for having two Wives and afterwards advertised and put in Chester Goal, and sold out for his Fees. He was born in Ireland, but has been a considerable Time in this Country.

Had on when he went away, a homespun redish brown Cloth Jacket, Tow Trowsers,[1] a strong new Shirt of Russia sheeting, old Shoes, with Brass

---

[1] A coarse, heavy linen in 18th century use for clothing.

Buckles, and a middling good Furr Hat, about half worn.

He had no Money, and it is thought he will steal other Apparel.

Whoever takes up and secures said Servant, in any of his Majesty Goals, so that his Master may have him again, shall have the above Reward, and reasonable Charges, paid by JOHN BALDWIN.

'Will Be Sold Out for Their Fees'

State-Sponsored Slave Trader MATTHIAS BUGH Caught Himself Some Boys

June 4, 1767, The Pennsylvania Gazette (Penn.)

Lancaster, May 27, 1767.

WAS committed to my custody, the 21st of last April, on suspicion of being runaway servants,

Richard Merryman, a low set fellow, about 5 feet 4 inches high, red hair, much freckled, and speaks much with the Irish accent;

says he served his time in George Town, on Potowmack, Maryland, with one James Divin, and has the counter part of his indenture with him.

And Thomas McVenny, about 5 feet 6 inches high, well built, dark brown hair, of a dark complexion, and says he came in here from Ireland last fall with Captain Davis, and that he paid him for his passage, but can produce no receipt for the same.[1]

Their masters, if any they have, are desired, in four weeks after the date hereof, to come, pay their charges, and take them away, or they will be sold out for their fees by MATTHIAS BUGH, Gaoler. [1]

---

[1] If one did not have a document on his person that gave a receipt for having paid his passage, he would have been assumed to have run away and would be sold, even if he was not owned, for the simple reason that travelling without a pass was a capital offense in Plantation America. Not that such a document couldn't have been destroyed by the gaoler for personal gain.

Nicholas Forster Hughes

Runaway School Teacher

May 28, 1767, The Pennsylvania Gazette (Penn.)

RUN away, in the Evening of the 15th Instant, from the Subscriber, living in Nockamixon Township, Bucks County, an indented Servant Man, who writes his Name Nicholas Forster Hughes, but is likely he may change it, born in Ireland, but speaks good English, of small Stature, slender built, thin Face, a little marked with the Small pox, has thin blackish Hair, which he endeavours to curl and has a Scar (it is thought) over his Right Eye brow:

Had on, when he went away, an old Beaver Hat, blue Broadcloth Coat, half worn, greyish napped cloth Jacket lined with red, without Sleeves, and Breeches of the same, lined with Check, Check and white Linen Shirts, black and blue ribbed Worsted Stockings, and Calfskin Pumps, with

Buckles. He has followed keeping School[1] since he came in the Country, and is apt to brag of his learning, when in Liquor, which he will be as often as he can get it.

Whoever takes up and secures said Servant so as his master may have him again, shall have Three Pounds Reward, and reasonable Charges, paid by JAMES LOUGHREY. N.B. All Masters of Vessels are forbid to carry him off at their Peril.

---

[1] The first slave teacher on record was Thomas Hellier of 1678. The increased number of runaway teachers after the French and Indian Wars might indicate prosperity in Philadelphia and other major towns but might also reflect a perceived need for literacy among the frontiersmen with whom such men as Hughs might seek refuge in return for tutoring.

'Both Good Scholars'

With the Literacy to Forge a Pass

May 14, 1767, The Pennsylvania Gazette (Penn.)

RUN away from the subscriber, in Cecil county, Maryland, 10 miles from Christiana bridge, on Saturday night, the 2d of this instant May, two indented servant men,

one named Patrick McKogh, a native Irishman, about 20 years of age, came in last fall from Ireland, talks much on the brogue, and is by trade a cooper;

had on, when he went away, a snuff coloured coat and jacket, half worn, with mohair buttons, blue country made cloth breeches, lined with linen.

The other named Thomas McNeely, came in last May from Ireland, about 20 years of age, by trade a cooper; had on, a light coloured country made coat, with blue and white drugget[1] lining, and

---

[1] Drugget: a heavy, felted fabric of wool or wool and cotton used as a floor covering.

white metal buttons, a double breasted scarlet jacket, and snuff coloured cloth breeches, stockings uncertain, as he had several pair with him, old and new shoes, with Pinchbeck buckles.

Both about 5 feet 5 inches high, and wore their own short brown hair;

they are both good scholars, and it is like may forge a pass.[2]

Whoever takes up and secures said servants, so that the subscriber may have them again, shall have three Pounds reward, or thirty Shillings for either, and reasonable charges paid by AMOS ALEXANDER.

N.B. Said McNeely has followed the soap boiling business.

---

[2] Again, increased numbers of runaways were literate and literacy was beyond the police state measures of the day to combat. Note that upon being purchased by a former runaway slave as an act of mercy, Peter Williamson, in the 1740s, was sent to school by his master in order that he might maintain his freedom.

'Until Reduced by Sickness'

Pursuit of an Ailing Convict Slave

Virginia Gazette (Purdie & Dixon), Williamsburg, June 1, 1769 (Boucher)

THREE POUNDS REWARD WILL be given to any person who will apprehend and have conveyed home to the subscriber, living near Fredericksburg, a runaway convict servant named James Lee, of about 35 years of age, born near Manchester in Lancashire, the dialect of which county he speaks to great perfection.

There is good reason to believe that he got on board a small eastern shore vessel that left Fredericksburg about the 22d of April, commanded by one Sterling, from Prince's creek, in Pocomoke. Any Gentleman who may happen to live in this man's neighborhood are requested to make inquiry of him.

Lee is a tall stout fellow, and, until reduced by sickness, remarkabley strong and brawney; but, having been long afflicted with a cachexical complaint,[1] he still has a dropsical appearance,[2] his belly and legs being swollen, and his face sallow and bloated. He is very much pitted with smallpox, round shouldered, and has lost the first joint of the thumb of his right hand.

He had on a blue short coat, or jacket, like a seaman's, but also took with him a drab coat, which he will probably put on, as making a better appearance, a double breasted swanskin[3] waistcoat, blue breeches, and mottled yarn hose, though he had several other pair, both thread and worsted, sand shoes with uncommon thick soles.

He is a very tolerable practical farmer, and in particular an excellent ploughman. Being a very clownish ignorant fellow, and neither able to read nor write, I can hardly suppose him to frame a very plausible account of himself, and that therefore any person who happens to question him must easily discover him to be a runaway.

The above reward shall be faithfully paid to any person who will deliver him to Mr. Charles

---

[1] "A condition in which the body is evidently depraved. A bad habit of body, chiefly the result of scorbutic, cancerous, or venereal diseases when in their last stage." (Dunglison) p. 154.

[2] Dropsy is a condition wherein a person's body or body part has swelling or excessive accumulation of fluid. In modern medical terms, it is called "edema." Dropsy isn't a disease in itself but may be a symptom of various illnesses or diseases.

[3] A fabric resembling flannel and having a soft nap or surface.

Yates, in Fredericksburg, or to JONATHAN
BOUCHER.[4]

---

[4] A good example of a well-to-do master seeking a
servant, whose running away besmirches his honor and
standing.

'Pretends to Be a Shoemaker'

The Classic Invalidation Advertisement from Plantation America

May 16, 1765, The Pennsylvania Gazette (Penn.)

RUN away from the Subscriber, living in Mount Bethel Township, in Northampton County, on the 17th Day of March last past, a Highland Servant Man, named Donald McDonald, about the Age of 25 Years, about 5 Feet 6 Inches high, of a fresh Complexion, fullfaced, pretty much pitted with the Small pox, has a Scar on the fore Finger of his Left hand, speaks between the Highland and Irish Dialects;

having lived about three Years and an Half in Ireland, and pretends to be a Shoemaker by Trade;

Had on, when he went away, a old blue Broadcloth Coat, stained with Tar, with carved Brass buttons, an Orange coloured Thickset Jacket, with blue Lining, good Buckskin Breeches;

had two Pair of pale blue Stockings, one pair ribbed, with a Darn in the Middle of one of the Stockings, having cut it, with his Leg, last Winter;[1]

it is supposed he will change his Name and Clothes the first Opportunity;

he enquired the Way to Baltimore Town.[2]

Whoever takes up and secures the said Servant, in any of his Majesty Goals, so that his Master may have him again, shall receive Five Pounds Reward, and reasonable Charges, paid by me WILLIAM MILLER.

N.B. All Masters of Vessels, and others are warned on their Peril not to take the said Servant off.[3]

---

[1] His injuries and garments suggest land clearance work, the primary use of rural white slaves, where blacks were used indoors and in working cleared land.

[2] This indicates a network of slave master informers to rival 20th century communist nations.

[3] Working onboard ships in the Age of Sail is universally recognized as among the most perilous occupations in and out of military service. Yet, something about servitude in Plantation America made serving as a slave sailor preferable to large bodies of men. Donald's tar-stained clothes might indicate previous service as a sailor.

'Given Much to Swearing'

Convict Transport, Claudius Taylor, Branded with Gunpowder Letters and on the Run

June 6, 1765, The Pennsylvania Gazette (Penn.)

RUN away, the 26th of May last, from the Subscriber, living in Philadelphia, an Apprentice, named Claudius Taylor, a native of Ireland, about 23 Years of age, 5 Feet 5 or 6 Inches high, round visaged, Pock marked, and marked on his Left hand, by his Thumb, with Powder C T, brown Hair;[1]

had on, when he went away, a blue Saggathy Coat, brown Cloth Jacket, black knit Breeches, new Castor Hat, and new Pumps, with Steel Buckles;

---

[1] This gunpowder burned C T brand means "Convict Transport" and marks young Claudius as a convicted felon who has previously escaped and is therefore most likely to be serving 14 years or life. Despite Claudius' admitted legal status as condemned chattel, he is yet called an "apprentice" in this advertisement, one of myriad indications that terms such as indentured servant and apprentice were often assigned as sham labels for human cattle.

it is very likely he may endeavour to get Work at the Carpenter Trade, he says he served some Time to it in Ireland;

he is fond of Liquor, very talkative, and given much to Swearing.

Whoever takes up and secures said Apprentice, so that his Master may have him again, shall have Three Pounds Reward, and all reasonable Charges, paid by EDWARD BONSALL.

N.B. It is thought he is gone to New York, as he was seen going that Road, in Company with another Man the same Day, and it is likely he will call at Amboy Ferry. All Masters of Vessels, and others, are forbid to harbour or carry him off at their Peril.[2]

---

[2] Slavery was such an important aspect of Plantation America economics that private citizens like Edward Bonsall had been empowered by the British Admiralty [1743] to threaten British Naval Officers with court marshal and possible death for hiring on escaped chattel!

'An Indented Servant Man'

ARCHIBALD THOMPSON Wants His Irishman Back

July 23, 1767, The Pennsylvania Gazette (Penn.)

July 3, 1767.

RUN away last night from the subscriber, living in Norrington township, Philadelphia county, an indented servant man, named John Diermond,[1] a native of Ireland, about 22 years of age, about 5 feet 8 or 9 inches high, of a pale complexion, a little pitted with the small pox, has a down look, near sighted, brown hair, sometimes tied;

had on, when he went away, a brown jacket, made sailor fashion, a fustian ditto, with the back blue cloth, a pair of blue cloth breeches, check shirt, blue yarn stockings, and half worn shoes, with brass buckles; he took with him a pair of two trowsers, and some other wearing apparel.

---

[1] It brings to mind the Robert E. Howard horror story, *Dermond's Bane*.

Whoever takes up said servant, and secures him so as his master may have him again, shall have Four Dollars reward, and reasonable charges, paid by ARCHIBALD THOMPSON, junior.

N.B. All masters of vessels are forbid to carry him off at their peril.[2]

---

[2] The Seven Years' War had recently ended, sparking not only a spike in runaways [often service men who had been sold after discharge] but an increase in threats to sea captains who might take them off. With the only logic for a sea captain taking a penniless runaway onboard being the employment of that man as a sailor, the most dangerous job of the day, this indicates that maritime trade was on the upswing and that a servant's life had either gotten worse [unlikely] or had simply become unbearable in the wake of military service.

'Aged about Sixteen'

Roger Hagon, White Slave and Runaway

August 27, 1767, The Pennsylvania Gazette (Penn.)

RUN away from the subscriber, living near Sasquehanna Lower Ferry, on Sunday, the second instant, a servant lad, named Roger Hagon, lately come from Ireland, aged about 16 years, about 5 feet high;[1]

had on when he went away, an old felt hat, a flax and tow shirt, a pair of old leather breeches, no shoes or stockings, neither coat or jacket, his hair of a black colour, and lately cut off, pretty fair complexion.

He speaks with something of the brogue, and is very talkative. It is thought he went in company

---

[1] Roger is obviously still physically a child, yet he is a slave. How exactly does a child of the favored race of a self-proclaimed white ethnostate end up enslaved at age 15? Fifteen was his probable term of enslavement, a term which may well not have been his first, as many boys were first sold between ages 9 and 12, often by their parents or guardians, and then resold!

with a certain James Barns, a young man, about 18 years old, 5 feet 10 inches high, and well set;

he had on and took with him, when he went away, a castor hat, check shirt, black calimanco jacket, blue breeches, thread stockings, a pair of shoes or pumps, having both kinds with him he had also two coats, one of blue cloth, bound with ferreting the other of country cloth, of a lightish colour, two fine shirts, and a black silk handkerchief;

it is very probable they will keep together as much as possible.

Whoever takes up the above Roger Hagon and secures him, so that his master may have him again, shall have FOUR DOLLARS, reward and reasonable charges, paid by JAMES PORTER.

'By Trade a Gardiner'

The Lowest of the Low Is on the Run in Plantation America

September 3, 1767, The Pennsylvania Gazette (Penn.)

Uwchland township, Chester county, August 28, 1767.

RUN away last night, from the subscriber, a native Irish servant man, named Patrick Brown, lately arrived from Ireland in the snow Sarah, Captain Taylor,

by trade a gardiner, is of a fair complexion, looks sickly, having had the ague for some time past, is a thick well set fellow, about 5 feet 7 or 8 inches high, wears his hair tied behind:

Had on an old fine linen shirt, blue jacket, without sleeves, a frize jacket,[1] of a grey colour,

---

[1] Middle English term for a coarse woolen, plain weave cloth. In the period under question, this indicted a woolen garment with a long, normally uncut nap.

striped ticken breeches,[2] yarn stockings, good shoes, with brass buckles, and a half worn hat.

Whoever takes up and secures said servant, so as his master may have him again, shall have FORTY SHILLINGS reward, and reasonable charges, paid by DENNIS WHELEN.

---

[2] "Ticken" breeches is the same word as "ticking", associated with mattresses. Ticking is the heavy blue-and-white striped cotton material that was used for bedding, now and then.

'Remarkably Slow in Speech'

Runaway Retard, Timothy Downey, Should Be Easily Caught

October 1, 1767

The Pennsylvania Gazette

THREE POUNDS Reward.

RUN away, on the 20th ult. from the subscriber, an apprentice servant man, born in Ireland, by trade a taylor, of a dark complexion, black short hair,

had on, when he went away, a red cloth jacket, without sleeves, a beaver hat, bound with tape, check flannel shirt, check trowsers, half worn pair of shoes, with yellow metal buckles, a pair of buckskin breeches;

he is about 5 feet 4 inches high, about 27 years old,[1] his name Timothy Downey, remarkably slow in speech, and seemingly very quiet.

---

[1] In the Plantation Era, child slaves were typically resold as adults between the ages of 15 and 20. It is of interest

Whoever takes up and secure said apprentice,[2] so that his master may have him again, shall receive the above reward, paid by DAVID PARRY.

---

that the owners of these people never seem to be certain how old they are, and that this runaway white man should have completed any conceivable term of indenture and be enjoying his white privilege, grateful for having given the best years of his life in service to good Christian folk.

[2] In writing nearly a dozen books on this subject, I have found no documented evidence that servants, apprentices and convicts were treated differently. In this ad, David Parry does not seem to be able to decide whether or not his chattel is a servant or an apprentice.

'In the Ship Rose'

A 23-Year-Old Man, Set to Give the Seven Best Years of His Life Away, Takes His Future in Hand and Runs

October 8, 1767, The Pennsylvania Gazette (Penn.)

FORTY SHILLINGS Reward.

RUN away, the 27th day of September last, at night, from the subscriber, living in Leacock township, Lancaster county, a servant lad, named Samuel Askin,

came in the ship Rose last fall from the north of Ireland, a little set fellow, about 5 feet 3 inches high, 23 years old, of a dark complexion, small dark eyes, long thin nose, wears his own long brown hair, cut at top, and tied behind;

had on, and took with him, a good cloth coat, brown coloured buttons round the cuff, and up the sleeve, trimmed full, with yellow gilt buttons, a jacket nearly of the same, the back parts dull coloured twilled flannel, not so long as before, half worn drab breeches, with black horn buttons, half worn felt hat, cocked up with pins, two new tow shirts, and one of flax, good thick new shoes, with one steel, and one carved yellow buckle.[1]

Whoever takes up and secures the said servant, so that his master may have him again, shall receive the above reward from MOSES BRINTON.[2]

---

[1] Note the gross materialism of the culture, with the things worn and carried by the runaway always of more and more precisely worded note than the person.
[2] The Old Testament sanction for slavery rings loud and clear throughout the history of Plantation America.

'An Arch Fellow'

A Combat Veteran with Severe PTSD Has Run Away with His Fellow Slave and They Must Be Returned to Their Master

Wilmington, Delaware was the shipment center for white chattel bound to serve in Pennsylvania, Delaware, New Jersey and Northeast Maryland.

October 15, 1767, The Pennsylvania Gazette (Penn.)

SIX POUNDS Reward.

RUN away, on Monday, the 17th of August, from the subscriber, living near Newark, New Castle county, the following servants, viz.

John Bryn, an Irishman, aged about 25 years, 5 feet 7 or 8 inches high, an arch fellow,[1] being an old soldier in the American expeditions, both to the westward and northward, a ropemaker by trade,

---

[1] An arch fellow, in this context, is taken to mean a leader among his peers, based on his skills, experience and learning.

given much to drink and s[w]earing, and trembles very much with his hands, blind of the left eye, but open and clear;[2]

and as he is a tolerable good scholar, probably will write passes for himself and the others, and will be apt to talk about New Castle and Wilmington, as he is well known in both places, has short black hair, lately cut short before, a midling slim built fellow;

had on a tow shirt, striped linen trowsers, on old spotted jacket, no shoes nor hat known of.[3]

The other an Irishman, named John Milighen, aged about 26 years, 5 feet 9 or 10 inches high, given to drink, and swears when in liquor, is a good butcher, having served a time to that trade in Ireland, a midling set fellow, thin faced;

had on a tow shirt, tow petticoat trowsers, striped linen jacket, and a pair of new shoes, tied with thongs, has a down look when spoke to, with

---

[2] It seems that war has taken a terrible toll of this young man.

[3] No hat or shoes, homeless, on the eve of winter, during the Little Ice Age. If white slavery was the benign trade school of the New World that establishment historians continually babble about, why would a man who has suffered much escape into the cold night with neither shoes nor hat?

often repeating the word Sir, and stroking his hair back, with this hat off, and looking downwards.[4]

Whoever takes up and secures said servants, so as their master may have them again, shall have the above reward, paid by JOSHUA McDOWELL.

These runaways were merely some of tens of thousands who escaped under harsh conditions from something Americans have been led to believe was humane and beneficial, a voluntary employment contract signed—mostly by those who could not read or write.

---

[4] These are signs of a man who has suffered severe corporal punishment and verbal abuse at the hands of his betters.

'Has a Freckled Face'

A Gold-Hoarding Leprechaun Is on the Run with a Renegade Cloth-Maker

February 18, 1768, The Pennsylvania Gazette (Penn.)

Gloucester county, New Jersey, February 13, 1768.

TEN POUNDS Reward. BROKE out of the goal of the county of Gloucester, this morning, the following prisoners, viz.

HUGH WILSON, born in Ireland, about 30 years of age, a tanner by trade, 5 feet 3 or 4 inches high, well set, has black hair, a pleasant countenance, marked with the small pox, has lived lately in Chester and New Castle counties;

had on, a good blue surtout, a light coloured broadcloth jacket, and swanskin waistcoat with black spots, a pair of good leather breeches, and a good hat. It is thought he has a large quantity of money with him, chiefly gold.

And

DAVID COCHRAN, born in Ireland, about 25 years of age, 5 feet 6 inches high, has a freckled face, and red short hair, a fuller[1] by trade, and has lived in Allentown and Haddonfield

had on, a light coloured homespun cloth coat, a striped jacket, cloth breeches, a pair of half boots, and an old hat;

also took a pair of shoes with him;

it is supposed he is gone towards Lancaster.

They are both much inclined to strong liquor, and apt to be intoxicated.

Whoever takes up the above prisoners, and secures them in any goal in New Jersey, Pennsylvania, or the lower counties on Delaware, and gives notice to the subscriber, so that he may have them again, shall receive for Hugh Wilson, Six Pounds reward, and for David Cochran, Four Pounds, and reasonable charges from SAMUEL BLACKWOOD, Sheriff.

---

[1] Fulling, also known as tucking or walking, is a step in woollen clothmaking which involves the cleansing of cloth (particularly wool) to eliminate oils, dirt and other impurities and making it thicker. The worker who does the job is a fuller, tucker or walker.

'Whoever Will Take Up Said Run-Away'

Another White Slave Flees the Slave Depot of Wilmington

Robert Kilby

Essex Gazette – Salem, Massachusetts, Tuesday, July 18, 1769 (New Castle)

Wilmington, July 17, 1769

LAST Saturday night at 10 o'clock ran away from his master Cadwallador Ford, of Wilmington, an indented servant Lad, named Robert Kilby, of short stature, and well fet, of a light complexion and brown hair, near 18 years of age – a new cut upon the fore finger of his right hand.[1]

---

[1] There is no grounds for supposing this was a wound from a beating, as work wounds to the right hand would be more common among servants of all descriptions than those sustained during their regular beatings [beatings being the norm], which, if defensive wounds, would be found primarily to the left hand. Since most beatings were delivered while the servant was tied to a post or ladder, these would fall on the back and secondarily to the head.

Had on when he went away, a brownish colour'd camblet coat, lin'd with red, pretty well worn, strip'd linen and woolen jacket, double-breasted, green worsted plush breeches, a pair blue seam'd stockings, one pair light blue worsted stockings, a pair of thick pumps and brass buckles, two tow shirts and one garlic, 2 pair of tow trowsers, and a felt hat.

Whoever will take up said Run-away, and convey him to, or secure him, so that his master may have him, shalt have TWO DOLLARS Reward and all necessary charges paid, by said CADWALLADOR FORD.

N. B. All masters of vessels and others, are hereby cautioned against harbouring concealing or carrying away said servant on penalty of the Law.

There was with him one Joseph Ross, as he called himself, something taller, and about the same age, supposed to have run away from Ipswich, and to have inticed the said Robert to go with him; they had with them two brownish doges each about as big as a fox.

'Whoever Takes Up Said Boy'

An Injured Sixteen Year-Old Slave Boys Hobbles Off in Search of Liberty

March 31, 1768, The Pennsylvania Gazette (Penn.)

RUN away from the subscriber, living in Leacock township, Lancaster county, on Wednesday the 23d of March, an Irish servant boy, named Francis Davenport, or Divers, about 5 feet 3 inches high, about 16 years of age, a thick fellow, with short brown hair, dark complexion, with a down look, full faced;

had on, when he went away, a blue coat, with black buttons, a white double breasted jacket, made of an Indian blanket, with metal buttons on the one side of it, a pair of leather breeches, one pair of white woollen stockings, a pair of shoes, tied with strings, and an old wool hat;

he has his right ancle strained, so that he walks lame, and the broad side of his foot foremost;

he has a cut on said leg, below his knee, 3 inches cross;[1]

he pretends to have had the palsey on said side, he has travelled most parts in Ireland, and pretends to be a hemp heckler[2] by trade.

Whoever takes up said boy, and secures him in any of his Majesty goals, shall receive FORTY SHILLINGS reward, and reasonable charges, paid by me BENJAMIN VERNOR.

N.B. All masters of Vessels, and others, are forbid to harbour or carry him off at their peril.

---

[1] Very possibly a land clearance injury, as such "boys" were used primarily to clear land to be worked by more valuable human property.
[2] To heckle is to split and straighten flax or hemp fibers for spinning.

'Of a Black Complexion'

Was John Meshefrey the First Irish Negro?

April 7, 1768, The Pennsylvania Gazette (Penn.)

RUN away from his Bail, out of New Castle, on the 30th of March last, one John Meshefrey, born in the North of Ireland, a thick well set Fellow, about 5 Feet 7 Inches high, of a black Complexion,[1] and talks broad:

Had on, when he went away, a blue Coat, whitish Jacket, Buckskin Breeches, grey Stockings, a Pair of Brass Buckles, and an old Felt Hat, tarred on the Top of the Crown.

Whoever takes up said Runaway, and secures him in any Goal in this Province, so that I may have him again, or brings him to me in New Castle, shall have Forty Shillings Reward, paid by JAMES CAMBLE.

---

[1] Was John a mulatto or a full African Irishman? He had a thick Gaelic accent. During the 18th century, the term "black" was used to describe Irish of darker hair and eyes than the typical blond or redhead.

'Has with Him an Indenture'

James Welch and Alexander Sweeny Escape
with James Wilson's Slave Paper

April 21, 1768, The Pennsylvania Gazette
(Penn.)

RUN away from the subscriber, an Irish
servant man, named James Welch, born in Kilkenny
in Ireland, about 23 years of age, about 5 feet 6
inches high, fair Complexion, fair curled hair, by
trade a carpenter and wheelwright;

took with him, an old blue coat, buckskin
breeches, 3 jackets, 1 ratteen, 1 striped cotton, and 1
little red ditto, a sheepskin apron, two shirts, one
fine, the other coarse, two pair of ribbed stockings,
one pair blue, the other brown, and a felt hat, with
white looping;

he can play well on the German flute, or any
other instrument of music; has with him an

indenture of James Wilson, which name it is supposed he will go by.[1]

Likewise went in company, a certain Alexander Sweeny, about 5 feet 10 inches high, fresh coloured, much pitted with the small pox, short hair, of a darkish colour;

had on, a brown coat, a spotted flannel jacket, grey worsted stockings, a check shirt, and buckskin breeches.

All masters of vessels are forbid to carry off the above persons, at their peril.

Whoever secures the above named persons, in any of his Majesty goals, shall have the sum of Eight Pounds, and reasonable charges, paid by CHARLES OHARO, living in the Barrens of York county, near Stevenson Ferry. April 4, 1768.

---

[1] Whenever possible, runaways took their paper, some else's paper or forged one, which is an indication that early America was a comprehensive police state.

'Committed for Felony'

One Sure Way to Become a Slave in Plantation America

April 21, 1768, The Pennsylvania Gazette (Penn.)

FIVE POUNDS Reward.

MADE his escape from Caecil county goal, on Wednesday, the 6th of this inst. April, Edward Johnson (committed for felony)[1] born in Ireland, about 27 years of age, 5 feet 3 or 4 inches high, wears his own dark brown hair, tied behind, a long sharp nose, a little pitted with the small pox, fresh complexion;

---

[1] Edward would certainly be sold for his crime, as the criminal justice system was inextricably linked to slave labor, .a practice that did not end with the so-called Reconstruction Amendments. Indeed, Section 1 of the Fourteenth Amendment provides for the denying of "life, liberty and property" under "due process of law."

it has been reported that he went formerly by the name of Edward Carney;[2]

had on, when he went away, a short brown cloth coat, with large metal buttons, old buckskin breeches, grey yarn stockings, but no shoes.

Whoever apprehends the said Johnson, and brings him to the goal in Charles Town, in the aforesaid county, shall receive the above reward, and reasonable charges, paid by W. MITCHELL, Sheriff of said county.

---

[2] Carney is a neighborhood in South-Central Baltimore County. It is not known if there is any connection between the Carney family and the locale.

'Pretends to Be a Schoolmaster'

A Fugitive Advertisement with an Excellent Description of a Horse

May 26, 1768, The Pennsylvania Gazette (Penn.)

THIRTEEN POUNDS Reward.

ABSCONDED from his usual place of Abode, in East Bradford Township, Chester County, on the 6th of April last, a certain Dennis Salmon, born in Ireland, about 21 Years of Age, 5 Feet 7 or 8 Inches high, wears his own dark brown Hair, inclining to curl, has thick lips, long Nose, his Forehead wrinkled, ruddy dark Complexion, down Look, slim, but pretty fleshy:

Had on, when he went away, a fine half worn Hat, a fine Shirt, ruffled at the Bosom, a light Country made Cloth Coat, and Jacket, without Sleeves, made plain, with Mohair Buttons, good Buckskin Breeches, the Buttons covered with Leather, half worn Shoes, with Pinchbeck Buckles;

and took with him several fine Shirts, and several Pairs of fine Thread and Worsted Stockings, and two Silver Watches;

he pretends to be a Schoolmaster, and has been in that Employ:[1] It is supposed he is gone to Virginia or Carolina, and very probably will change his Name, and may likely pass for a Quaker.

He clandestinely took with him, a valuable large dark bay Mare, supposed to be with Foal, a natural Pacer, about 15 Hands high, in good Order, well built, shod before, has a switch Tail, and hanging Mane, curled. about ten Years old, goes fast and easy, and carries herself lofty, has two remarkable Curls, or Twists, in her Forehead, right

---

[1] This is a fascinating statement, that he "pretends" to be a teacher and has been a teacher, which indicates that, although he was employed [which may mean being owned or paid as a free man as the terminology was dual-use and came from the French "to use"] as a teacher, he had recently been owned as a slave in some other capacity [possibly to pay off a debt], was then free and had stolen a horse. Whatever the story behind Dennis Salmon, if captured, he would have been sold. It may be that he was a grifter and recently came from Ireland with an education but no money. His youth and education suggest a middle- to upper-class parentage. The tone of the ad certainly paints him as a confidence man and criminal. However, based on many previous ads reviewed by this reader, it was common for a person who was owned in one employ, but who had previously been free in another employ, to be accused by their recent owner of "pretending" to be a person experienced in that pursuit—a classic method of invalidation.

between her Eyes, without Brand or Ear mark; likewise an old breasted Saddle, and Curb Bridle.

Whoever takes up and secures the said Man, and Mare, so that the Man may be brought to Justice, and the Owner of the Mare gets her again, shall receive the above Reward; or Three Pounds for the Man, and Ten Pounds for the Mare, with reasonable Charges, if brought home to the Subscriber, living in the Township and County aforesaid.

MARY GRUBB.

N.B. The said Dennis Salmon was advertised last Month in both the Pennsylvania Chronicle, and Gazette.

'Took Away from His Master'

Two Irishmen on the Run

June 16, 1768, The Pennsylvania Gazette (Penn.)

Wednesday, June 8, 1768.

RUN away last Sunday night, from the subscriber, living in East Nantmell, Chester county, two Irish Servant Men;

one named WILLIAM CUMMINGS, about 35 years of age, 5 feet 9 inches high, full faced, large nose, black hair, fair complexion, his head bald, and very subject to drink, if he can procure it;

he took away from his master, a white cloth coat and jacket, a fine shirt, two pair of stockings, and a pair of silver buckles belonging to his mistress; he may appear in coarse cloathing, such a tow linen shirts, and trowsers, black stockings, &c.

The other a young man, named JAMES IRELAND, about 17 years of age, of slender stature, about 5 feet 3 inches high;

had with him, a ragged blue coat, tow petticoat trowsers, &c.

Whoever secures the said servants in any Goal, so that their master may have them again, shall receive for the said William Cummings, the sum of Forty Shillings, and for the said James Ireland, the sum of Twenty Shillings, and reasonable charges, paid by JOHN THOMPSON.

Men of varied experience, age, skills and race were more often teaming up to run away together. Also, the number of runaways in Maryland and Pennsylvania increased by a large margin between 1765 and 1775, with as many runaways in the last ten years of the Colonial Era than in the previous 40.

'A Very Artful Fellow'

A Runaway Jockey 'Who Pretends to be a Carpenter' and Stands almost Six Feet Tall, is Worth 200 Shillings [1]

July 7, 1768, The Pennsylvania Gazette (Penn.)

Chester County, June 30, 1768.

TEN POUNDS Reward.[1]

LAST night, broke out of the goal of said county, a certain JAMES DICKEY, born in Ireland, but came to this country very young, with his parents, and lived in Oxford township, in said county of Chester, is a very artful fellow, and speaks with the Irish accent, and very mild, is long visaged, wide mouthed, is about 5 feet 10 or 11 inches high, wears his own strait hair;

---

[1] With 20 shillings to the pound and a shilling being the going day labor rate, this man is worth 200 days' work. Whatever his crime, if any, he would have been sentenced to at least 200 days of labor when sold to pay off his reward cost.

had on, when broke goal, a felt hat, blue cloth jacket, without sleeves, leather breeches, white yarn ribbed stockings, coarse shoes, and brass buckles;

pretends to be a carpenter and weaver by trade, has been a great horse jockey, and has been often in New England, and at Carolina, in Roan county, where he has a brother living, who broke out of said goal some years ago,[2] and it is imagined he will make there again, with one Robert Smith, who was to see him the evening before he broke out.

Whoever apprehends the said James Dickey, and secures him in any of his Majesty goals, or brings him to Chester goal, shall have the above reward, and reasonable charges, paid by JOSEPH THOMAS, Goaler.

---

[2] Is this a clan of criminals or have both boys run away from slavery? In the end, these were not useful distinctions in Plantation America.

'Both Apt to Be Drunk'

A Portrait of Two Day Laborers from Plantation America

July 14, 1768, The Pennsylvania Gazette (Penn.)

TEN POUNDS Reward.

ESCAPED from the Constables, some Weeks ago, the following Persons, viz.

ANDREW CRAWFORD, late from Ireland, about 25 Years old, 5 Feet 11 Inches high, stoop shouldered, Pock pitted, pale faced, has black Hair, tied behind, his Cloathing uncertain,

ROBERT SCOTT, 24 Years old, 5 Feet 9 Inches high, full faced, Pock pitted, has light brown Hair.

Both apt to be drunk, and to swear, generally work together, and commonly reside in London Britain Township, near Newark; but now are supposed to be gone to Maryland, to Harvest.

Whoever secures the said Fellows, and delivers them to Mr. JOSEPH THOMAS, Goal Keeper, of Chester County, in Pennsylvania, shall have the above Reward, or Six Pounds for Crawford, and Four for Scott.

It is anyone's guess what these two did, but they did it together. They were two big, strong men, the kind of men who would make a shilling a day competing with slave owners for the farmers who rented, rather than bought, their help, and also likely worked alongside unfree slaves doing the same thing. There is no indication that Crawford and Scott had ever been slaves. However, they represent the future threat of wage work to the institution of chattel slavery and may have been physical enough— both specimens of the age—to outwork the typical slave, who was malnourished and about 5' 6".

Also note that they travelled together, as men without documents must do to protect themselves from abduction and sale. According to the ad, these men had been travelling through Chester County when arrested, telling the gaol keeper that they were headed to Maryland for the harvest. Perhaps they did not have travelling papers, a crime even if they were free laborers? Odds are, they got drunk and had a fight against some local boys and got arrested.

Overall, these fellows and their conduct give the reader an idea of one kind of people a runaway slave might encounter on the road.

'Hearty Looking Servant Maid'

A Five Dollar Man and a Forty Shilling Maid

July 21, 1768, The Pennsylvania Gazette (Penn.)

TEN POUNDS Reward.

BROKE out of the workhouse, in the borough and county of Chester, on the 14th of the Sixth Month, the two following servants, viz.

HENRY SMITH, an Englishman, about 23 years of age, of a fair complexion, grey eyes, light straight yellowish hair, a little marked with the small pox, a scar on his cheek, like a large pock mark, about 5 feet 7 or 8 inches high, a carpenter or wheelwright by trade, but his employ in this country has been attending a saw mill;

stole since he went away,[1] a light coloured camblet jacket, lined with cinnamon coloured

---

[1] The clothes they were wearing are included in the list of stolen goods, as their every stocking and shoe was owned by their owners. Thus, escaping by any means other than naked would incur theft charges as well as runaway fees and time owed the master.

tammy, a red twilled flannel waistcoat, a new beaver hat, with two stains on the brim, near the crown, of a redish colour, a pair of English ticking trowsers, two pair ditto striped linen, several fine shirts, one check ditto, a black neckcloth, several pair of thread stockings, and a new pair of neats leather shoes.

The other, a healthy, hearty looking servant maid, named MARY KENNEDY, came from Ireland, and hath pretty much of the brogue in her talk, broad face, somewhat pock fretten, black complexion, and black hair;

had on, and stole since she went away,[1] a linsey striped gown, a short check ditto, a check apron, a red and blue striped petticoat, one ditto of walnut coloured tammy, one riding ditto of walnut colour and black tammy, a black cloth cloak, with a velvet collar, no cape, one Irish linen shift, one ditto of Irish sheeting, cambrick caps, with lawn borders, a plain lawn Handkerchief, one ditto of silk, a white peeling hat, puckered over, with a white silk ribbon about the crown, a pair of calfskin pumps, one ditto of neats leather;

much more clothes they have stolen.

She is in company with the above servant, and it is thought they will pass for man and wife; they have been lurking about Thomas Waters for some weeks, in order to furnish themselves with clothes, and will now be for making off; they lie by in the day, and travel slowly in the night, breaking open spring houses and smoke houses as they go.

Whoever takes up and secures said servants in goal, so that their masters may have them again, shall have FORTY SHILLINGS for the woman, and FIVE POUNDS, reward, and reasonable charges, for the man, if taken up within 25 miles of Chester, or the above reward for both, if further off, paid by WILLIAM PETERS, and THOMAS WATERS.

'Lockings O!'

'At the Sign of the Breeches' John Jones' Master is Missing His Services

July 28, 1768

The Pennsylvania Gazette

FIVE DOLLARS Reward.

RUN away from John Jones, breeches maker, at the sign of the Breeches, near the prison, an apprentice lad, named JOHN NELSON, about 21 years of age, 5 feet 6 or 7 inches high, of a sandy complexion, sandy hair, born in Ireland, has a little of the brogue on his tongue, very apt in his talking to make use of the expression, Lockings O!

Had on, when he went away, a dark fustian coat, a broad check shirt, brown thread stockings, new shoes, leather breeches, new wool hat.

It is supposed he is either gone up Lancaster road, or into Bucks county. Whoever takes up and secures the said apprentice, so that his master may have him again, shall receive the above reward, and all reasonable charges, paid by JOHN JONES.

N.B. All masters of vessels are forbid to carry him off, at their peril.

I'd like to think that John made that pair of breeches specifically for his escape. This has been often reiterated but bears repeating: being a seaman was the worst job in the world and was not engaged in freely but represented a bond, either forced or voluntary, to serve. That so many men with relatively easy jobs would be expected by those who knew them best to head to sea is telling and at the least demonstrates that being an apprentice or servant was not an act of social or economic mobility but a payless pit.

'Scalped Before'

Busted up Survivor of the Indian Wars Is on the Run

July 28, 1768

The Pennsylvania Gazette

RUN away the 22d of this instant July, from ROBERT HAYS, in Rapho township, Lancaster county, an Irish servant man, named JOHN BERRY, a short thick fellow, about 25 years old, with a large lump on the fore part of one of his shoulders, like a windgall,[1] has short bushy brown hair, scalped before,[2] and a flat cocked up nose.[3]

He took with him a little black mare, six years old, white face, glass eyes, one white hind foot, and hollow backed; also an old saddle and bridle;

likewise a dark brown snuff coloured coat, bound with tape, almost new, a silk and cotton jacket, with yellow, red and green stripes, and small silver buttons, an old green velvet jacket and breeches, with hair buttons, a Thirty Shilling hat, not much worn, a god linen shirt, a pair of black worsted stockings, and a pair blue yarn ribbed ditto, calfskin pumps, with large square silver buckles,

---

[1] A windgall is a small painless swelling observed in horses' legs.

[2] The fact that he had been previously scalped indicates that he had been to America before as a teenager and was most likely involved as a combatant in the French and Indian War. It is telling that so many servants made their way back to Ireland or England, only to be sold and shipped back again. If America was viewed by all as the land of opportunity, if servitude was the opportunity to get an economic footing in the new world, as we Americans have so often been taught, why did so many seek to return to the Old World or escape to live with the Indians in the oldest world possible? A member of Peter Williamson's regiment was scalped in action near the beginning of the conflict, as was at least one Mountain Man who survived scalping. Even a woman is known to have survived a scalping at the Musselshell during a battle with the Sioux a hundred years later.

[3] Who knows if the broken nose was caused by Indian club, Irish fist or English horsewhip?

and a pair steel ditto. He came from Ireland this summer, and talks on that accent.

Whoever takes up and secures said servant and mare, so as his master may have them again, shall have THREE POUNDS reward, and reasonable charges, or Forty Shillings for the servant paid by me ROBERT HAYS.

'An Arch Cunning Fellow'

Another Pennsylvania Horse Thief on the Run

August 11, 1768, The Pennsylvania Gazette (Penn.)

Carnarvon Township, August 4, 1768.

RUN away, last night, from the subscriber, a servant man, named James Murray, an Irishman, came from Ireland two years ago; he is about 5 feet 5 or 6 inches high, an arch cunning fellow, well learned as to reading and writing, and may possibly forge a pass;

had on, when he went away, an old shirt and trowsers, a home made jacket, middling large, of light colour, a pair of good neat leather shoes, with a pair of narrow rimmed buckles, of a yellowish cast, a new felt hat, of William Jenkinsmake:

He stole and took with him, a dark brown horse, of a middling size, well set, in good order, and an old saddle, and possibly has the marks of the gears, as he went in the waggon one of the hind horses, his shoes are newly removed.

Whoever takes up and secures said servant, and horse, so that the owner may have them again,[1] shall have Three Pounds reward, or Four Dollars for each, and reasonable charges, paid by EDWARD HUGHES, in Carnarvon township, Lancaster county, or WILLIAM GRAHAM, at the sign of the Black Horse, in Market street, Philadelphia.

N.B. All masters of vessels are forbid to carry him off at their peril.[2]

---

[1] "Whoever takes up and secures said servant, and horse, so that the owner may have them again..." says everything the past needs to tell us about the value of working white men in Plantation America. In fact, James and the horse—and the horse is barely fit for use—are both assigned the same 3–4-pound value.

[2] By this point in my research, I am of the opinion that, being threatened with peril by shopkeepers had gotten sea captains, men of a higher masculine order and higher social status, in such an ire that they were hiring on runaways out of spite.

'Lately Come From the Ship'

Two Irish Slaves on the Run

August 18, 1768, The Pennsylvania Gazette (Penn.)

RUN away from the subscribers, living in Hanover township, Lancaster county, on Sunday, the 7th of August inst. an Irish servant man, named PETER CONOWAY, of a middle stature, speaks with the brogue, is about 5 feet 6 or 7 inches high, has a down look, his hair is of a darkish pale colour, cut short off, except a little behind, as he is lately come from the ship;[1]

had on, when he went away, a wool hat, about half worn, striped shirt, old white trowsers, a spotted flannel jacket, an old pair of shoes, and midling large brass buckles.

---

[1] Just as soul drivers who sold blacks "down the river" to New Orleans would groom their chattel before sale, even using shoe polish to dye gray hair, white slave merchants would similarly clean up and even makeup their cargo before prospective buyers boarded their ship to see the human wares. Most white slave purchases took place onboard ship.

Also, went in company with the above, another servant man, a native of Ireland, named THOMAS DOIL, speaks more with the brogue than the other, about 5 feet 4 or 5 inches high, his hair also cut, but black, and somewhat curly;

had on, an old wool hat, striped shirt, old white trowsers, an old light blue jacket, much worn, the upper part of the back parts another kind of cloth, and dark blue, and a new pair of calfskin shoes with straps, but were tied with thongs.

Whoever takes up said servants, and secures them in any of his Majesty goals, so that their masters may have them again, shall have Forty Shillings for each, if taken separate; if taken together, Three Pounds for both, and reasonable charges, paid by us DANIEL SHAW, SAMUEL ALLEN.

N.B. All masters of vessels, and others, are forbid to carry them off, at their peril.

'Pockpitted'

An Irishman and a Scott on the Quarrelsome Run Near 2 Months

These boys were first advertised as having escaped in July, see: 'Both Apt To Be Drunk'

September 1, 1768, The Pennsylvania Gazette (Penn.)

TEN POUNDS Reward.

ESCAPED from the constables, some weeks ago, the following persons, viz.

ANDREW CRAWFORD, late from Ireland, about 25 years old, five feet eleven inches high, stoop shouldered, pockpitted, pale faced, has black hair, tied behind, his cloathing uncertain.

ROBERT SCOTT, 24 years old, 5 feet 9 inches high, full faced, pockpitted, has light brown hair;

both apt to swear, and get drunk, and very quarrelsome; they generally make their home at one Ralston, near Newark.

Whoever secures said fellows, and delivers them to Joseph Thomas, Goalkeeper, for Chester county, shall be intitled to the above reward, or Six Pounds for Crawford, and Four for Scott, paid by JOSEPH THOMAS, Goaler.

The reward prices and the shipping note on Crawford suggest that both men were escaped servants who committed a crime [which might have constituted or included running away] and then broke free of the constables.

'Very Little Hair upon his Head'

Twenty-Two Years and Worth Only 40 Shillings

September 15, 1768

The Pennsylvania Gazette

RUN away from his Bail, JOHN BURK, a young Man, about 22 Years of Age, born in the Country of Gallway, in Ireland, is about 5 Feet 7 Inches high, smooth faced, and a little freckled, of a slender Stature, with very little Hair upon his Head.

Had on, when last seen, an old white Flannel Waistcoat, a Check Shirt, old blue Breeches, and a small round Hat, with a Piece cut of one Side of it; and, it is supposed, went for New York Yesterday Morning.

Whoever apprehends said BURK, and secures him in any of his Majesty Goals, shall be paid a Reward of Forty Shillings,[1] and reasonable Charges, by JOHN TAYLOR.

---

[1] Forty days' pay.

'A Servant Boy'

Sixteen-Year-Old Chattel Barney Campbell Stole Himself

September 29, 1768, The Pennsylvania Gazette (Penn.)

Lancaster, September 20, 1768.

RUN away from the subscriber, a servant boy,[1] named BARNEY CAMPBELL, born in the north of Ireland, about 16 years of age, about 5 feet high, well set, black hair, is pitted with the small pox, and hath a scar on his right cheek, near his eye.[2]

He hath for some time past been at the tanner business, and hath no other clothes with him (it is thought) than such as are much dirtied, and appear as if worn by a person accustomed to work at that business, which are thought to be a light coloured

---

[1] *Boy* is the original English term for a male slave. Servant is a term designating any unfree person, adopted for use in the King James Bible to denote a variety of slave types.
[2] He has likely been beaten by his master.

cloth coat, a coarse linen shirt and trowsers, shoes, and an old hat.[3]

It is supposed he is gone towards Carlisle, as he hath been seen on the road leading from Lancaster to that place.

Whoever takes up the said servant, and secures him in any goal, so that his master may have him again, shall have Twenty Shillings reward; but if brought home to his master, the subscriber, in Lancaster, Thirty Shillings, and reasonable charges, paid by CASPER SINGER.

N.B. It is supposed he is with one John O'Brian, a runaway, an artful fellow, and knows most parts of the country.

---

[3] He has one change of worn, dirty clothes and no shoes.

'On Suspicion of Being Runaway Servants'

Two Whites Arrested and Held for Not Having Freedom Papers—and a Sooty Colored Negro Too!

November 17, 1768, The Pennsylvania Gazette (Penn.)

York Town, in York County, October 30, 1768.

TAKEN up, and committed to this Goal, some time ago, two Men, on Suspicion of being Runaway Servants;

one goes by the Name of WILLIAM ROBESON, pretty well set, about 5 Feet 7 or 8 Inches high, of a fair Complexion, has brown Hair, tied behind, and has a Lump on one of his Eyebrows.

The other calls himself THOMAS WILKINSON, a thick short Fellow, about 5 Feet 5 Inches high, of a fair Complexion, round visaged, and has long Hair, tied behind.

They are lately from Ireland, but poorly clothed, and cannot be described from their Dress;

they are both young Fellows. Also a Negroe Man, about 28 Years old, named Joseph Butler, who says he is a Freeman; he is a stout likely Fellow, of a sutty black Colour. Any Person, or Persons, claiming said suspected Persons, are desired to come and prove their Property, pay their Fees, and take them away, otherwise they will be sold out for the same, in 4 Weeks from this Date, by JACOB GRAYBELL, Goaler.

These men were abducted by law officers and would have been sold no matter what, for they did not have paperwork on their persons declaring that they had been freed, which means all poor whites and all blacks were assumed to be runaway property. Perhaps Joseph Butler's freedom papers where soaked in a rain storm. Perhaps William Robeson's freedom papers were taken from him by the gaol keeper.

'Pale Faced Pock Marked'

A Shoemaker Slave Turned Criminal in His Old Age

November 3, 1768, The Pennsylvania Gazette (Penn.)

TWELVE DOLLARS Reward.

RUN away from his bail, the 23d of October last, a certain JOSEPH POST, born in Ireland, about 28 years old, by trade a shoemaker, about 5 feet 3 inches high, pale faced, pock marked, dark curled hair, and blind in one eye;[1]

had on, when he went away, a castor hat, short blue coat, striped linen trowsers, chocolate coloured stockings, half worn neats leather shoes, with buckles. He took with him, a small black mare, about 12 hands high, 5 or 6 years old, some white on one hind foot, with a switch tail;

---

[1] Twenty-eight-year-old persons of the working class in this age had generally aged and accumulated injuries equivalent to a modern American laborer in his late 50s.

also took a new hunting saddle, with old stirrup irons, and no housings.

He appears to be a still quiet fellow, except he has taken too much strong drink, which he is apt to do.

Whoever takes up and secures the said fellow, with the mare and saddle, so that the subscriber may have them again, shall have the above reward; or Three Pounds for the man alone, and Thirty Shillings for the mare and saddle, paid by WILLIAM KERLIN, living in Birmingham, Chester county.

'Has Ungenerously Left a Wife and Child'

A Deadbeat Dad Makes off on the Brink of Winter

December 15, 1768, The Pennsylvania Gazette (Penn.)

ABSCONDED from the constable of Plumsted township, Bucks county, a certain James Montgomery, a short, well set, smooth faced young man, about 5 feet 3 or 4 inches high, born in Ireland, is very talkative, has black curled hair, fond of singing and dancing, in both which is something of a proficient. It will be impossible to give an exact description of the cloaths he will wear, as he had on, and took with him, a blue duffil great coat, bound round with brown binding, a brown stuff, and a blue cloth tight bodied coat, several jackets, but more than a green and swanskin one are not remembered, a pair of plush, and a pair of new leather breeches. It is supposed he intends going off in some of the first vessels for Ireland. He has ungenerously left a wife and child at home, stripped of every thing which could have any ways contributed towards their sustenance.[1]

The good character he has always borne in the neighbourhood, has given him an opportunity, a few days before his going away, of being guilty of several very gross impositions, in particular to the great distress of a poor widow, whose circumstances can by no means bear it. All masters of vessels are forbid carrying him off, and it is hoped so great a villainy will excite the resentment of all well disposed persons to endeavour taking him up.

Three Pounds reward, and all reasonable charges, will be given for securing said Montgomery, so that he may be had again.[2]

WILLIAM HOUGH, Constable.

---

[1] A positive aspect of Plantation America was that it was against the law—most of the colonies actually being governed under religious sects beholden to the British crown—to abandon wife and child. The most tragic aspect of this situation was that, if Montgomery was not captured and restored to his family, the widow and child, one or both, would very likely be sold into slavery.

[2] If Montgomery had been recovered, he would have been sold to pay off this fee, as it would become his debt and debts were immediately settled with forced labor. He would have been sold within—or even to—the municipality and also tasked with supporting his family and paying off his wife's short-term debts, as did the father of Thomas Hellier back in England in 1678.

'He Serv'd His Time'

A Black Slave Escapes with the Aid of a Former White Slave

Virginia Gazette (Rind), Williamsburg, June 15, 1769. (Brockenbrough)

Hobb's Hole, June 6, 1769. RUN away from the subscriber, on the second of May last, a Negro boy named BILLY, about 16 years old, a likely, stout, well made lad, and not very black:[1]

Had on, when he went away, a brown cloth coat, with red sleeves and collar, and green plains waistcoat and breeches. He was seen in Richmond county;

going upwards with one David Randolph, a cooper by trade, who ran away from this town about the same time. He is a stout well made fellow; and had on a blue lappell'd serge coat, with yellow buttons, a blue and white striped waistcoat, (which appear'd to be country made) and leather breeches:

---

[1] In other words, he's a mixed-race person.

He had other clothes with him, and some coopers tools:

He work 'd some time ago at Mr. James Hunter's; but I am inform 'd he serv'd his time in Philadelphia,[2] and am apprehensive he will carry the boy to Maryland, or Pennsylvania, and sell him.[3] Whoever takes up the said boy, and secures him, so that I may get him again, shall receive FIVE POUNDS, if taken in the colony; if out of the colony, TEN POUNDS. JOHN BROCKENBROUGH.

---

[2] Randolph had worked off his sentence or indenture in Philadelphia and was now working as a wage laborer. Such men often helped slaves and servants escape and it was risky to have hired help around your servants and slaves.

[3] The market for black slaves in Pennsylvania was never good. It is more rational to suspect that David and Billy had teamed up.

'Supposed to Be a Runaway'

The Intrinsic Injustice of Plantation America

January 19, 1769, The Pennsylvania Gazette (Penn.)

Burlington, January 9, 1769.

WAS committed to the goal of the county of Burlington, on the 5th day of this instant January, a certain man, supposed to be a runaway,[1] a Cooper by trade, about 29 or 30 years of age,[2] says he was born in the county of Derry, in Ireland, and came to this country with Captain Corwell, 7 years ago;[3]

he goes by the name of JOSEPH BENNIN, alias BENNETT, very much pockmarked, with short black hair; has on an old brown nap jacket,

---

[1] This first note and those that follow are the glaring contradictions implicit in this document when set against the fanciful historical "record."

The only evidence required to be judged a runaway was that a person did not have freedom papers.

[2] Typically, white slaves were sold for the first time between ages 14 and 18.

[3] According to establishment historians, white slaves were all indentured servants doing seven-year terms.

with a blue under ditto, black velvet breeches, and black stockings, and check shirt.[4]

His master, if any he has,[5] is hereby desired to come, pay charges, and take him away, in five weeks from the date hereof, otherwise he will be sold for the same,[6] by me EPHRAIM PHILIPS, Goaler.

---

[4] Joseph had no shoes and was found at large in the coldest month of one of the coldest eras on record. When runaways and convicts had shoes, this was always noted and in detail.

[5] It is not known if this man was a slave, but it was assumed by a local jailer, with that assumption immediately becoming uncontested legal fact.

[6] No matter whether this man was an escaped slave or not, he would have been sold as one.

'He Has a Foul Disorder'

John Wilson, Runaway Weaver

January 19, 1769, The Pennsylvania Gazette (Penn.)

Chester county, January 9, 1769.

RUN away from the subscriber, in Uwchland township, Chester county, on the 8th instant, a servant man, named JOHN WILSON, by trade a Weaver,[1] about 22 or 24 years of age, 5 feet 6 or 7 inches high, about 5 months from Ireland,[2] well set, fair hair, cut short before, has a scar on one of his cheeks, and is of a dark brown complexion;[3]

had on a short coat of a dark yellowish colour, a blue and white striped jacket, with old blue stockings for sleeves, new cloth breeches, of a whitish colour, white ribbed yarn stockings, an old

---

[1] What was it about weaving that drove so many to run away?
[2] Just being transported at the age of 22–24 marks John as being sold for the second time at least.
[3] Dark complexion among Irish is noted more often in later years.

374

check shirt, a new felt hat, bound with tape, half worn shoes, and carved brass buckles.

Whoever takes up said servant, and secures him, so that his master may have him again, shall have Forty Shillings reward, and reasonable charges, paid by me WILLIAM DENNY.[4]

N.B. He has a foul disorder, which appears on his right arm and side, which will be an indisputable mark that he is the person described, for which he was under a course of physick.[5]

All masters of vessels are forbid to carry him off.

---

[4] Forty shillings, or merely 2 pounds, is a small reward for a man with six years and more left to serve. Might his ill health have affected his value?
[5] Afflicted by a skin disease of some kind, John seems to have been getting treatment, which would have been paid for by his owner, indicating a certain compassion.

'A Very Good Scholar'

A Long-Term War Veteran Turned School Teacher Runs Away? How Bad Must Colonial Children Have Been?

March 16, 1769, The Pennsylvania Gazette (Penn.)

SIX DOLLARS Reward.

RUN away, about the 16th of November last, a servant man, named JAMES DAVENPORT, about 30 years of Age, 5 feet 8 or 9 inches high, a dark complexion, hollow eyes, long black hair, tied behind;

had on, when he went away, a good castor hat, a grey lappelled coat, a blue waistcoat, buckskin breeches, old shoes, and pinchbeck buckles;

also took with him, a claret coloured coat and waistcoat, and a red silk waistcoat;

he says, he was born in London, and has been 11 years in the service, and got his discharge in Cork, in Ireland;[1]

he is a very good scholar, and has taught school two years and a half in Sadsbury township, Chester county, and took with him a certificate, signed by several of his employers.

Whoever takes up and secures said servant,[2] in any goal, or brings him to the subscriber, living in the township aforesaid, shall have the above reward, and reasonable charges, paid by me JAMES BOYD.

---

[1] Discharged British servicemen were almost always destitute, many having been simply kidnapped or otherwise impressed into service to begin with. During this period, across Europe, armies and navies were used in place of extensive prison systems to dispose of men of the lower classes.

[2] From the mid-1760s, it becomes for any servant to be referred to as an indenture, only rarely were allusions made to them having sold themselves or been sold by their parents. Simply being unemployed or homeless was a capital crime.

'Doctor Thomas Ogle'

A Runaway Physician in a Bearskin Coat

April 27, 1769, The Pennsylvania Gazette (Penn.)

Salem, West New Jersey, April 29, 1769.

TWELVE DOLLARS Reward.[1] ABSCONDED from his usual Place of Abode, on the 16th Instant, a certain Doctor THOMAS OGLE, born in Ireland, about Five Feet six or seven Inches high, pitted with the Smallpox,[2] is give to Liquor, and when in Drink talks much of his Skill in Physic and Surgery;

---

[1] "Took with him/her" is always indicative of theft. This fact, taken along with the number of men signing the advertisement for his recovery as well as his steep $12 reward, suggests that his bondage may have been a joint investment of the three men named. It is of note that increasing numbers of servants in post French and Indian War America were highly skilled and presumably better educated than their masters, possibly indicating increased economic dislocation at the end of hostilities.

[2] This man seems a wreck, hardly likely to instill confidence in his patients.

has had one of his Legs broke, and commonly wears a Handkerchief about it;[2]

had on, when he went away, a half worn Beaver Hat, Bearskin Coat, Buckskin Breeches, Worsted Stockings, and good Shoes, with Pinchbeck Buckles.

He took with him a Silver Watch, a Silver Face, MakerName Wm. Clayton, London, No. 2450, rode a sorrel Horse, with a Blaze in his Face; and had a Couple of Boxes, with Medicines in them (like a Pedlarpack) and a Suit of Fustian, not made up.[1]

Whoever takes up the said Dr. Ogle, and secures him in any of his MajestyGoals, shall receive the above Reward. THOMAS HARTLEY, DANIEL LITHGOW, PETER AMBLER.[1]

N.B. All Watch Makers are desired to stop the said Watch, if offered for Sale, or otherwise.

'Of A Swarthy Complexion'

Another Runaway School Teacher

June 8, 1769

The Pennsylvania Gazette

May 27. 1769.

RUN away from the Subscriber, living in Warrington township, Bucks county, a servant man, named James Henderson, born in Ireland, about 26 years of age,[1] about 5 feet 5 inches high, long black hair tied behind, of a swarthy complexion,[2] and pitted with the small pox;

he has taught school some time in Maryland, and afterwards in Bucks county;[1]

had on and took with him, a half worn brown coat, a cotton jacket, striped with yellow silk, nankeen breeches, Germantown and white cotton stockings, good shoes, and square steel buckles.

---

[1] It seems that James is working on his third term of servitude and has been in America for at least six years, suggesting that professional servants were held for shorter terms of three years.

[2] Another dark-skinned man out of Ireland and of the professional class at that.

Whoever takes up said servant, and secures him in any goal, so that his master may have him again, shall receive Forty Shillings reward, and reasonable charges, paid by JOHN CRAIG.[1]

N.B. As it is thought he intends for Ireland, all masters of vessels are desired not to carry him off, but to secure him in goal, for which they shall have the above reward.

There remains the possibility that there were a great deal of cheap servants of the manual trades who were not valuable enough to warrant an advertisement, fee and a reward and were simply let go, particularly if there were a glut of them. By the 1780s, Benjamin Franklin was concerned that as many runaways were on the loose as there were servants on plantations.

'Speaks Good Dutch and English'

A Mysterious White Slave

It is quite interesting that at age 20, Christopher is noted as speaking good English and Dutch [the languages of slave traders operating in North America in the age], when many servants this young from Ireland have been described as speaking poor English. There is also the fact that the description of this man is unusually brief, especially for an educated person, leading one to suspect more than the usual foul play in Plantation America.

June 29, 1769, The Pennsylvania Gazette (Penn.)

THREE POUNDS Reward.

RUN away, about a month ago, from the Subscriber, in Earl township, Lancaster county, a certain CHRISTOPHER OWENS, a tall slim made young fellow, about 20 years of age, born in Ireland, speaks good Dutch and English, of a dark complexion, has black hair, and has a scar in one of his legs, from a kick of a horse.

Whoever takes up said Owens, and secures him in any goal in this province, shall have the above reward, paid by ROBERT WALLACE.

'Two Indented Servant Men'

Two Permanent Occupants of the Indentured Servant Racket

The advanced age of these two men, and lack of mention of military service, suggest that they are running from their fourth or fifth terms of service, from a lifetime of slavery.

July 27, 1769, The Pennsylvania Gazette (Penn.)

EIGHT DOLLARS Reward.

RUN away from the subscriber, two indented servant men,

one named MICHAEL DAVIS, 5 feet 6 or 7 inches high, born in Ireland, has a little of the brogue on his tongue, short black hair, thin visage, a little bald headed, and near 40 years of age;

had on, when he went away, a swanskin red spotted jacket, double breasted, with sleeves, a coarse white shirt, a pair of tow trowsers, with double fall, half worn shoes, and old felt hat.

The other named THOMAS JONES, born in Dublin, professes horse breaking and jockying, about 5 Feet 6 inches high, very slim made, about 40 years of age, and blind of one eye;

had on, when he went away, an old fine broadcloth coat, of a purple colour, old white cloth jacket, and old white shirt, wears a wig with one row of buckle, and is a little bald headed, has black worsted stockings, black breeches, and half worn shoes;

he loves drink, and swears much. Whoever apprehends said servants, shall have the above reward, or for Davis Forty Shillings, and Jones Twenty Shillings, and reasonable charges, paid by me JOSEPH ANDERSON, in Philadelphia, near the Blue Bell, in Front street.

'Wears His Own Short Ill Grown Hair'

Two Slaves of the Middle Class

It was a fact that any man who lost his fortune or faltered in his trade was liable to be sold as a first principal. As illustrated by these fellows below, skill and promise were no security against enslavement. One must be lucky as well to remain free.

August 3, 1769, The Pennsylvania Gazette (Penn.)

Philadelphia, August 3, 1769.

RUN away from the Subscriber, on Sunday, the 16th of July last, two indented servants, viz.

JAMES SAMUEL GORDON, by trade a jeweller,[1] was born in Scotland, but went to England with his parents when a child, so that he retains

---

[1] Clearly, artisans were more often enslaved in later colonial times than in earlier periods, which was no indication that slavery would ever be abolished. Indeed, the very first slaves in English America were Welsh survivors from Roanoke, used as jewelry-making slaves by an Indian tribe.

nothing of the Scots dialect; he has been long in France, the language of which country he speaks well; he said he is about 24 years old;

he is a small neat man; about 5 feet 1 inch high, small lively black eyes, smooth face and fresh coloured;

had on, and took, with him, a good coat, jacket and breeches, of superfine laylock coloured cloth, besides a striped damascus jacket, lapelled; the coat is rather large for him than otherwise, and is trimmed with 4 buttons on each pocket flap, 4 on each hip, and 4 on each sleeve, wears a half worn castor hat, lately dressed and cocked smart, wears his own short black hair, but sometimes a false tail, which he has now taken with him, a white shirt, the sleeves finer than the body, a white cravat, brown thread stockings, a pair of halfworn turned pumps, with plain Pinchbeck buckles.

The other named JAMES LOGAN, a well set boy, about 16 years of age, was born in the North of Ireland, is fond of liquor and dancing, very talkative, has a sour down look, and is exceedingly impudent, wears his own short ill grown hair, of a yellowish colour, sometimes tied, and sometimes loose;

had on, when he went off, a castor hat, much worn, but lately dressed, and cocked smart, the one which he wears foremost is remarkably broad, a snuff coloured cloth coat, with yellow metal buttons, a white linen jacket, leather breeches, a check shirt, blue and white cotton stockings, half worn, shoes and a pair of carved Pinchbeck, buckles; he has worked some time at the silversmiths[1] business, and will, no doubt look for employment at said business, though no wise qualified for it.

Whoever takes up the above two servants and secures them in any goal, so as I may have them, again, shall receive as a reward the sum of FORTY SHILLINGS for each, besides reasonable charges, paid by EDWARD MILNE.

N.B. All masters of vessels are hereby forbidden to take the above servants off, at their peril.

'A Servant Lad'

Sold at Age 16, William Ralston Runs Away at Age 19

August 3, 1769, The Pennsylvania Gazette (Penn.)

FORTY SHILLINGS Reward.

RUN away from the Subscriber, living in Oxford township, Chester county, a servant lad, named William Ralston, about 19 years of age, 5 feet 4 inches high, came from Ireland about 3 years ago, no doubt he will pretend to be a blacksmith,[1] as he has been some time at the trade;

had on, when he went away, a new brown coat, with flat metal buttons, new shoes, new coarse shirt, petticoat trowsers, an old felt hat, a striped silk

---

[1] As stated by the master posting this advertisement for his human property, a person was not what he had done or aspired to do but exactly what his master said he was and nothing else. The frequency of servants hijacked from one life to toil in another by force, being said to "pretend" at their trade, exposes the white slave trade in plantation America as more than economic exploitation but as a systematic assault on human identity.

handkerchief, and a fine shirt, marked on the breasts with S. S. he is very talkative, and will swear and lie.[2]

Whoever takes up said servant, and brings him home, or secures him in any goal so that his master may have him again, shall have the above reward, and reasonable charges, paid by me THOMAS WHITE.

---

[2] The astonishing fact about runaways through most of the history of white slavery in Plantation America was that so few of them were willing to lie to protect their interest in freedom once caught and were so habitually honest that a slave who would lie about having run away was an oddity.

'Is Almost Well'

Freeman Turned Slave, William Shannon, Runs Away

August 17, 1769, The Pennsylvania Gazette (Penn.)

RUN away, the 10th of August instant, at night, from the Subscriber, living in Salisbury township, Lancaster county, an indented servant man, named William Shannon, born in the north of Ireland, about 24 years of age, about 5 feet 8 or 9 inches high, stoop shouldered, wants one of his upper fore teeth, has light brown hair, has a cut of a sickle across his right ankle, but is almost well, he has been four years in the country, and says he came in a freeman,[1] if he can get liquor, he is very apt to get drunk:

Had on, a light coloured country cloth coat, a russia sheeting shirt, an old spotted flannel jacket, striped trowsers, new black grained shoes, brass

---

[1] The implication is that he lost his freedom due to drunkenness.

buckles, and an old felt hat; it is thought he may have a pass.[2]

Whoever brings him home or secures him in any of his Majesty goals, so that his master may have him again, shall have Eight Dollars reward, and reasonable charges, paid by me JOHN SHELLENBERG.

---

[2] Any person not carrying a pass, freedom papers or countersigned indenture form could be taken into custody by a sheriff or gaolor and sold.

'A Good Deal of the Brogue upon His Tongue'

A Breeches Maker on the Run

Making breeches was hardly land clearance, cane farming or even cotton picking, which brings one to wonder from what so many workhouse tradesmen and apprentices were running. Note that David is not "'indentured" but rather simply a "servant," the term used by 19th century slave owners when referring to their back chattel.

September 14, 1769, The Pennsylvania Gazette (Penn.)

Philadelphia, August 31, 1769.

RUN away from John Correy, of Philadelphia, an Irish servant man, named DAVID CARDEW, by trade a breeches maker, of a middle size, about 30 years of age,[1] wears his own black hair, generally tied behind, he came from Limerick,

---

[1] David is most likely fleeing his third term of service, as slavery began at 14–16 and generally consisted of seven-year terms.

in Ireland, and has a good deal of the brogue upon his tongue;

had on when he went away, an old blue coat, a striped jacket, lappelled, black leather breeches, Russia linen shirt, an old castor hat, bound round the edges with silk ferreting, calfskin shoes, middling high in the quarters.

He went in company with a red haired woman, much freckled, and out mouthed, and may perhaps pass for man and wife.[2]

Whoever secures said servant, so that his master may have him again, shall have Four Dollars reward, and reasonable charges, paid by JOHN CORREY.

---

[2] If David was captured along with the woman, if she happened to be a free woman with a pass or freedom papers, she would no longer have been free but would have been sold for the crime of abetting a runaway.

'Old Shoes and Stockings'

William Ferguson, Runaway Servant[1]

November 9, 1769, The Pennsylvania Gazette (Penn.)

RUN away from the Subscriber, living in East Marlborough, Chester County, the 22d Instant, at Night, a Servant Man, named William Ferguson, born in Ireland, and lately from thence, about 20 Years of Age, middle Stature, a Down look, fair Hair and Complexion;

had on a blue Cloth Coat and Jacket, without Sleeves, olive coloured Plush Breeches, Check Shirt, old Shoes and Stockings.[2] Whoever takes up the said Servant, and secures him in any Goal, or brings

---

[1] Servants, sold straight away by a third party rather than signing indentures, were at this point coming steadily from Ireland as well as indigenous debtors.
[2] Though persons were routinely being sold to sell their grocery or clothing debts, the instances of runaway barefoot slaves were at this point quite rare. Thirty years earlier, to be shoed had been a notable thing for a runaway.

him home, shall have Forty Shillings Reward, and reasonable Charges, paid by JOSEPH PENNOCK.

'Galled about His Ancles'

A Housebreaker Breaks Goal Also

November 9, 1769, The Pennsylvania Gazette (Penn.)

THREE POUNDS Reward.

BROKE out of the goal of the county of Gloucester, in New Jersey, the morning of the 30th of October last, a certain ROBERT JONES, born in Ireland, about 6 feet high, strong made, has a rugged look, large black beard, short black curled hair, about 30 years of age, round shouldered, and stoops in his walk;

he has had a remarkably bad sore leg, was confined for house breaking, and is galled about his ancles, with being ironed;[1]

---

[1] Being ironed or shackled at the ankle was common with criminals like Jones, while servants would be collared about the neck to facilitate work, which would have been Jones' fate if he had been captured, for unless he had been executed for his crime, he would have been sold, and as a convict laborer of great strength and known spirit, he would certainly have been collared.

had on, when he went away, a black jacket, without sleeves, two white shirts, long check trowsers, half worn shoes, and an old hat;

he is very fond of strong drink.

Whoever takes up the said Robert Jones, and secures him in any of his Majestygoals, so that he may be brought to justice, shall have the above reward, and reasonable charges, paid by me JOSEPH HUGG, Sheriff.

'At the Sign of the Highland Man'

An Attempt by a Man to Find His Servant, Brother or Son

December 28, 1769, The Pennsylvania Gazette (Penn.)

WHEREAS there came into this province, last summer was a year, from Cork, in Ireland, a certain Patrick Callaghan, it is supposed indented for 4 years, with one James Kenny, blacksmith, in Salisbury township, Lancaster county;

he is about 18 or 19 years of age, pock marked, about 5 feet 4 or 5 inches high, by trade a weaver;

the subscriber would be very glad if he would send a letter, directed to James Huston, at the Sign of the Highland Man, and Bear, in Second street, Philadelphia, between Market and Chestnut streets, for DANIEL CALLAGHAN.

It is notable that Daniel Callaghan and his male relative—brother, cousin or son—were both literate, which suggests hard times in Ireland among the literate. This also provided evidence that Patrick was sold at 14 or

15 and had been working for some time before that, possibly as a servant or apprentice weaver.

'Full Faced, and Fresh Coloured'

Thomas Linch, A Non-Indented Servant Man[1]

January 11, 1770, The Pennsylvania Gazette (Penn.)

FORTY SHILLINGS Reward.

RUN away, the first of this instant January, from the subscriber, in Montgomery township, Philadelphia county, a servant man, named THOMAS LINCH, who arrived from Ireland about three months ago, is between 19 and 20 years of age, about 5 feet 8 inches high, well set, brown curled hair, full faced, and fresh coloured;

had on, a felt hat, good blue cloth coat, turned collar, mohair buttons, a cloth jacket, the fore part brown, and mended, the back part of a different colour, with a strip of white down the back, homespun shirt, good buckskin breeches, with brass buttons, and strings to the knees, two pair of

---

[1] Non-indented servants were generally folks auctioned off to pay debts at county courts under the British system up through 1776.

yarn stockings, one blue and white, the other a light brown, neats leather shoes,[2] and steel buckles.

Whoever takes up the said servant, and brings him home, or secures him in any goal, so that his master may have him again, shall receive the above reward. EVAN JONES.

---

[2] Neatsfoot oil is still used by some boxing coaches to maintain sparring gloves and headgear made of leather.

'Liable to A Certain Redemption'

The Commander of the *Snow Friendly Adventure* Would Have His Human Cargo Returned

February 15, 1770, The Pennsylvania Gazette (Penn.)

RUN away from on board the Snow Friendly Adventure, whereof I am Commander, and now lying at Annapolis, the following persons, who came Passengers in said Snow, liable to a certain Redemption, as specified in their several Agreements, viz.

John Goodwin, Edward Murphy, Edward Loney, James McCarty, and William Niness:

They are gone towards Baltimore, and pretend that they have complied with their Engagements to me, which not being the Case, they are still answerable for the same;

and, I am informed, by the Laws of this Province, may be taken and secured, as if they were indented Servants, until they comply with their Engagements. (I therefore promise a Reward of Twenty Shillings Currency, for each of the abovementioned Persons, besides what the law allows, to have them, or any of them, secured in any public Goal, in Maryland, or brought to me, at Annapolis, where the Reward will be paid by Messieurs James Dick and Steward; or, if secured in any Goal, and the abovementioned Gentlemen being acquainted therewith, the Reward will be duly paid. WILLIAM SNOW.

John Goodwin, about 5 Feet 7 Inches high, a brown Complexion, wears his own Hair, and wore a white Jacket and Trowsers.

Edward Murphy, about 5 Feet 8 Inches high, a dark Complexion, wears a brown Coat and Waistcoat, a Native of Ireland.

Edward Loney, about 5 Feet 7 and an Half Inches high, a dark Complexion, wore a white Coat, turned up with blue.

James McCarty, about 5 Feet 6 Inches high, a brown Complexion, wore a blue Coat, and red Waistcoat, a Native of Ireland.

William Niness, about 5 Feet 8 Inches high, wore a brown Coat and Waistcoat, and a Wig, a Native of England.

Redemptioners were people who sought passage to America in return for a promised payment by a third party [relative, prospective husband, etc.] once landfall was made or in return for the captain selling these people for a term of service. This is the type of arrangement that historians would have us believe was entered into by servants and indentured or indented servants, when in fact these folks were often kidnapped or sold by an existing master, parent or sibling in the old country. What we have been lead to believe was the lot of a servant was actually the lot of the redemptioner, who might well become a servant.

Barefoot, March 1, 1770

Brief Sketch of a Criminal

All chattel and other persons of the "lower orders" were regarded in fugitive advertisements as being barefoot unless otherwise noted.

There is no reason to suppose that James Welsh was an escaped servant, although he was probably once held in servitude, simply based on his ancestry and condition.

The fascinating aspect of this ad is the fact that with no regular police force—especially outside of the few cities—that the apprehension of fugitives was farmed out to the public at large.

March 1, 1770, The Pennsylvania Gazette (Penn.)

FOUR DOLLARS Reward.

MADE his escape, the 16th of February last, from the Constable of Norrington township, Philadelphia county, a certain man, named JAMES WELSH, born in Ireland, a taylor by trade, about 30 years of age, black hair, tied behind, about 5 feet 2 inches high, thick legs;

had on, when he went away, a short blue coat, spotted swanskin jacket, white cloth breeches, blue ribbed stockings, and old fine hat.

Said fellow was charged with felony, and made his escape on the road, in going to goal.

Whoever secures him, in any of his Majestygoals, so that he may be brought to justice, shall have the above reward and reasonable charges, paid by SAMUEL PEASLEY, Constable.

'Judged Out of New Castle Goal'

Another Barefoot, Irish Runaway Weaver in Plantation America

March 29, 1770, The Pennsylvania Gazette (Penn.)

THREE POUNDS Reward.

RUN away the 16th instant, from Isaac Bailey, living in West Marlborough, in Chester county, one THOMAS LITTLE, who was judged out of New Castle goal, for a debt due to one John Underhill, living in Kennet;

he was born in Ireland, is about 5 feet 8 or 9 inches high, of a sandy complexion, wears his own hair, of a sandy colour, cut short on the top of his head, a thick well set fellow, and talks good English;

can do something at the weaving business;

had on, when he went away, a grey homespun jacket, grey yarn stockings, velvet breeches, and supposed to have with him a velvet jacket, and light coloured broadcloth coat, a lapelled striped jacket, black knit breeches, and a grey surtout;

he is supposed to have gone towards the Lower counties, or the Jersies.

Whoever takes up the said Thomas Little and brings him to the said Bailey, or Underhill, shall have the above reward, and reasonable charges, paid by JOHN UNDERHILL.

Translation to modern English: Thomas Little was in debt to John Underhill.

According to a speech by Benjamin Franklin given a few years later, these debts were most often owed to grocers and clothes importers, as most goods were imported from England and were too expensive to purchase outright. At whatever time a county court came into session, all of those owing debts for such everyday purchases would be auctioned off as servants at the county courthouse. In such a manner might Thomas have been judged rentable by the magistrate, whereby he fell into the service of Mister Bailey, who seemed to have been on good terms with Mister Underhill and had no money himself to purchase a servant or to pay for his return.

One wonders what would have come of Mister Bailey if he did not profit enough off of employing [from the French for "use"] Thomas.

Would he be gaoled and sold as well?

'Old Leather Heeled Shoes'

A Runaway Irish Slave Girl

May 3, 1770, The Pennsylvania Gazette (Penn.)

FOUR DOLLARS Reward.

RUN away, the 24th of April last, from the subscriber, living in Salisbury township, Lancaster county, a servant girl, named Anne Mackey, about 18 or 19 years of age, born in Ireland, speaks much on that country dialect, a stout chunky girl, dark brown hair, a coarse homespun shift, an old black and white striped linsey short gown, two linsey petticoats, one striped, the other a walnut colour, old leather heeled shoes.

Whoever secures said servant, so as her master may have her again, shall have the above reward of Four Dollars, and reasonable charges, paid by JARRED GRAHAM.

'Apt to Play at Cards'

Born in Ireland and on the Run in America

There is no telling why James was being held on bail. It is, however, note that by 1770, many more fugitives from jail and service are described as having been "born in Ireland" rather than having just come over, indicating that by this point in history there were large numbers of adult Irishmen who had completed one or more terms of service and were now either in jail for a crime or on the run from a second, third or fourth owner.

April 12, 1770, The Pennsylvania Gazette (Penn.)

FIVE POUNDS Reward.

ABSCONDED from his bail, about the middle of last February, one James Pursel, born in Ireland, but it is supposed he has changed his name to James Cumins,

full red face, a thick well set fellow, about 5 feet 6 or 7 inches high, and had two suits of apparel along with him, one a snuff colour, and the other a brownish colour, bound with tape, has black hair, and he is a lover of strong liquor, and apt to play at cards, and fight when drunk;

he has a pass wit him from the Mayor.[1]

Whoever takes up said James Pursel, and secures him in any goal, so as he may be had again, shall have the above reward, and reasonable charges, paid by us, HUGH STEWARD, RICHARD FAWKES, living in Newtown township, Chester county.

---

[1] The fact that James has a pass means that he had most likely recently finished a term of servitude and was free at whatever time he committed the offense that required bail put up for him to remain at large. As private individuals put up bail, someone in Newtown Township trusted him to be able to earn enough money in his trade to pay off the bail and to do so in good faith.

'Mistrusted for a Servant'

With A Suspiciously Rich History

May 17, 1770, The Pennsylvania Gazette (Penn.)

THREE POUNDS Reward.

RUN away from last New yearday, from the subscriber, in Montgomery township, Philadelphia county, a servant man, named THOMAS LYNCH, who was born in Queencounty, in Ireland, and took shipping at Dublin, with Captain Story, and arrived at Philadelphia last September,

is between 19 and 20 years of age, about 5 feet 8 inches high, well set, full faced, and fresh coloured, brown curled hair;

had on, when he went way, a felt hat, a good blue cloth coat, close bodied, with a falling collar, mohair buttons, a jacket without sleeves. The fore part of a brownish colour, the back part of a different colour, with a strip of white down the back, very remarkable, good buckskin breeches, with brass buttons, and strings to the knees, homespun flaxen shirt, two pair of stockings, one of a blue and white, the other a brown colour, neats leather shoes, and steel buckles,

has been brought up to the farming business, and says his father was a considerable farmer in his time, who died the fall before he came away;[1]

as he is a likely fellow, and has but little of the brogue on his tongue, and had good cloaths on when he went he went away, it is likely he has not been mistrusted for a servant.[2]

Whoever takes him up, and brings him home, or secures him in any goal, so as his master may have him again, shall have the above reward, paid by EVAN JONES.[3]

---

[1] Thomas may have sold himself after his father's farm was taken by creditors or may have been sold to cover any debts left by his father.

[2] In Plantation America, it was every free person's duty to question strangers and determine if they were runaways and take appropriate action against them if they were "'mistrusted," as running away was an inherently deceptive business which necessitated adoption of a false identity.

[3] Mister Jones seems to have had a high opinion of Thomas' personal qualities and oddly used the term "home" in referring to his recovery, which is the first such instance I have noted.

'A Smart Look and Lofty Carriage'

A Runaway Employee?

October 11, 1770, The Pennsylvania Gazette
(Penn.)

Buckingham, Bucks County, September 15,
1770.

RUN away from my Employ,[1]

a certain John Trusdel, by Trade a Weaver,
born in Ireland, about 24 Years of Age, 5 Feet 8 or 9
Inches high, has short black Hair, a smart Look and
lofty Carriage;[2]

had on when he went away, a brown coat,
with Mohair Buttons, brown Jacket, the Fore Parts
English Plains, with blue Lincey Backs, half worn,
Buckskin Breeches, with a small Piece in the Crotch,
two Shirts, one or both fine, a Stock with a Buckles,
white ribbed Thread Stockings, much broke in the

---

[1] From the French "to use." In Plantation America, the
term *employee* designated a servant, an unfree person.
[2] Arrogant, confident.

Feet, half worn Calfskin Shoes, with Pinchbeck Buckles, and a half worn Castor Hat;[3]

has a Scar on his Left Cheek;[4]

writes a good Hand;

he had a Silver Watch, with a China Face, much out of Order; he also had two Half Johannes, and 6 or 7 Pounds in other Money, part thereof stole;

has a Clearance from Captain Cheevers,[5]

and a Certificate from the [...];[6]

he has been near two Years in the Country, and [...] and Chester County Part of last Winter.

Whoever [...] said Trusdel (who is suspected of stealing) shall have [...] Shillings Reward, when brought to Conviction, paid by MATTHEW KELLEY.

N.B. The Public are cautioned from taking an Assignment of a Note of Hand of L 11 17 1, passed by me to said Trusdel about the 10th of July last, as no

---

[3] The wardrobe is ostentatious, if ragged. However, the common man of the age, if he had the means, would heap on clothes as do the homeless of our age, for all they owned was upon their back, in their pockets or bundled to a stick.

[4] Either from discipline or adventure. Scars to the left side of the face almost always indicate an antagonistic stroke.

[5] Trusdel's passage to America was paid and he disembarked a free man.

[6] The above freedom paper would be used to acquire a travel pass from the local magistrate.

Part thereof will be paid, until the Conditions on which said Note was given are complied with by said Trusdel.[7]

MATTHEW KELLEY.

---

[7] Perhaps a line of credit promised if Trusdel accomplished a certain work order?

'Near the Head of Elk'

A Non-Indentured Servant Runaway

October 18, 1770, The Pennsylvania Gazette (Penn.)

RUN away last night from the subscriber, living near the Head of Elk,[1] in Caecil county, Maryland, a servant man, named PETER HUGHES;

had on, when he went away, a blue coat, red waistcoat, black breeches, black stockings, new shoes, with large brass buckles;[2]

lately from Ireland, and speaks pretty good English.

---

[1] The numerous place names related to the extinct eastern elk gives an indication of how richly eastern Maryland was stocked by God with creatures that disappeared within three generations of European settlement.

[2] The increasingly well-dressed servants—attired like princes compared to those of the 1730s—indicates an expanding debt society, as does the lower rewards offered for recently acquired and escaped human property.

Whoever takes up said servant, and secures him, so as his master may have him again, shall have Thirty Shillings reward, and reasonable charges, paid by ANDREW FRAZER

October 2, 1770.

'Something of a Down Look'

A Runaway Mason Apprentice, Just Another Name for Slave

January 17, 1771, The Pennsylvania Gazette (Penn.)

RUN away, from the subscriber, living in Bart township, Lancaster county, the 2d day of January inst. an apprentice to the Mason trade, named James Tumblety,

about 5 feet 8 inches high, has dark brown curled hair, something of a down look, black eyebrows, and small legs;

had on, when he went away, an old light brown coat, linsey jacket, with black horn buttons, light blue breeches, two pair of stockings, one a light blue grey, the other a dark blue worsted, a felt hat, an old pair of shoes, and a black silk handkerchief;[1]

---

[1] The attention to clothing details by the owners of men and women seems astonishing. However, everything worn would be noted upon the purchase of a person, so that any additional clothes worn might indicate theft and additional time to serve. However, the primary

took also, a considerable sum of money, wherein was one Half Johannes, the rest in silver and bills;

he might be apprehended in changing the bills, as he cannot read;

it is likely he may change both name and apparel.

Whoever takes up, and secures said apprentice, so as his master may have him again, shall have Three Pounds reward, and reasonable charges, paid by JOHN BIGHAM.

N.B. Masters of vessels are forbid to carry him off at their Peril, as he was seen going towards Philadelphia, and it is thought intends for Ireland.[2]

---

reason for recording all articles worn was for identification in case of escape, something that was expected.

[2] Imbedded in the usual threat to sea captains is an indication that "said apprentice" never wanted to be in the country of his master to begin with.

'More Sulky than an Oliverian Countenance'

'RUN Away, in the Night': A Convict Servant Man, Slave by Another Name

February 7, 1771, The Pennsylvania Gazette (Penn.)

FOURTEEN DOLLARS Reward. RUN away, in the night of the 6th of November last, from Marlborough Forge, in Frederick county, Virginia,

a convict servant man, named John Campbell, born in Ireland, is a thick well set fellow, appears to be between 35 and 40 years of age, 5 feet 7 or 8 inches high, has short black curled hair, double chin, and somewhat wrinkled face, rather more sulky than an oliverian countenance;[1]

he has a remarkable scar on the outside of his right leg, occasioned by a cut with a scythe, also, on the shin of the left leg, a scar, by a cut with an axe;[2]

---

[1] Looking stern, like a Puritan in the mold of Oliver Cromwell.
[2] Common land clearance injuries. A convict servant's time was generally reckoned at 14 years.

had on, when he went off, a light or ash coloured fly coat, lined with red, white and blue linsey, waistcoat outside of the same, lined with red shaloon, shirt and trowsers of country made linen, a flag silk handkerchief about his neck, an old hat, and steel buckles in his shoes.

Whoever takes up said Campbell, if out of the colony, and brings him home, shall have the above reward; or if secured in any of his Majestygoals, so that his master may have him again, shall have Ten Dollars, paid by WILLIAM HOLMES.

N.B. If taken in or near, or to the northward of Philadelphia, by acquainting Isaac Zane[3] thereof, that he may have him secured, or delivered to him, shall be intitled to the last mentioned (Ten Dollars) reward.

---

[3] The Zanes would be prominent in West Virginia in the next generation.

'Rocks in His Walking'

A White Slave by Another Name Escapes from the Slave Entrepot of New Castle Delaware

March 7, 1771, The Pennsylvania Gazette (Penn.)

Christiana Bridge, February 13, 1771.

RUN away from the subscriber, last Sunday, a certain EDWARD McCOLGAN, born in Ireland, aged 32 or 33 years, about 5 feet 6 inches high, fresh coloured, has long blackish hair, a little marked with the smallpox, and rocks in his walking:

Had on, when he went away, a light grey napped duffil coat and waistcoat, bound and lined, tape the same colour as the coat, the waistcoat wore a good deal below his breast, light coloured cloth breeches, old blue yarn stockings, new shoes, one buckled with a broad brass buckle, the other tied with a leather string.

Whoever takes up and secures said servant, so that his master may have him again, if within the county of New Castle,[1] shall receive the sum of Forty Shillings, or out of said county, Three Pounds, and reasonable charges, upon delivering him to PATRICK McGONNEGAL.[2]

---

[1] New Castle Delaware was the mid-Atlantic hub of white slavery from the 1710s.

[2] Increasingly, Irish were trafficked by other Irish as the years wore on in brutal Plantation America.

'Whoever Takes Up the Said Servants'

Two Human Sewing Machines, Barefoot and on the Run

April 4, 1771, The Pennsylvania Gazette (Penn.)

March 24, 1771.

RUN away from the subscribers, living in Salisbury township, Lancaster county, two servant men, natives of Ireland, both taylors by trade;[1]

one of them named Matthew Carney, about 5 feet 9 inches high, of a fair complexion, wears his own hair, cut short;

had on, a short whitish coloured bearskin coat, a spotted flannel jacket, and a coarse white shirt. [2]

---

[1] These involuntary servants were natives of Ireland but not newly arrived and had probably been auctioned off for debts incurred after gaining freedom, a common practice of the late colonial period in English America.
[2] Both men were barefoot and on the run, apparently as soon as the ground had thawed.

The other names John Corbett, about 5 feet 8 inches high, of a dark complexion, sulky look, talks with a good deal of the brogue, and wears his own short hair, sometimes curled;

had on, a whitish coloured coat and breeches, a black linsey jacket, a coarse white shirt, and a wool hat.[2]

Whoever takes up the said servants, and secures them in any goal, so as their masters may get them again, shall have FOUR POUNDS reward, and reasonable charges, paid by JAMES LEECH, and JAMES McDILL.[3]

---

[3] Again, Irish ownership of Irish points to economic drivers for servile conditions rather than racial hatred. Just as blacks who gained freedom trafficked in blacks, Irish also trafficked in Irish.

'Who Calls Himself WILLIAM WILSON'

When a False Identity Steals Itself in Plantation America

April 25, 1771, The Pennsylvania Gazette (Penn.)

Philadelphia, April 22, 1771.

EIGHT DOLLARS Reward. RUN away from the subscriber, living in Waterford township, Gloucester county, a servant man, who calls himself WILLIAM WILSON, but his right name is WILLIAM McCOLLUN, born in Ireland.[1] He is about 30 years of age, 5 feet 5 or 6 inches high, of a sandy complexion, his hair almost red, tied behind, and is a well set, full faced, fresh coloured fellow, with a large under lip, grey eyes, and has a sour look.

Had on, and took with him, a good felt hat, a broadcloth jacket, of a blue grey colour, without sleeves or lining; two shirts, one ozenbrigs, the other sheeting; old black knit breeches; one pair of

---

[1] He was born in Ireland and arrived as a child, putting William on his third seven-year term.

good blue stockings, and an old grey pair; a pair of neats leather shoes, half worn, with brass buckles.[2]

Whoever takes up said servant, and secures him, so that his master may have him again, shall receive the above reward, and reasonable charges, paid by BENJAMIN INSKEEP.

All masters of vessels are forbid to carry him off at their peril.[3]

---

[2] Additional time would be added to his term for theft and running away.

[3] From 1741, the British Admiralty had been sworn to enforce the property claims of plantation slave owners over merchand and Navy captains who might take on such runaways as crewmen—a form of slavery often more brutal than that of negroes in Antebellum Virginia. What soul-eating condition impels a man to seek life as a brutalized slave sailor?

'An Artful Fellow'

An Irishman Helps a 'Virginia Born Negro Man Slave' Escape

Virginia Gazette (Purdie & Dixon), Williamsburg, February 21, 1771. (Martin)

Twenty five Pounds Reward.

RUN away from the Subscriber, in Cumberland County, Virginia, the 3rd of June last, a Virginia born Negro Man[1] Slave named WILL, near six feet high, thirty five Years old, and well made; his Face is often full of bumps.

He was seen with a forged Pass, signed by Charles Clark, at John [illeg.], on Roanoke River, near Jefferson's Ferry, and passed for a Freeman,[2] by the Name of Austin Cousins.

---

[1] The idea that blacks were regarded as less than human is often given the lie by such statements that recognize the humanity of negro slaves, as well as the dual distinction, that of being both a negro and a slave, in a context of brevity.

[2] Not only was a white man willing to aid him, but there were enough free negroes in Virginia to permit an escaped one to pass as a freeman.

He endeavoured to get another Pass, to go into Carolina; which if he did it is probable he may have changed his name, as he is an artful Fellow.

Whoever apprehends the said Slave, and brings him to me, shall have the above Reward; or if secured in any Jail, and advertised in the VIRGINIA GAZETTE, TEN POUNDS Reward.

As he is outlawed, I will give TEN POUNDS for his Head,[3] or for a proper Certificate to entitle me to be allowed for him by the Country.

FEBRUARY 1, 1771. ANTHONY MARTIN.

N.B. GEORGE KELLY, an Irishman, about six Feet high, stout made, who talks big and loud, and is of mean Character, had some Dealings with the above Slave before he ran away, and I have Reason to think harboured him some Time after. The said Kelly, with his Wife and one Child, ran away in August, and crossed the Roanoke River, at Jefferson's Ferry. It is probable the Slave had some Place appointed to meet him in Carolina; and if they are together, I have no Doubt will endeavour to make him pass for a Freeman.[4]

---

[3] Scalp bounties were always suspect, whereas a head could be identified. He will take his slave's head for 10 pounds if the County does not drop the slave's outlaw status. I once worked for a man of similar character and am not shocked by the suggested decapitation.
[4] George Kelly is obviously a servant, who not only escaped with his hostage family, but seems to have helped Will escape as well.

'A Native Irish Servant Man'

A Non-Indentured Servant Runs from a Master Named Abraham

May 23, 1771, The Pennsylvania Gazette (Penn.)

FOUR DOLLARS Reward.

RUN away from the subscriber, living at the Sign of the Bear, in Donegall township, Lancaster county, the 12th of this instant May, at night, a native Irish servant man, named ARTHUR DONELY, about 21 years of age, pockmarked, short black curly hair, about 5 feet 4 or 5 inches high;

has been accustomed to drive a carriage in Ireland;

had on, and took with him, when he went away, a light coloured napped coat, made frock fashion, and a snuff coloured jacket, with brown backs, likewise one striped and flowered calicoe ditto, a pair of buckskin breeches, 3 coarse shirts, 1 fine ditto, grey ribbed stockings, and old shoes;

went off with a servant man belonging to James Young, near Carlisle, named Alexander, of a pale complexion, and had on a brown coat, a convict.[1]

Whoever takes up said servant, and secures him, so that his master may have him again, shall be entitled to the above reward, with reasonable charges, paid by ABRAHAM HOLMES.

N.B. All masters of vessels and others, are forbid to harbour or carry him off, at their peril.

---

[1] Not serving James Young, not in the service of James Young, but belonging to James Young.

'Since He Served His First Time'

John Curtin, an Indented Servant

May 30, 1771, The Pennsylvania Gazette (Penn.)

FORTY SHILLINGS Reward.

RUN away on the 20th of this instant May, an indented servant man, named JOHN CURTIN, born in Ireland, is about 5 feet 8 inches high, well set, full and fair faced, about 23 or 24 years of age;

has served 4 years in Chester county already; is artful in his speech, and has travelled a good deal in the back parts of this province, since he served his first time, also in Maryland and Virginia,[1] and It is supposed he has made that way;

had on, and took with him, a good brown broadcloth coat and jacket, both lined with durant of the same colour, the jacket lappelled, and more

---

[1] His first term served was split under at least two owners, along with his age indicating that he was probably 14–16-years old when sold into the plantations. This seems to be a case of a released servant then selling himself to a new master.

worn than the coat, an English castor hat, about half worn, tow trowsers, and new shoes, without stockings.

Whoever takes up said servant, and secures him in any of his Majestygoals, so as his master may have him again, shall have the above reward, and reasonable charges, paid by JOHN RANKIN.

'May Forge a Pass'

Three Plus One Runaway Servants

June 13, 1771, The Pennsylvania Gazette (Penn.)

TWELVE DOLLARS Reward.

RUN away, from the subscriber, living in Carlisle, the three following servants, viz.

WILLIAM KING, a native of Ireland, a stout well made fellow, about 30 years of age, near six feet high, wears short brown hair, fair complexion, speaks good English, understands Latin, and is fond of talking about it, writes a good hand, and may forge a pass;

he came into the country the 27th of June, 1770, with Capt. Robert Miller, and went off in company with one Michael Stewart, a servant to Andrew Holmes, near Carlisle, who carried a short rifle gin with him, and having been in the army, had a printed discharge from the same;[1]

---

[1] An officially discharged veteran has managed to find himself property to a man, another example of the 18th

they were seen at Susquehanna, enquiring the way to Reading;

said King had on a felt hat cocked, a striped silk handkerchief, a light cloth coloured jacket with sleeves, lined with cross barred stuff, almost new, a white flannel waistcoat, a hempen linen shirt, striped linen trowsers, good shoes, with round iron buckles, not fellows.

CHARLES PARKER, an Irishman, has been about four years in the country (but by his frequent running away is still a servant)[2] about 20 years of age, 5 feet 6 inches high, a little pitted with the small pox, and has a down look, when challenged;

had on, and took with him, a small felt hat slouched down, a coarse fly coat, of a dirty blue colour, an old olive coloured velvet waistcoat, an old nankeen ditto, tow linen shirt and trowsers, blue and white cotton stockings, and old shoes, with round brass buckles, not fellows;

he sprained his right ancle, which was not well, when he went away.

HENRY DAVIS, born in Ireland, but says he lived 16 years in England, talks good English, and speaks Welsh, about 30 years of age, 5 feet 10 inches

---

century British veterans administration—privatized slavery.

[2] It seems that a fair proportion [not known as records have been destroyed and suppressed] of non-indentured servants served terms of only three years. The range of service was 3–31 years.

high, a clumsy made fellow, bandy legged, wears short brown hair, and has a red beard;

his cloathing not now known, having run away the 27th of June, 1770; writes a good hand, and may forge a pass;

he was seen at Bedford and Juniata last spring, enquiring his way for Fort Augusta, and Wyomokin, on Susquehanna.

Whoever apprehends said runaways, and secures them in any of his Majestygoals, so as their masters shall have them again, shall have the above reward, or FOUR DOLLARS for each, and reasonable charges, paid by Carlisle, May 27, 1771. JOHN GLEN.[3]

---

[3] An Irishman trafficking in Irishmen.

'When in Liquor'

Drunkenness, One of Many Justifications for Enslavement

September 5, 1771, The Pennsylvania Gazette (Penn.)

RUN away from his Bail, on the 24th of August, a certain John Mooney, by Trade a Weaver, about 28 Years of Age 5 Feet 8 or 9 Inches high, pale Face, wears his Hair, which is cut short, and very black, is a well made Fellow, and has a Stammering in his Speech when in Liquor, which he is very fond of;

he came from the County of Armagh in Ireland, about 7 Years ago, and served his Time with John Vaneleave, at Cranberry, near Bush Town, in Baltimore County, and speaks pretty good English, but is a very idle drunken Fellow;

had on and took with him, a Castor Hat, newly dressed, two Jackets without Sleeves, one a greyish Nap Broadcloth, with white Metal Buttons, the other a red and white shoot-about Lincey lapelled, Country made Shirt and Trowsers, a black

Silk Handkerchief, and old Shoes, with round carved yellowish Metal Buckles.

He was taken up as a Runaway last October was a Year, and committed to New Castle Goal, out of which he was redeemed by the Subscriber, with whom he has lived till about three Weeks ago.

Whoever secures and brings him to the Subscriber, living near Bush Town, or commits him to Goal, if taken in Baltimore County, shall have Eight Dollars Reward, and if out of the Province, Five Pounds, and reasonable Charges, paid by JOHN MEGAW.[1]

---

[1] The 5-pound reward for escaping a goal while being held on charges of idleness may only be redeemed by the gaol keeper in one fashion: by the sale of Mooney.

'Thick Made, and Pockmarked'

A Conspiracy to Commit the Penultimate Colonial Sin—To Live Free

For all you folks who are against conspiracy theories, how do you explain these two Irishmen conspiring to run away? If these two knuckleheads could pull off a conspiracy, don't you think powerful internationalists might also be able to succeed in duplicitous plots?

August 29, 1771, The Pennsylvania Gazette (Penn.)

FIVE POUNDS Reward.

RUN away from the subscribers, living in Carnarvon township, Lancaster county, two Irish servant men,

one named James Sheehy, about 5 feet 7 or 8 inches high, dark complexion, short black curled hair;

had on, and took with him, a brown saggathy coat, with mohair buttons, striped silk lappelled waistcoat, light coloured knit breeches, white cotton stockings, 2 pair of pumps, and 1 pair of shoes, with square silver buckles, 2 fine shirts, 1 coarse ditto, a beaver hat, and white trowsers.

The other, named John Glashien, about 5 feet 6 or 7 inches high, thick made, and pockmarked;

had on a blue coat, white linen waistcoat, leather breeches, grey ribbed stockings, white linen waistcoat, leather breeches, a coarse home made linen shirt:[1]

Both native Irishmen, and speak with the brogue; they lately came from Waterford, in Ireland, with Captain Curtis.[2]

Whoever takes up said servants, and secures them in any goal within this province, or brings them to the subscribers, shall receive Three Pounds for Sheehy, and Forty Shillings for the other, with reasonable charges.

DAVID MORGAN, JOSEPH JENKINS.

---

[1] As John was barefoot, perhaps one of the two pairs of pumps he carried off was to be used to shoe his fellow runaway.

[2] A ship's captain would own and conduct a sale of indentures, redemptioners, convicts, kidnapping victims and ordinary servants. The only thinking certain about this listing is that neither of these men was an indenture or a convict, which would have been noted as these were categories of forced labor whose condition was aggressively backed by the state.

'At Their Peril'

An Indented Servant Lad Named JAMES CARNEY

October 17, 1771, The Pennsylvania Gazette (Penn.)

THREE DOLLARS Reward.

RUN away, on the 13th day of this instant October, from the subscriber, living in West Caln township, Chester county, an indented servant lad, named JAMES CARNEY,[1] a native of Ireland, about 18 years of age, 5 feet 7 inches high, with fair hair, fair complexion, thin faced, out mouthed;

had on, when he went away, a plain white flannel jacket, and breeches of the same, greyish yarn stockings, almost new, a pair of half-souled shoes, with a piece on one of the heel quarters, and tied with thongs, one tow linen shirt, one check ditto, a felt hat, and had a half-worn linen wallet.

---

[1] Baltimore County is home to a small town, now long reduced to a neighborhood, named Carney. It would be nice to think that James or one of his descendants made good five miles from this desk.

Whoever takes up the said servant, and secures him in any of his Majestygoals, so that his master may have him again, shall receive the above reward, and all reasonable charges, paid by me WILLIAM BENNETT.

N. B. All masters of vessels, or others, are forbid to conceal or carry off servant, at their peril.

'A Native of Ireland'

An Indented Servant Man

November 14, 1771, The Pennsylvania Gazette (Penn.)

RUN away, on the 23d of July last, from the subscriber, living in Cumberland county, Letterkenny township, an indented servant man, named MARTIN McKINNEY, but probably may change his name, he is a native of Ireland, and talks much with the brogue, about 25 years of age, 5 feet 5 or 6 inches high, slim built, tawny complexion, dark brown hair;

had on, and took with him, an old grey sailor jacket, an old fur hat, pieced in the crown, 3 shirts, one about a 9, another about a 7, and the other about a 600 linen, two pair of coarse trowsers, one pair old, the other new, a pair of new shoes, with metal buckles, a pair of black yarn stockings, ribbed;

he also took a sickle with him, marked ION.[1]

---

[1] Sickles were commonly stolen by runaway blacks in Carolina and used as swords by those intent on living as maroons.

Whoever takes up said servant, and secures him in any goal, so that his master may get him again, shall have THREE POUNDS, reward, paid by November 8, 1771. ROBERT McCONNEL.

'A CERTAIN Servant Man'

Slaver-Schoolmaster Andrew Porter Wants His Irishman Back

November 21, 1771, The Pennsylvania Gazette (Penn.)

Philadelphia, November 16, 1771.

A CERTAIN servant man, named ROBERT MOORE, by trade a Weaver, who came from Ireland in the brig Dolphin, last May, and, on the 28th of September, went from this city towards Christiana Bridge, under pretence of finding a friend to release him,[1] is desired to return to Philadelphia, before the 30th of this instant;

otherwise be will be advertised as a runaway.

The Subscriber has opened an EVENING SCHOOL (with a well qualified assistant) at his School House, in Union Street, near Second Street;

---

[1] The conduct of owner and slave here indicates that it was not unusual for a servant to be bought out of bondage by friends. There is precious little indication that servants were bought out of bondage by family, but rather that families often sold their own into bondage.

where are taught writing, arithmetic, and book-keeping, geometry, trigonometry, algebra, mensuration, gauging, surveying, navigation, geography, &c. &c. ANDREW PORTER.[2]

---

[2] This advertisement, taking up as much space as the runaway complaint, might be an indication that industry rather than slave mastery was becoming contagious, at least in Philadelphia.

'A Person of Ill Fame'

Portrait of a Plantation Era Criminal

December 19, 1771, The Pennsylvania Gazette (Penn.)

TEN POUNDS Reward.

MADE his Escape from the Sheriff of Bucks County, a certain Person, named Barnabas McCullough, born in Ireland, about 5 Feet 6 or 7 Inches high, 35 Years of Age, but may be taken to be younger by his Look, well set, of a fair or rather pale Complexion, sandy Beard, black Hair, but not tied behind, as described in some other Advertisements, by Misinformation;

had on, when he went away, blue Clothes, but perhaps may change Dress;

he lived some Time in the Falls Township, at Bordentown Ferry, in the aforesaid County of Bucks, and since moved to Plumsted Township, in said County, from whence he absconded about the 4th instant.

Whoever will secure the above Barnabas McCullough, in any of his MajestyGoals on this

Continent, shall receive the above Reward of TEN POUNDS, by giving Notice thereof to

December 11, 1771. GEORGE WALL, Sub-Sheriff.

N. B. It is supposed the above McCullough is gone off in Company with one Henry Tremble, who lived with him last Summer, and followed butchering, is a Person of ill Fame, was also born in Ireland. All Masters of Vessels are forewarned, at their Peril, to take McCullough aboard.

There is no indication that McCullough was a runaway or had ever been a servant. However, if he was caught and escaped execution, there was only one other fate in Plantation America: to be sold. Which brings up one other aspect of life in that age: how would you want to own this bad man, whose close associate was a butcher of "Ill Fame." With a certainty, on some occasions, slave masters must have purchased their own robber, rapist or murderer.

'Formerly the Property of Mr. Hugh Houston'

Another in the Legion of Non-Indentured Servants Enslaved in Plantation America

Virginia Gazette (Pinkney) Williamsburg, October 20, 1774. (Johnston)

RUN away from the subscriber, in Fredericksburg, a servant man named TAOMAS OGLE, by trade a shoemaker, about 5 feet 6 inches high, of a pale complexion, speaks soft and low, says he is an Englishman, but by his make he appears to be an Irishman, his hair (if any on) is short, and of a brownish colour, has a scar in his face, or forehead, not larger than a straw, and, as well as I remember, about an inch long, he is very artful, and capable of imposing on most people;

took with him a Virginia cloth coat of cotton, filled with red, a red jacket, leather breeches, and several other cloaths. He has a burn on his right leg, near his knee.

The said fellow was formerly the property[1] of Mr. Hugh Houston, of Fredericksburg.

Whoever takes him up, if out of Spotsylvania county, shall receive a HALF JOE[2] reward, on delivering him at my house; or if at a distance too far to convey him for that money, reasonable charges will be allowed. BENJAMIN JOHNSTON.

---

[1] Like most runaway servants, this man was not indentured.

[2] A gold coin formerly used as currency in Portugal, first issued in the early 18th century after King John V. Uncertain of the exchange rate into pounds.

'Most Diabolical Practices'

Revolutionary War Runaway

Virginia Gazette (Dixon & Hunter), Williamsburg, November 22, 1776. (Zane)

THIRTY DOLLARS REWARD.[1] FREDERICK County, VIRGINIA, Nov. 20, 1776. RUN away on the Night of the 17th of June last, from Marlborough Iron Works, CHARLES WHITE, an English Convict, born in Rutlandshire, by Trade a Stocking Weaver, had been both in the Land and Sea Service,[2] is about 28 Years of age, 5 Feet 10 or 11 Inches high, a stout able Fellow, rather square built, has short dark brown Hair, a pug Nose, high Cheek Bones, and small Eyes;

had on a narrow brimmed Felt Hat, a short Fearnought Coat, coarse Country Linen Shirt and Trousers, old Shoes, with pewter Buckles, but, being

---

[1] This is an astoundingly high reward.
[2] A two-time British military veteran and two-time servant, who has refused to fight for one side and is agitating against the other. I cannot discern from the wording if he has sided with the Loyalists or Revolutionaries.

a notorious Villain, he may steal other Clothes, and change his Dress. The Mare it was supposed he had stolen, and advertised with him[3] in June last, is recovered, and the Villain himself has been twice apprehended, the first Time at Fredericksburg, where he had entered on Board an armed Vessel[4] by the Name of Johnson, from whence he made his Escape, and has since forged a Pass;

afterwards taken at Manchester, in the County of Chesterfield, where he confessed the Theft of the Mare above-mentioned, and was committed to the Gaol of the County, but made his Escape, and is now at large. It is supposed he will endeavour to enter into the Service of some of the southern Governments, as there was a recruiting Party in the Neighbourhood from whence he last made his Escape; or, if possible, to the Enemy, as he had used the most diabolical Practices to corrupt the Minds of his fellow Servants before he first ran away.

Should he be again taken, it is requested that he may be well secured; and whoever does so secure him, provided I get him, shall have the above Reward, and if brought Home, all reasonable Charges will be allowed by ISAAC ZANE [symbol]

---

[3] He was listed as livestock next to a horse.
[4] Conscripted as a sailor.

'The Property of Said Berry'

The History as Commodity of a 'Negro Man Named Peter'

Pennsylvania Packet – Philadelphia, Pennsylvania, Tuesday, October 30, 1781 (New Castle)

Peter AKA Dick Butcher

Two Half Johannesses Reward.[1]

RAN away from the subscriber, living in New Castle county, St. Georges hundred and Delaware state, a Negro Man named PETER, about 20 years of age, and about 5 feet 6 or 7 inches high, is marked with the small pox, straight limbed and well made;

was raised in Kent county, Delaware state by a certain Peter Cooper, and afterwards given to a certain Joseph Berry, and after said Berry's decease, sold by the sheriff of Kent county as the property of said Berry, to Nehemiah Tilton at Dover, of whom

---

[1] From the context, this researcher is inclined to value the half-Johannesses at a British pound but has been unable to find any historic valuation of this coin.

the subscriber purchased said negro, who ran away from me the 22d of February, in the year 1780;

he has been formerly seen in Kent county, but since has been in Philadelphia, and was out the last cruise in the ship Congress, captain Geddes commander, and passed by the name of DICK BUTCHER.

Whoever takes up said Negro and secures him in any goal on the continent, or brings him to the subscriber, shall have the above reward.

GEORGE CROW Port-Penn.

While the sources indicate that the life of a white slave and of a black slave generally followed this same course of being owned multiple times by various owners, the runaway negroes seemed to have the affection of the owners, who value the history of their life as a commodity above the discarded pasts of their white property, which was dismissed out of hand, as if the owners wished to know nothing concerning the past of a white slave. Indeed, most listings that mention a white slave's claim of previous stations in life are accompanied by claims that this person is a boastful drunkard and a liar. Hence, the history as commodity of the Negro Peter, who preferred life as Dick Butcher, is so illustrative of the unrecorded lives of the nearly anonymous white slaves who died in their millions to build the same iniquitous place that consumed them and the collective memory of their earthly damnation.

'So That Their Master May Get Them'

A Negro Fellow and a White Boy on the Run

Orange County, May 16th 1788
[Poughkeepsie Journal (Poughkeepsie, New York);
10 Jun 1788, Tue] (Hawkins)

Ten Dollars Reward

Run away from the subscriber living in Orange County near Goshen, on the 13th instant, a likely NEGRO Fellow named PRIME, about 18 years of age, thick set, about 5 feet 4 or 5 inches high;

had on when he went away a brown homespun short coat, and homespun under jacket something patched, Tow Trowsers, but might have changed his clothing, as he took others with him; blue yarn stockings, very old shoes and new felt hat.

Also went off the same time, an Apprentice boy, named NATHANIEL ROCKWILL, about 15 years old, small of his age, of a fair complexion—- had on an half worn short light brown homespun coat, an old jacket of the same colour.

James LaFond

Has taken with him both linen and woolen shirts, both of which he has worn at the same time - brown tow cloth Trowsers, half worn shoes and a new felt hat.

Whoever takes up the said run aways, so that their master may get them again, shall have the above reward for both, or the

same for the Negro only[1]—and a reasonable charges paid by David Hawkins.

---

[1] Throughout Plantation Era, negroes were always valued more highly than whites as slaves, primarily because of the high importation cost, which did much to encourage the policy of lifetime enslavement under the same master, whereas the cheaper white slaves were continually castoff and replaced by younger chattel. Keep in mind, that in a total slave society, the slave is better off than the free poor, who have to feed and house themselves from wages earned in competition with slave labor, while at the same time being legally bound to act as unpaid slave catchers. Any person who stood by and did nothing to stop an escaping slave was theoretically guilty of treason, for which some men stood trial.

'Broken Down'

A Two-Dollar White Slave on the Run

Delaware Gazette (Wilmington, DE) Saturday, January 30, 1790 (New Castle)

TWO DOLLARS REWARD.[1]

RAN away from the subscriber, on the 5th inst., a Servant Man named William Walker, of a pale complexion with short light colored hair,

had on when he went away, a fur Hat, and old Great Coat, a new Hunting Shirt, and old light colored Jacket, a Pair of Stockings, web Breeches, and tow Trowsers over them, brown yarn Stockings and a Pair of new Shoes—

Went off by night from James Phillips's house, he had two particular marks - one of his legs was broke down almost at his ankle, and a scar on his breast which appear as if he had been wounded.[2]

---

[1] Eleven years later, the negro Adam Right was worth 30 dollars.

[2] A runaway with a visibly broken shin bone suggests that the scar on William's chest was from a wound, as it

Any person securing said Servant so that I get him again shall have the above Reward, and reasonable charges if brought home to

Thomas Lee.

Milltown, Jan. 9.

---

is said to appear. Thomas lee, in his own words, strongly suggests his own savagery.

'Has Rather a Down Look'

A Four-Dollar Man Runs Away from America's Primary Slave Depot

Gazette – Wilmington, Delaware, October 6, 1792 (New Castle)

Foure Dollars Reward.

Ran away from the subscriber, living in Christianna hundred, New-Castle county,[1] on the 2d inst. An Irish indented servant man, named MICHAEL DOUGHERTY;

he is about 20 or 21 years of age; 5 feet 7 or 8 inches high, of a light complexion, with middling large grey eyes;

he is a fresh hearty looking well set fellow, and when spoken to, has rather a down look.[2]

---

[1] The port of New Castle brought in between 2,000 and 5,000 white slaves per year for most of the 1700s.

[2] It is often noted that white slaves had broken wills in this manner, from either beatings or downward social pressure. It is a wonder that so many of these emotionally shattered people found the will to run away.

461

Had on when he went away, a good wool hat, a linen coat, sustain waistcoat, and tow linen trowsers, all of an olive color an old shirt of common linen, old shoes with strings in them; but he may change his dress.

Whoever takes up and secures said Servant in any Goal; so that his Master may get him again shall have the above reward, and reasonable charges.

Thomas Chandler, jun.

4th of the 10th mo., 1792

'Four Feet Ten Inches High'

White American Slave Boy on the Run

Delaware Gazette – Wilmington, Delaware, June 30, 1792 (New Castle)

FOUR DOLLARS REWARD.

Ran away from the subscriber, living in Wilmington, an Apprentice lad, named SAMUEL STARR, by trade a Taylor, between 15 and 16 years of age, about four feet ten inches high, of a Sandy complexion, and pretty much Freckled;

is of a forward, talkative disposition, and has a great inclination of going to sea[1] (therefore all masters of vessels and others are forbid to harbor or carry him off)

he had on and took with him a sustain Coatee[2] and trowsers, a waistcoat and trowsers of

---

[1] This inclination for the sea seems to have represented among bold white slaves a deep upwelling for freedom, as they sought to escape even the physical clutches of a slave nation.

[2] A military cutaway coat with shortened coat-tails.

plain olive colored cotton, two shirts, a pair of shoes with large plated buckles, and an old wool hat.

Whoever takes up and secures said apprentice, so that his master may get him again, shall receive the above reward, and i[f] brought home reasonable charges, paid by

Henry Troth.6th mo. 28th, 1792[3]

---

[3] Educational institutions in states which have preserved such record of white enslavement have been loath to preserve documents, and especially to make available such ads that post-date 1776, trying to implicate America as a White Nation for Whites, when in fact it was not; rather, it was a class-based slave society. Thanks so much to Mary Kay Krogman for publishing this find.

'Red Hair and Freckled'

A Print Shop Boy Seeks His Freedom

Delaware and Eastern-Shore Advertiser – Wilmington, Delaware, Saturday, July 5, 1794[1] (New Castle)

Wilmington, July 5.

TWO DOLLARS REWARD.

RAN away from this Printing-Office, a lad named ALEXANDER KILPATRICK, 15 years of age,[2] about 5 feet 3 inches high, red hair and freckled, is of a pert and talkative disposition, and has a down look when closely questioned. – Took with him an olive green cloth coat, nankeen jacket, and ruffia sheeting trowsers.

---

[1] The United States had been a free nation for 11 years. However, many of its citizens were still predominantly unfree. Of roughly 3 million persons, 500,000 were unfree negroes and a million were unfree whites.
[2] After being sold once as a child to serve as a houseboy between the ages of 8 and 14, many boys were sold again at age 14–15, often to pay a parent's debt.

The above reward will be given for apprehending him.

'So That the Subscriber Get Him Again'

Another Runway Apprentice Lad

Delaware and Eastern-Shore Advertiser–Wilmington, Delaware, Saturday, April 25, 1795 (New Castle)

THREE DOLLARS REWARD.

RAN away from this Printing-Office, an Apprentice Lad,[1] named ELEC KILPATRIC,[2] about 17 years of age, and 5 feet 6 or 7 inches high; has red hair and freckled face; is talkative, and has a down look when closely questioned. He has a long nose

---

[1] Could this be the older brother [one year older] of runaway Alexander Kilpatrick? If so, might they have been bought as a package or was Elec serving the rest of Alexander's time? In 1678, the father of Thomas Hellier sold himself to a village as a community servant to satisfy a debt his son had incurred.

[2] In actual practice an apprentice had no more rights than an indenture, redemptioner or transport. Indeed, there is evidence, including the brutal enslavement of young Benjamin Franklin by his older brother, that apprentices—since they did not fall under servant statutes—were beaten more often than servants.

and chin. Had on when he went away, coating trowsers and coatee, round had – took with him a bundle of other clothes –

The above Reward will be given for apprehending him, so that the subscriber get him again, and reasonable charges if brought home, paid by

SAMUEL ADAMS.

All masters of vessels, and others, are forbid harbouring him, at their peril.

April 14, 1795

The 30-Dollar Man

Comparing White and Negro Slave Prices

Mirror of the Times and General Advertiser – Wilmington, Delaware, Saturday, May 16, 1801 (New Castle)

SIXTY DOLLARS REWARD.[1] –

Ran away from the Subscriber, living near Middletown, New-Castle County, in the State of Delaware, on the 17th of April last, a negro man, ADAM, and has surnamed himself Right. About 34 years of age, and about 5 feet 4 or 5 inches high, is well set, middling black, thin and moves lively, altho' very large feet for his size.

---

[1] This man has put in over half of his life's value in work. If he were as young as the 18–21-year-old whites that were being sought for 2–10 dollars apiece during this period, he would be valued at $60. Negro prices during this period ran from $30 to $100. Why? Were they really supermen, or were there better reasons to own a man of that race? These reasons are obvious and implicit in the advertisement. At 34, Adam was an old man for his era.

Had on when he went away, a tow linen shirt, much worn, a surtout, a round jacket, and trowsers, all of these made drab colored cloth, better than half worn; he had a dress suit, a blue broad-cloth coat, a vest and breeches of black velvet, he may have other clothing unknown to me. He has a great turn to the Methodist religion, and makes a very good prayer.[2]

He took with him his wife named RACHEL, a fat woman, somewhat on the yeallowish cast;[3]

also three children, the oldest a girl named SARAH, about eight years old, the second a girl also, named ELIZA, about three years old, and the third a boy named JOHN, about 4 months old.

He took them from a widow Price, near Fredericktown, Cecil County, Maryland.

Their clothing is unknown to me. It is expected they are gone up the Country some where, either Wilmington, the Turk's Head, Philadelphia, the Jerseys or perhaps New-York; but they are so remarkable that they must be easy taken notice of.

Whoever secures them in any jail so that the owners shall ge[t] them again, shall receive the above reward, and all reasonable charges if brought

---

[2] Adam is regarded as a good Christian and that gets him no succor.

[3] Adam's wife is obviously mixed race, with her complexion indicating she is half white rather than a "high yellow" quadroon or octoroon.

home, or one half for the man only, paid by me, JOHN COCHRAN.

May 8th, 1801.

Adam has three children with his mixed-race wife. Now, imagine if you will, buying a black pickup truck that, if you parked it next to your neighbor's yellow pickup truck, would produce three brown pickups which could be used and/or sold. This was the value of the black slave over the white slave, ever since the 17th century laws which tied his condition to his parent's race. He could be bred, eliminating virtually all labor costs and shipping uncertainties that complicated the white slave trade and the transatlantic black slave trade, as opposed to buying a man who was an embittered prisoner of war from some terrible conflict and got no sleep at night while he sharpened his tools in the barn...

Adam, a Christian man, separated from his family, escaped from his master in Middleton Delaware and stole his wife and children from their owner, the Widow Price, without doing the widow any harm. For those who view the current astonishing levels of black male child abandonment [75%–80%] and levels of interracial, cross-gender violence [13,000 to 7 in 2013] on their race and a reversion to type, let us consider Adam, a blacker man than most postmodern African-Americans, with more African DNA, and with a true reason to be hateful, and be reminded that he gathered his family and ran. We might also want to consider the reason why negroes were preferred slaves over whites, why whites paid four times the price for blacks whenever they could, because they were reportedly more docile, less violent and less likely to runaway than their savage Irish and English convict counterparts.

"Will Pass for a Free Man ..."

Andrew Jackson's Half-Breed Runaway

Here you go James. I thought you might find this Washington Post article about Andrew Jackson's classified advertisements for runaway black slaves interesting. No mention of ads for runaway white slaves posted in the papers over the years, such as you have diligently chronicled, however.

Of course, the point of the article is to take a cheap shot at God-Emperor Trump for paying homage to the Jackson, evil slave owner that he was, as a populist president. What was he thinking about, huh? (Brown)

-Jeremy Bentham

The runaway slave ad placed by Andrew Jackson ran in the "Tennessee Gazette," on Oct. 3, 1804. The ad was published on Page 3, column 4.

"Stop the Runaway," Andrew Jackson urged in an ad placed in the Tennessee Gazette in October 1804. The future president gave a detailed description: A "Mulatto Man Slave, about thirty years old, six feet and an inch high, stout made and active, talks sensible, stoops in his walk, and has a remarkable large foot, broad across the root of the toes — will pass for a free man ..."

The above ad is indistinguishable from ads for runaway whites of the same period, such as this one:

The Adams Centinel, Gettysburg, PA (Wray)

May 20, 1801

Eight Dollar Reward

Ran away from the subscriber on Sunday, the 17th inst., a German indented servant man, named John Godfrey Daniel Fidler, by trade a shoemaker, about thirty-two years of age, five feet eight or nine inches high; he is stout made and has short black hair.

Had on a lead colored homemade thick cloth coat, brown thick cloth pantaloons, a white dimity waistcoat, and half boots. It is expected he is making towards Philadelphia. Whoever takes up said Servant and secures him in any jail so that his Master gets him again, shall have the above reward, and all reasonable expenses if brought by me.

Robert Wray

Furthermore, the remark that the runaway can pass for a free man admits that numerous free men shared his appearance. Whether he appeared to be mixed race or white does not matter in terms of discovering the limits of bondage in this evil nation at its birth. If he appeared to be white, then it is clear that many whites were being held in bondage. If he appears to be mixed or black, then clearly, many non-whites were in a position of freedom, which is denied by our current narrative. Interestingly, the illustration on the ad at the top right of the listing is an illustration of a black man with hobo stick and pouch tied to its end, which is based on an earlier illustration of a white boy with such a stick, being led along out of bondage by the Devil himself!

Editor's Note: The Washington Post article makes mention of the Freedom on the Move project, a database of runaway slave advertisements. The database appears to omit any advertisements for paleface slaves, except when they are listed together with negroes or mulattoes. My inquiry as to their plans to include advertisements for slaves of European origin went unanswered.

'Has a Remarkable Twisting in His Hip'

Handicapped Carpenter John Cunning is Worth as Much as a Negro!

Mirror of the Times, and General Advertiser – Wilmington, Delaware, Saturday, August 13, 1803, (New Castle)

Twenty Dollars Reward[1]

RAN away from the subscriber an Irish lad, an apprentice to the carpenter's trade, calls himself John Cunning, and sometimes Cunningham, about 19 years of age, five feet seven or eight inches high, very dark hair and eyes, stoops when he walks and has a remarkable twisting in his hip.[2]

---

[1] The high reward offered for this physically handicapped apprentice indicates a slim supply of construction slaves and/or a long term of service, with 4 dollars normal for slaves in other trades doing seven years. The Constitution of the United States did indicate that importation of "'such persons" would only continue until 1804, which might be a reason for holding onto the slaves you had.
[2] Such injuries and conditions were unusual among black runaways and far more common among whites, possibly indicating that free white people who became

Took with him two pair of nankeen dark striped pantalets, 2 pair of check trowsers, 2 russia sheeting shirts, 1 black nankeen waistcoat, one yellow crossbared dimity do – 2 pair of shoes, one fur hat, one light nankeen outside jacket, one blue cloth do. &c. &c.

Whosoever takes up said apprentice and delivers him to the subscriber shall have the above reward and reasonable charges.

BENJAMIN MASON.

Wilmington, August 8th.

---

injured and unable to pay debts might have been sold to satisfy their financial commitments.

'Said Boy'

Runaway Apprentice Jacob Murphy Illustrates the Falling Values of Runaways from the 1790s through 1830s

Mirror of the Times and General Advertiser – Wilmington, Delaware, May 25, 1805,

TWO DOLLARS REWARD.

Ran away on Thursday last the 16th inst., an apprentice to the stone cutting business, named Jacob Murphey, about 15 years of age, fair complexion, dark hair, had on a grey round over Jacket & green tow trowsers, Whoever returns said boy to me shall have the above reward.

MICHAEL VANKUICK

Brandywine Mills, May 18, 1805

Before American independence, runaway whites brought 4–5 dollars. Twenty years later, in 1804, just as the last generation of trafficked whites out of Europe were newly bonded, the price had dropped to 2–3 dollars. By 1812, the price would drop to 12 cents and by the 1830s 5 cents! Why was the return value of white slaves so much lower at the very time one would expect their lack of importation to raise their value? The answer is debt slavery, with youths such as William Garrison exchanged for a parent's debt or sold, such as Andrew Johnson, by a widow unable to provide for a man's surviving child. However, the largest factor was that fugitive slave laws increasingly demanded that free, uninterested citizens must act as slave state deputies and return runaways, even at the penalty of treason.

The 1793 Fugitive Slave Act did not pertain only to chattel of African descent but also to any mixed-race or white servant, slave, apprentice, redemptioner, convict or transport. A white bystander to the 1851 Christiana Riot was charged with treason for not siding with slave catchers.

'So That I Get Him Again'

A Runaway Who Has Maintained His Value

Mirror of the Times and General Advertiser – Wilmington, Delaware, February 2, 1805 (New Castle)

FIVE DOLLARS REWARD. Ranaway from the subscriber living in the Borough of Wilmington, County of New Castle, on the 20th of January inst. An apprentice boy named David Porter, above 5 feet 7 or 8 inches high, slender made, dark complexion.

Had on when he went away, a brown Round about coat and trowsers, striped swansdown waist coat, and took with him two Russia sheeting shirts, and two blue and white neck handkerchiefs, and one white one, 2 pair of dark gray stockings, and fur hat. Whoever brings home said apprentice or secures him in any jail so that I get him again, shall be entitled to the above reward, and reasonable charges paid by

BENJAMIN MASON.

Wilmington, Jan. 30, 1805.

It is of interest that we still have a runaway commanding such a high price at this date. And Benjamin Mason seems quite the grasping miser by his eager wording. David better make tracks.

The Slave Media, 1805

Another Fleeing Newspaper Apprentice

Mirror of the Times and General Advertiser – Wilmington, Delaware, June 1, 1805 (New Castle)

Benjamin Franklin, foremost printer of his era, had once fled from his brother's newspaper shop and started up his own, where he eagerly placed advertisements for runaways and even paid out reward money for their return as a slave-catching agent.

TEN DOLLARS REWARD. Ran away on Sunday morning last the 26th inst. An apprentice to the printing business, named SAMUEL REA, nineteen years of age in October next. One of his eyes has been hurt, the effect of which is still visible.[1] His cloathing are a nankeen coatee and trowsers, a short round striped, or cross bared jacket

---

[1] It was within the rights of a master of an apprentice to beat him during this era, so there was no need to be squeamish about reporting injuries.

and trousers of home made plaid, a new hat, and shoes nearly new.

Whoever will return him, or secure him in jail so that I get him, shall have the above reward, and reasonable expences paid if brought home.[2]

It is hoped and requested that no printer will give employment to said apprentice. Masters of vessels, and others, are warned not to harbor, employ, or carry him off, under penalty of the law.

Printers or newspapers in the U. States are requested to insert this notice as often as convenient, and command a similar favor when necessary.[3]

JAMES WILSON.

Wilmington, Del. 29 May, 1805.

---

[2] The high reward is apparently coupled with [see 3] an expectation that such notices would be printed for free, in return for the printer who owns Samuel offering to do the same.

[3] This indicates that a certain number of runaway apprentices and servants were expected in the print business. I worked in a print shop in 1979 and wonder if these men could be running away due to boredom or due to the type of severe beating that Benjamin Franklin's printer-brother inflicted on him 75 years earlier. Also, could the fact that newspapers had been central to slave catching over the previous century have something to do with their use of unfree staff?

A Runaway, Cross-Dressing Hatter

Apprentice Boy, Thomas Bailey, Is Worth 12 Cents

Do note that the title of apprentice *grants the enslaved person but one thing a typical servant does not have: a promise that his master will teach the apprentice his trade so that he may have marketable skill. Otherwise, the apprentice would be beaten at will and worked as his master sees fit.*

Delaware Gazette and State Journal – Wilmington, Delaware, April 29, 1814 (New Castle)

Twelve Cents Reward.

RAN away from the Subscriber, in Wilmington, on the 19th of February last, an apprentice boy to the Hatting business, named THOMAS BAILEY, About nineteen years of age;

had on when he went away, a dark brown coatee and pantalets,[1] and a new fur hat; his other clothing not recollected.

He is five feet 8 or 9 inches high, and stout made, of very loose habits, and is remarkable for his ignorance and impudence.

The above reward (but no charges) will be given for securing [the apprentice] by

John Sellars.

April 19

[Submitted to geologytrails.com by Mary Kay Krogman]

---

[1] Long underpants with a frill at the bottom of each leg, worn by women and girls in the 19th century.

'To Digest a Plan of Escape'

A Runaway Stock Clerk Makes Off in the Company of a Scheming Hatter

Delaware Gazette and State Journal – Wilmington, Delaware, April 29, 1814 (New Castle)

STEWART HENDERSON,

who ran way on the 19th of March last;

he is twenty years old, had on when he went away, a brown coatee and new fur hat;

his other clothing not known, is five feet 9 inches high, of a slender make, fair complexion, and thin visage;

his face much broken out in small lumps, it is supposed that he has gone to Baltimore in company with a hatter by the name of THOMAS LAMBDEN,[1] who, it is probable, enticed him away, as he was

---

[1] This hatter apprentice appears to be a fellow advertised for on the same date by the name of Thomas Bailey.

frequently lounging about my shop[2] previous to their going away; in order, I suppose, to digest a plan of escape.

The above reward (but no charges)[3] will be given for securing both the above Runaways, or six cents for either of them, by

John Sellars.

April 19

---

[2] Stewart appears to have been a clerk in the good old days before one could quit one's thankless job and before one was paid for his labors.

[3] Although laws still served the master in regard to securing runaway whites, said masters, for reasons this reader is not yet able to determine, had become loathe to pay charges to presumably professional slave catchers.

'The Law Will be Put in Force'

Native Born Mulatto Man Wanted

Delaware Gazette and State Journal –
Wilmington, Delaware, Thursday, February 9, 1815
(New Castle)

10 DOLLARS REWARD.

RAN away from the subscriber, a mulatto
man, named Charles Hamilton, about five feet 10
inches high, a very good looking fellow, black eyes,
and about 22 years of age born in the State of
Delaware.[1]

He is supposed to be shipped on board of the
Mary Ross, at New Castle – All masters of vessels
and other persons are warned from harboring said

---

[1] This indicates that Delaware was a slave state in 1815
and is also of importance as it demonstrates that the
only legal chattel in America after 1804 was native born!
For the U.S. Constitution forbade the shipment of such
people into the country as of 1804. America had truly
become a people farm rather than a convict labor
colony.

mulatto, as the law will be put in force against them if they harbor him.[2]

The above reward will be given to any person who will return him to the subscriber in Philadelphia, or John Janvier, New Castle,[3] or confine him in New Castle Jail.

Capt. Joseph Robinson.

---

[2] This is evidence that free, mixed-race men were employed as sailors. Charles also has a surname and is not known as "Negro" Charles, for he is recognized as half-white.

[3] For over 100 years, New Castle had stood as the center of white human trafficking in English North America, with as few as 50 negroes held in bondage at any given time, but typically shipping in 2,000–5,000 white slaves per year. E ven after the ban on human trafficking, it seems to have remained a center for the sale of native-born Americans.

'A Mulatto Lad'

Worth Fifty White Men!

Nov 7. [The National Advocate, Friday, November 08, 1816] (Newkirk)

$20 Reward

Ran away from the subscriber, residing in the town of Montgomery, Orange county, state of New York;

a mulatto lad, about 17 or 18 years of age, by the name of JACOB, but commonly called JAKE; he is about 5 feet 8 inches high;

had on a deep blue cloth coat and pantaloons, striped cotton jacket, he has two pair of shoes, a fine and a course pair, a fur hat, a brown great coat, with a large cape, he is a talkative fellow, brought up to farming;

it is likely he will endeavour to pass himself as free.[1]

---

[1] This very valuable young man, with decades of backbreaking work ahead of him, is a slave, even though he is half white. Furthermore, the suspicion that Jake will pass himself off as free indicates that a sizable

A reward of Twenty Dollars will be paid[2] to any person apprehending said runaway, and returning him to the subscriber or confining him in any prison. Charles Newkirk.

---

population of free mulattoes was to be found in New York in 1816.

[2] Rewards for runaway whites of this period, who would work for 3–7 years instead of 20–30 years, were around 10 cents. The huge disparity in value per years left to serve, at 1–2 cents per year for whites to 50 cents to a dollar a year for blacks, is difficult to fathom, unless blacks were so much more highly valued due to the fact that they could be bred to produce more free labor— even bred with a white girl.

'Fourteen Years Old'

A Rare Case of a White Slave Whose Age is Known

Delaware Gazette and State Journal – Wilmington, Delaware, August 8, 1823 (New Castle)

$5 REWARD.

RANAWAY from the subscriber on the 22d of June last, an indented servant[1] boy named William Taylor. He is a light coloured mulatto, fourteen years old, four feet three inches high,[2] and is subject to a swelling on his right jaw.

He took with him one pair of blue gray cassimere trowsers, one do. plaid, one do. olive green tow, one striped round about, one finsey do. Three thin waist coats, straw hat with black lining, and one wool do.

---

[1] The definite claim of age and that he is an indenture a generation after such people were being tricked and kidnapped into the nation from overseas indicates that his parent or parents owed a debt and gave up their son to satisfy it.

[2] William is physically a child.

Whoever will return him shall receive the above reward, with reasonable charges.

Jeremiah Harker. July 22.

'Slender Made, and Not Very Black'

Delaware Gazette and State Journal, Wilmington, Delaware, Tuesday, November 24, 1829 (New Castle)

Notice

Was committed to the Public Goal of New Castle County, in the State of Delaware, on the 2d day of Nov instant, as a runaway, a black woman[1] who calls herself

SARAH SMITH

She appears to be about twenty-five years of age, rather slender made, and not very black. She is dressed in a Calico Frock, a Silk Coat of an olive coloar, and a black straw hat, trimmed with ribbon; and rings on her fingers. She has no cloathing except what she has on.

---

[1] We see the police state of early America in action again with the capture of this mixed-race woman, who is said to be black a few lines above where she is said not to appear to be black, marking blackness as a social state, not a biological one.

She says she served part of her time with a certain William Gilmore of Baltimore, and the remainder with Owen Huffington, of the same place, and that she is now free.[2]

The owner or owners are hereby notified to come prepared to prove their property, pay charges and take her away, otherwise she will be discharged from prison in six weeks from the date, agreeably to an act of Assembly in such case made and provided.[3]

William Herdman, Sh'ff.

New Castle, Nov. 4, 1829. 10 6.

---

[2] This woman claims to have been a time-serving slave, now free, and although the authorities do not believe this, they hold that it may be true and that if no one comes for her she will be set free.

[3] In the cases of runaway whites from the previous generation caught travelling without freedom passes, these were sold "for their keep" if not claimed, whereas Sarah would be freed.

'An Indented White Boy'

A White Boy Worth Six Cents in 1830

[Delaware Gazette and State Journal – Wilmington, Delaware, Friday January 29, 1830 (New Castle)

6 Cents Reward

ABSCONDED from the Subscriber, living in Mill Creek hundred, New Castle county and state of Delaware, on the 5th of January inst., an indented white boy,[1] by the name of ALBERT ASHBY; between 19 and 20 years of age.

Any person taking up said runaway and securing him, or if brought home, shall receive the above reward, but no charges will be paid

All persons are forewarned not to harbor or employ said boy at their peril, as they will be dealt with as the law directs.

James Giffin. January 19-4p

---

[1] Note the term "boy," used in 1830 to describe an unfree white man.

As of 1804, the United States, as delineated in the Constitution, accepted no more white slave shipments from Europe. However, the Anglo-American addiction to selling and buying children and debt-enslaving men and women, kept the practice going in an even cruder form, with the value of white slaves now at less than 10% of their former standing under British rule.

Five Cents of Chattel

'Indentured, Black Boy' in 1830

Delaware Gazette and State Journal – Wilmington, Delaware, Friday January 29, 1830 (New Castle)

5 Cents Reward

RANAWAY from the Subscriber, living in New Castle hundred, near the Red Lion Hotel, on Monday the 4th of January 1830, an indented black boy,[1] named ABRAHAM W. BROWN, goes by the name of Abe.

Had on when he went away a new drab cloth roundabout, drab trowsers, white yarn stockings, coarse lace boots and a new wool hat; took with him two domestic muslin shirts, and one drab bumbazette coatee.[2]

---

[1] Clear proof that dispels the myth that all unfree blacks were slaves for life and that indenture "contracts" were a form of white privilege.

[2] A thin plain or twill-woven worsted cloth with smooth finish used for dresses and coats.

Said Boy is between the ages of 19 and 20. All persons are forbid harboring him at their peril.[3]

John D. Turner

January 19-4t

---

[3] This is what finally brought slavery to an end, the fact that in a free-range slave society, every single person is enslaved, as all are liable to be called upon to capture the runaway [who now brings almost no reward] and are also at risk for felony prosecution for harboring a fugitive. There were charges of treason brought against upstanding citizens who merely declined to fight on the side of slave catchers.

Runnagates

Excerpts from:

Memoirs of the Late Dr Benjamin Franklin: with a review of his pamphlet, entitled "Information to those who would wish to remove to America."

By Thomas Day, Esq.

Annotated by James LaFond

Editor's Note: The author came across this book while researching the use of the word *cracker* as a slur for paleface Americans. He came across a quote the following quote in the Wikipedia entry for *Cracker*: "a race of runnagates and crackers, equally wild and savage as the Indians" who inhabit the "desert[ed] woods and mountains." The quote is attributed to Benjamin Franklin, in his memoirs published in 1790, but this is incorrect. The author tracked the quote to the book named above, which was written about Benjamin Franklin in the third person, and which is sometimes attributed to Benjamin Franklin, and sometimes to "Wilmer, a Maryland Loyalist." The scanned copy of the book made available by Google reveals a portrait of what must be the true author on the last page: Thomas Day, Esq., an English abolitionist with a history of criticizing American policies.

The complete work is included in the following section, with annotations by James LaFond appearing [in brackets] or *italicized paragraphs.*

Author's Notes

The following notes reference the pages as set in the original document, which is available online (Day).

Pages 30–32: Lecture transcription on the evils of British imports leading to debtor auctions and "thralldom."

Page 39: "chains, stripes and famine," on war as slavery.

Pages 63–69: Transcript and critique of Franklin's invitation to Hearty Young Men to come to America and homestead by Day. Page 67 has the runnagate quote:

"A race of runnagates and crackers, equally as savage as the Indians."

Day rails against the greater number of Knaves "pest[s] of society" who flourish in America and points out that most good land has long ago been bought up and that men must seek the deep interior.

On page 69, children are described as running nearly naked in the woods shooting and hunting rather than learning industry, as opposed to being enslaved in workhouses, fields, mines and other occupations from a young age as was the proper English child of the poor brought up.

Pages 70-71 describe debtors running away to the woods and the manner of their settlement and destruction of forest as well as their far-famed drunkenness.

Page 72 describes "The first settler in the woods" as a runaway debtor who builds a dirt floor log cabin with attached animal shed and plants corn around trees he has killed by ringing them around the base. This settler is described as "acquiring a strong tincture of [Indians]," being a violent, warlike hunter who feeds his family largely through hunting, while practicing limited herding and planting in his half-wooded parcel of "40 to 50 acres." Day is disgusted by the ragged clothes, rum-drinking and Indian-like sexual nature of the marriage between the woodsman and his wife. He goes on to discuss the realistic length of such a settler's stay as three to four years until he must move on due to population pressure on available game.

"He eats sleeps and drinks in dirt and rags in his little cabin," says Day of the despised cracker or runnagate who made up the bulk of the American frontiersmen.

Overall:

Thomas Day, Esq., of England wrote the body of the book. The quote about runnagates attributed to Franklin was his. His vision of runaway debt slaves in the back country was brutal and accurate, whereas Franklin's was optimistic and unreal, the myth our nation adopted.

Franklin's lecture on mercantile culture leading to a life of slavery is not refuted by Day's criticism, but buttressed.

Paragraph breaks have been added to the text below, as well as annotations by this author. It provides a keen insight into the life of the American laboring class as he journeyed beyond the reach of the landed aristocracy of the Tidewater and Piedmont regions and became something uniquely American and half Indian.

MEMOIRS OF THE LATE DR. BENJAMIN FRANKLIN

WITH A REVIEW OF HIS PAMPHLET ENTITLED "INFORMATION for those who would wish to Remove to AMERICA."

1 LONDON: Printed and sold for the Author, by A. GRANT, No. 91, Wardour 5 Street, Soho; sold also by J. Cunuuz, No. 38, New Bond Street; 5, C. STALKLR, Stationers' Court, Ludgate-hill 3 and W. RICHARDSON, Royal Exchange, M DCC XC [1790]

MEMOIRS, &c.

THE biographer who attempts to write American lives, will find their characters very complex, and of difficult dissection. Doctor BENJAMIN FRANKLIN, the subject of the present memoirs, affords a striking instance of the propriety of this remark. In him we may discern both the sagacious philosopher, and the subtle politician—well versed in the mazes of human life, he knew the best means of rendering the virtues and vices, the infirmities and follies of mankind subservient to his own purposes. Possessing naturally a deep and distinct perception, his judgment led him to soar above the prejudices of vulgar minds, and to look down, as from an eminence, on those who were confined by modes of education, systems of faith, or political institutions. Being self-taught, and free from the authority of great names, he boldly investigated every object of the creation, drew his deductions from the phaenomena, and thought for himself. This produced an active, vigorous intellect; a mode of reasoning concise, clear, and convincing.

This wonderful man, who surprized the schools, and became the admiration of the people, was born at Boston, in the State of Massachusets, in the year 1705. His father was a tallow-chandler, and the son served an apprenticeship to a printer in that city.

Benjamin's master was his oldest brother, who beat him every day, spurring Benjamin to flee to Philadelphia and begin his own life.

This occupation led him to the pursuit of knowledge; and in these younger years he manefested a love for science, and a particular attachment to subjects of a philosophical nature; of which his letters to Sir Hans Sloane are an evident testimony.

There have been different motives assigned for his leaving Boston, and going to Philadelphia; some have thought it was a love intrigue; but others say, that, having attacked the conduct of the General Court in some anonymous satyrical pieces, and being discovered, he was obliged to fly from his native country, to avoid the consequences.

His brother faced political censure for his and Benjamin's editorials.

However, his removal was the means of introducing him to a wider sphere of action, and gradually placed him in a more respectable situation; though, at his first appearance in Pennsylvania,

He was suspected of being a runaway and questioned, avoiding detection due to his great intelligence and maturity.

he was glad to get work as a journeyman printer; in which employ he exhibited a great example of frugality and industry. These virtues soon enabled him to commence business for himself. He began with printing Primers, Psalters, and spelling-books, for which there was a great demand in this infant country. At length he purchased, from its original proprietor, the Pennsylvania Gazette, the oldest paper in that province. It was in this paper,' and an almanac, which he annually published, that the superiority of his genius first burst forth from its humble obscurity, and displayed talents which have since astonished the world.

Mr. Franklin was now the admired editor of the Pennsylvania Gazette, and met with the warm encouragement of his fellow-citizens.

Franklin ran hundreds of wanted advertisements for runaways in The Gazette.

About this time he gained a valuable friend in the Rev. Mr. George Whitesield. This gentleman was then in the prime of life, possessed of all the charms and powers of oratory requisite to influence the passions, and captivate the hearts of the multitude. He was preaching throughout North America with great applause and success, and had just composed a volume of sermons, and also collated from Dr. Watts and others a hymn-book for the use of his followers, who were become very numerous.

Mr. Whitesield gave the copy of these to Mr. Franklin, who published them, and they had a rapid and extensive sale, the profits of which enabled him to enlarge his business to considerable advantage.

In proceeding on these memoirs, I would chuse to view Mr. Franklin at first in the amiable part of his character, as a philosopher and benefactor to mankind: it will then be time enough to reverse the medal, and to contemplate the shades and obscurities of his conduct as a politician.

Being now firmly settled in the printing business, no man could pay to it greater attention; and his prudence in pecuniary affairs was such, that he soon acquired, what any tradesman might consider, *a competency.* All the leisure time he could spare from other avocations, was spent in the acquisition of knowledge, and in his favourite study of natural Philosophy. Ever fond to be accounted a man of letters, he even applied himself to the acquirement of the Latin and French languages after he had arrived to manhood, and, by an unwearied perseverance, accomplished his purpose. It may be justly observed, that Pennsylvania has exceeded any other part of America in the number of its literary and charitable institutions; and several of them were first fuggested and promoted by Mr. Franklin. He was the principal agent in the foundation of the first public school of any note in that province; and the Philadelphians are originally indebted to him for their library.

In 1743 several gentlemen, in different parts of the colonies, formed themselves into a society for promoting useful knowledge in America: Mr. Franklin drew up the original plan or proposal, and it has been continued ever since, and is now known by the name of the *American Philosophical Society*, which has belonging to it, in Europe and elsewhere, many members of distinguished reputation.

The society greatly increasing in the number of its members, some years after, it was found necessary, for the more effectual advancement of their design, to distribute themselves into six committees, under the following heads, viz.

I.   Natural Philosophy, Mathematics, Optics, Astronomy, and Geography.

II.   Medicine, Chemistry and Anatomy.

III.   Natural History and Botany.

IV.   Trade and Commerce.

V.   Mechanics and Architecture.

VI. Husbandry and American Improvements.

This distribution was communicated to the several colonies by the public prints; and the friendly correspondence, in the fore going branches of knowledge, of all gentlemen of learning and ingenuity, was earnestly solicited. These means were crowned with success by an extensive correspondence, and the society became firmly and respectably established.

Mr. Franklin daily increased in reputation and science, and applied himself with uncommon assiduity to investigate the nature of electricity. In his experiments, it is said, he was assisted by the Rev. Ebenezer Kinnersly, prosessor of English and Oratory in the college and academy of Philadelphia, who was then reading weekly lectures on this curious and entertaining branch of natural philosophy, at the apparatus room in the college. He undoubtedly improved by the experience of this ingenious gentleman; but his own sagacious and active mind led him on to discoveries that will immortalize his name, and hand him down to the remotest ages.

The resemblance between the *Electric Spark* and *Lightning* is so obvious, that we find it among the earliest observations on the subject, but the proof of the important theorem of *their identity* was reserved for Mr. Franklin[1]; he first observed the power of uninsulated points in drawing off the electricity from bodies at great distances; and thence inferred, that a pointed metallic bar, if insulated at a considerable height in the air, would become electrical by communication from the clouds, during a thunderstorm. He gave this thought to the public; and several machines, consisting of insulated iron bars, erected perpendicular to the horizon, and pointed at top, were set up in different parts of France and England. The first apparatus that was favoured with a visit from the etherial matter, was that of Mons. Dalibard, at Marli la Ville, about six leagues from Paris; it consisted of a bar of the length of 40 feet, and was electrified on the 10th day of May, 1752, for the space of half an hour, during which time the longest sparks it emitted measured about two inches. Mr. Franklin, after having published the method of verifying his hypothesis concerning the sameness of electricity with the matter of lightning, was waiting for the erection of a spire in Philadelphia, to carry his views into execution; not imagining that a pointed rod, of a moderate height, could answer the purpose; when it occurred to him that, by means of a common kite, he could have a readier and better access to the regions of thunder than by any spire whatever. Preparing therefore a large silk handkerchief, and two cross sticks, of a

---

[1] Nicholson's Philosophy

proper length, on which to extend it, he took the opportunity of the first approaching thunder-storm to walk into a field, in which there was a shed convenient for his purpose; but, dreading the ridicule which too commonly attends unsuccessful attempts in science, he communicated his intended experiment to nobody but his son, who assisted him in raising the kite. The kite being raised, the end of the string was tied to a silk string, which he held in his hand, and a small key fastened at the place of junction.

A considerable time elapsed before there was any appearance of its being electrified. One very promising cloud had passed over it without effect, when at length, just as he was going to despair of his contrivance, he observed some loose threads of the hempen string to stand erect, and to avoid one another, just as if they had been suspended in a common conductor.—Struck with the promising appearance, he immediately presented his knuckle to the key; and judge of the exquisite pleasure he felt at the moment the discovery was compleat. He perceived a very evident electric spark; others succeeded, even before the string was wet, so as to put the matter past all dispute; and when the rain had wetted the string, he collected the electricity very copiously. This happened in June, 1752, a month after electricians in France had verified the same theory; but before he had heard anything they had done.

Having been thus fortunate with his kite, his success and pregnant invention prompted him to further contrivances. He insulated an iron rod, to draw the lightning into his house, for the purpose of making experiments, whenever there should be a considerable quantity of the electrical fluid in the atmosphere: and that he might not lose an opportunity of that nature, he connected *two bells* with his apparatus, which gave notice by ringing whenever the rod was electrified.

But this discovery was not only surprising and curious in its nature, but also of great benefit to mankind, as it led Mr. Franklin to the construction of his metalline rods, which have been found highly useful in preventing buildings from being damaged by lightning, and consequently must have saved many lives that would otherwise have been destroyed by this destructive element. For several years, while he was deeply engaged in these electrical experiments, he maintained an epistolary correspondence with Peter Collison, Esq. fellow of the Royal Society, to whom he communicated his various improvements and discoveries. These letters were published, and much admired both at home and abroad; and the English literati readily joined in giving every testimony of approbation to his merits and abilities.

In the month of April, 1762, the university of Oxford conferred upon him the honorary degree of Doctor of Laws; and being, as it were, in the zenith of his philosophical glory, many of the most eminent men of the age cultivated his friendship, and revered his name. In the letters on electricity afore-mentioned, there are many useful observations well worthy of notice, as they may, in some cases, tend to the preservation of life, one of which I cannot forbear laying before my readers. It being a very common practice in thunder-gusts, for Persons in the country to take shelter under a tree, the passage alluded to will claim their attention.

"As electrical clouds (says the Doctor) pass over the country, high hills, and high trees, lofty towers, spires, masts of ships, chimnies, &c. as so many prominences draw the electric fire, and the whole cloud discharges there; dangerous it is to take shelter under a tree, during a thunder-gust: it hath been fatal to many, both men and beasts. It is saser to be in the open field for another reason: when the cloaths are wet, if a flash on its way to the ground should strike your head, it would run in the water over the surface of your body. Hence a wet rat cannot be killed by the exploding electrical bottle, when a dry rat may."

These facts have been verified in several instances; two of which I shall relate for the information of such persons as may not have been conversant in such speculations. The first happened some years since near Lancaster, in the province of Pennsylania [sic], and is as follows:

515

"Three boys of that town, born within a few mouths of each other, and all in the thirteenth year of their age, went out on the 24th July, in the morning, to gather huckleberries. On their return about four o'clock in the evening, it rained pretty hard, which induced them, though already wet, to take shelter under a large black oak that grew in the middle of the great road, distant about forty yards from any other tree. *One of the boys sat close to the left side of the tree, and his head reclining upon the trunk.* The two others sat at some distance from the trunk, under a large spreading bough. Several claps of thunder broke from the westward; the explosions became sharper and more frequent; a flash of lightning at last struck the tree, killed the boy who sat next to it, together with a dog that had crept between his knees, and struck down the other two, so that they were insensible of their condition, and unable to move for several minutes. However, one of the two was at length able to get up; but found himself stunned, faint, weak and staggering like a drunken person. As soon as he came to reflect upon the cause of his distress, he turned round to examine the fate of his companions, and perceiving that the next one to him had some symptoms of life, attempted to raise him up; but not being able to effect this, he went to the other, whom he found in the same situation in which he had seen him alive, except that the stroke which he had received in the head had forced him into a more recumbent posture, His eyes were open, and in a staring position, and every limb and joint were stiffened. The boy, scarce recovered from the fright occasioned by his own misfortune, and now greatly terrified with the sight before him, took to his heels, and ran till he came to the house of a Mr. John Stoner, distant about a quarter of a mile, where he told the melancholy tale. Several people repaired immediately to the place; they found the second boy, who remained alive, lying upon his back, at the distance os about loo yards from the tree, where it is supposed he had fell, or rather crept, in attempting to get home. The other they found in the situation already described, with two large rents in his hat, where the lightning entered, and the hair upon the left side of his head, where he reclined against the tree, greatly singed; his left shoulder very livid, and several black spots upon his body. The day after, he was buried.

"The others were confined to their beds, in a dangerous and dreadful situation. In company with others I paid them a visit.—They are both sensible boys for their age, and were able to give satisfactory answers to all the questions that were proposed. Upon being asked whether they heard any noise, at the time they felt the stroke, they both agreed *that they did hear a noise, as if [many] guns were fired off together;*"— and as to their sensation of their stroke, *"it seemed as if a chord of wood, lighted up into one flame, had fallen upon them, and wrapped them up in fire."*

James LaFond

At this point in American history, circa 1750, the term boy, *once strictly meaning a slave of any age, was beginning to be used as a term for* lad, *meaning a male youth born into a family rather than owned by a family member. These boys may have been slaves or not. It is an indication as to how great the percentage of male youths in America had been referred to as* boys *rather than* lads *that* boy *became, after 150 years of planting English-speaking humans in North America, a term on par with* lad *in certain areas of America. It was rare indeed for a youthful male to be free, as he was often apprenticed or sold or rented to a master by his parents.*

"They were miserably burnt, (if philosophers will allow me to apply such a term to lightning) in several parts of their bodies, and the skin came away, as if by boiling water. The burn of one them reached from the shoulder to the hip, upon the left side, and was about six inches broad; in some places it ran in upon the belly, with a kind of ray, like those which painters give to the sun. But the most remarkable effects of this dreadful stroke were the following, equally and uniformly alike upon the three boys. Several holes, some capable of receiving a large bullet, some a pea, and some a grain of shot were made in the posteriors of each boy; occasioned, we supposed by the lightning's passing through the body by the shortest course, and so discharging itself here into the common

518

mass, through those parts which were most in contact with the earth; for each boy sat upon the ground. The legs of only one boy were burnt; this we endeavoured to account for, by supposing that this boy sat with his legs stretched out, which brought them in contact with the earth, as well as the breech; whilst the others had them drawn up, resting upon their feet; in which position the whole of the flash was discharged through the breech. We were encouraged in this supposition by observing that the boy who suffered in his legs, did not suffer so much in his posteriors as the others. Upon examining their breeches, we found that the destructive element had made and passed through several holes, corresponding exactly with those it had made in the flesh. The breeches of one of the boys were made of leather; the flame, in passing through these, left a burn to every hole, like that made by a spark in passing through a quire of paper in electrical experiments. The shirt and stockings of one boy were rent, without any marks of being burnt or singed, whilst the waistcoat and shirt of another had several holes, evidently burnt, as if done by the sparks of a smith's forge.

"In short, when we viewed the condition of these poor boys, and considered what a volume of lightning they must have been enveloped in, we were at a loss to conceive how they escaped with the breath of life, unless we may be allowed to attribute their preservation (next under God) *to their cloaths* being very wet before they came to the tree, which undoubtedly served *as conductors* to a considerable part of the destructive fluid.

The quotations indicate Franklins own words.

"The second instance happened at Savannah, in Georgia, in the month of July, 1773. A vessel bound to Providence, in the Bahama Islands, lying off one of the wharfs, had on her deck *twelve horses*: the Captain had cleared out at the custom-house, and was preparing to weigh anchor in order to sail, when, as is usual at this time of the year, a tremendous gust came on; the lightning struck the ship's mast, which conducted the fluid among the horses, and instantly killed ten of them: the two which escaped, were just taken on board, and a short time before had been swimming in Savannah river; hence we may conclude, that their *wet* condition protected them from the effects of the lightning.

Notwithstanding accidents by lightning are very frequent in North America, and the great usefulness of Dr. Franklin's rods are acknowledged, yet you will find them erected on very few houses. Many of the religious sectaries in Pennsylvania are averse to their use; they consider it as presumption, and say, they will trust to *the first great Cause*; though at the same time these very people are taking physic, and get cupped and bled, in order to prevent themselves from being sick and diseased.

Thus far we have contemplated the early life of Dr. Franklin, spent in philosophical investigation, in founding schools, diffusing knowledge, and producing a variety of useful inventions for the good of society.—In these we admire and revere him!—But we must now proceed to the political part of his character, the examination of which cannot afford so many pleasing sensations as we have already experienced. Indeed, we would express our sentiments on this occasion in the elegant language of a little poem, which is said to be inscribed on a chamber stove, in the form of an urn, invented by the Doctor, and so contrived, that the flame, instead of ascending, descended.

I.

Like a Newton sublimely he soar'd,

To a summit before unnttain'd;

New regions of science explor'd,

And the palm of Philosophy gain'd.

II.

With a spark that he caught from the skies,

He display'd an unparallel'd wonder;

And we saw with delight and surprize,

That his rod could protect us from thunder.

III.

Oh, had he been wise to pursue
 The path which his talents design'd,
What a tribute of praise had been due,
 To the teacher and friend of mankind!

IV.

But to covet political fame,
 Was in him a degrading ambition;
A spark which from Lucifer came,
 And kindl'd the blaze of Sedition.

V.

Let Candour then write on his urn,
 Here lies the renowned inventor,
Whose flame to the skies ought to burn,
 But inverted, descends to the centre.

Dr. Franklin had passed the meridian of life [classically thought to be age 35, see Dante's *Inferno*] before he rendered himself conspicuous as a politician. His opposition to the proprietary government, and his endeavours to introduce a *royal one*, first recommended him in this character to the notice of his fellow citizens: neither was it long until he got into favour with the then English ministry, by scheming new regulations for the management of the post-offices in America, and the increase of the post-tax. The display of his talents on these and some other occasions, procured him the place of joint postmaster-general, which gave him the super intendance of all the post-offices in the several provinces. Possessed of every accomplishment to acquire popularity, he obtained a seat in the Assembly, and united in his efforts, with Mr. Joseph Galloway, against the proprietary interest; and in 1764, was appointed agent to transact the business of the province at London: so extensive was his reputation at this period, that he was. nominated, soon after, agent for three other Provinces, New Jersey, Virginia, and Georgia.

The affair of the stamp-act coming on, the Doctor found full employment in opposing it; and exhibited likewise a specimen of the duplicity of his character; for though he was continually writing and arguing against it, yet he asked and obtained the place of stamp-master for one of his friends in Philadelphia; and recommended another for the state of Maryland;

The first use of the term "state" to designate a province is probably a reflection of the fact that ay wrote this book after the formation of the United States and represents an anachronistic slip of the pen.

but on the repeal of the act, that his Philadelphia friend might not be disappointed of a place, he got him provided for in the American customs; and, what crowns the whole, it has been said, that he advised this person to sell that place to the highest bidder, as soon as he could; alledging as a reason, that Great Britain would shortly have no custom houses in America.

The Doctor engaged in a friendly bit of what we would now call insider trading.

There are others who have asserted, that, though the Doctor opposed the stamp-act in England, yet he was the original projector of it. The history of the matter is, that, some years since, the Doctor happened to be at General Braddock's table, then in the province of Maryland;

This would have been the early stages of the French and Indian War, probably 1754, possibly 1755.

that the General was complaining of the backwardness of the Provinces to raise the supplies, and unite for the common good; when Mr. Franklin said, that a stamp duty, enacted at home, for all the colonies, would create an independent revenue to the Crown.—These words, or words to that effect, are well remembered by several persons of credit.

It further appears, that the stamp-act had been long a favourite scheme of his, from a manuscript written on the subject before he went to London as agent, which had been seen and read by several gentlemen at Philadelphia. In this performance, this patron of liberty projected a variety of ways and means, such as, a stamp-act, a poll-tax, circulating Exchequer bills upon mortgages bearing interest in the Exchequer in England; a general excise scheme, and a postage on ship-letters.—Thus we see he originally had no objection to internal taxes, provided he and his friends could have the management, and, consequently, derive emolument from them.

Day, here, presents this Founding Father as scheming to break away from the mother country in the manner of underbosses in a cartel attempting to seize control of a drug market distant from the center of power. Much evidence to the Founding Fathers as little more than aspiring tax farmers suggests that their notion of liberty simply meant the liberty to exploit lower forms of human life. This is stated flatly in the founding documents. See *The Greatest Lie Ever Sold.*

Having passed an examination before the House of Commons, at the time of the stamp act, he published a pamphlet of the same, which was circulated in every part of America, though it was much doubted whether the questions and answers are justly represented.

The use of anonymous or pseudonymous tracts, in the question and answer format, was a common tactic in the revolutionary era. Franklin, being a printer and a politician, was ideally positioned to manufacture consent for his designs.

However, he was indefatigable in his exertions, until a repeal of that act was obtained. But nothing tended more to widen the breach between the mother country and the colonies than the Doctor's inflammatory correspondence to his friends, who were men of revolution principles; and, notwithstanding their plausibility and pretensions of obtaining a redress of grievances and reconciliation, yet they were artfully employed to spread the flame of discord, excite an implacable hatred, and to propagate the Doctor's political nostrums throughout the country. These were the chiefs who afterwards embraced every opportunity to inculcate on the minds of the people, that America must one day or other become free and independent; that it was absurd to suppose such a vast continent could long be equitably governed by a little insignificant island, at three thousand miles distance, whose king could know nothing of them, but through the medium of corrupt and interested governors.

The repeal of the stamp act did not remove the jealousies of the Americans; it rather taught them to expect future concessions in their favour; hence they demanded the repeal of several other subsequent acts, until the destruction of the tea at Boston had matured the quarrel, and they began to throw off all disguise. A little before this period, the American newspapers were filled with the most virulent declamations against the king and ministry. For many of these, we were indebted to Mr. Samuel Adams, the Doctor's principal agent and correspondent, who was continually publishing extracts of his letters from London, though not with his name, yet as from a gentleman in a public character, and a warm friend to the Colonies. Among many others we shall give the following as a specimen:

"Now is the time of trial," says the Doctor; "now will all Europe see whether "the Americans are possessed of virtue: the eyes of all are turned to your part of the globe, in eager expectation of discovering your sentiments, in regard to the part you will act, since the partial repeal, the particulars of which, with the debates thereon, you will see by the English prints. Your conduct at this juncture will, in a great measure, determine your future fate, as the omission of the duty on tea in the repeal, is left as the test of American liberty. It is scarcely possible, my dear friend, for you to conceive the anxiety shall feel, till I hear of your determination, as on that the very existence of the ministry in a great measure depends: They flatter themselves with the expectation of seeing the provinces divided, that some will chose to import, which must in a little time induce the rest to follow the same steps; but your real friends think better of you, and I cannot be persuaded that you will now, after so noble a stand, sell your birthright for a mess of pottage. It is only necessary for you to be true to yourselves, and all will be well in the end, as your friends here are composed of the most sensible and important characters in the nation, who must in time bear down all opposition. Be steady, be virtuous and, as king Harry observed to his men, (just entering on action), dishonour not your mothers; now attest that those whom you called fathers did beget you."

Again, "It gives me great pleasure to hear that our people are steady in their resolutions of non-importation, and in the promoting of industry among themselves. They will soon be sensible of the benefit of such conduct, though the acts should never be repealed to their full satisfaction. For their earth and their sea, the true source of wealth and plenty, will go on producing; and if they receive the annual increase, and do not waste it as heretofore, in the gewgaws of this country, but employ their spare time in manufacturing necessaries for themselves, they must soon be out of debt;

Day should be commended for including this clause, which matter of factly indicts the English mercantile system as a creator of debt slavery. The logic for the continual segregation of black slaves from white slaves rested on the very real fact that any man but the king might, through misfortune, be reduced to slavery; that blacks and Indians had routinely owned Englishmen in 17th century Virginia; and that being held in bondage by people of another race was a condition declared against in the Book of Leviticus, which served as the Anglican and Congregationalist rule set for slave administration in English America.

Below, in Franklin's letter to Samuel Adams, he describes the mechanics of mercantile enslavement, a fate which awaited every man in a mercantile condition.

they must soon be easy and comfortable in their circumstances, and even wealthy. I have been told that in some of our country courts heretofore, there were every quarter several hundred actions of debt, in which the people were sued by shopkeepers for money due for British goods, as they were called, but in fact *evils*. What a loss of time this must occasion to the people, besides the expence! And how can freemen bear the thought of subjecting themselves to the hazard of being deprived of their personal liberty,

Freemen, that is, men who had their liberty and could bear arms yet owned no real estate holdings and were generally unable to vote in a provincial assembly— the very class that staffed the armies of Bacon's Rebellion in 1676—are here seen as highly susceptible to the British system, in terms of being put back into servitude, and are being promoted as the class of man who will make the Revolution viable.

at the caprice of every petty trader, for the paltry vanity of tricking out himself in the *flimsy* manufactures of Britain, when they might, by their own industry and ingenuity, appear in good substantial, honourable homespun!

In our current, global mercantilist economy, homespun goods and clothing cost more to produce than the cheap and abundant goods produced by largely Asian and largely unfree labor.

Could folks but see what numbers of merchants, and even shop keepers here, make great estates by American folly;—how many shops of A. B. C. and Company, with wares *for exportation to the Colonies*, maintain each shop three or four partners and their families, every one with his country house and equipage, where they live like princes, on the sweat of our brows; pretending indeed, sometimes, to wish well to our privileges, but on the present important occasion, few of them affording us any assistance; I am persuaded that indignation would supply our want of prudence; we should disdain the thraldom we have so long been held in by this mischievous commerce, reject it for ever, and seek our resources, where God and Nature have placed them, within ourselves."

Such were the lectures Dr. Franklin transmitted from London to his friend Adams, who made them the subject of his harangues at the Boston town-meetings; and communicated their contents, with his circular letters, to the Committees and Councils of Safety in the several provinces. The flame of liberty was now in a blaze, from New Hampshire to Georgia; and some enthuslasts attributed its ardour and extent to the special influence of Heaven; but sober reason may plainly discover, that the spirit of opposition to the mildest and best government in the world, originated with a *knot* of most subtle and designing men, whose abilities for the work are scarcely to be paralleled in any age or country.

The British Crown loyalist Day declares here that the Founding Fathers were, indeed, great, even unparalleled men. The value of such works as Day's, written in an age before the foe on the battlefield of ideas had to be the lowest vermin, is immensely valuable.

Thus did our philosophic Doctor appear an enemy to the government, manufactures and Commerce of a nation, from whom he had received distinguished honours and great emoluments.—But we shall not accuse him with ingratitude; though it cannot be denied, that, instead of sincerely recommending such meafures as were of a conciliatory nature, his pen, his tongue, his every faculty, were sedulously engaged to encrease the fears, and to inflame the minds of his countrymen: nothing less than Independence would satisfy this Machiavel; and independence was at length obtained, with Bankruptcy and Disgrace.

This boasted independent sovereignty has now been in the hands of a democracy for thirteen years; and so far have the people been from obtaining the manifold blessings for which they contended, that they have universally declared, that they could not be in a worse situation; and therefore, as an experiment, have consented to a change of their first Confederation. Their persons, property and Commerce have lost that security which they enjoyed as British subjects; and they are now humbly imitating a constitution, which Franklin, and other theoretical politicians taught them to despise. The manufactures of Great Britain are called "flimsy;" but the people know them to be good, necessary, and substantial; and, since the peace, have given them a decided preference; for these despised manufactures, at this day, make three-fourths of the American importations.

But to return.—Being dismissed from his office of post-master, for some mal-practice therein, he left London, and went speedily to America, with a firm purpose of supporting the cause of liberty, as it was then called, and to give his advice and information to the numerous Whig Associations, then formed in every colony. In the spring of 1775, the Doctor had an opportunity of electrifying the whole continent with the news of the battle of Lexington. Many were his pathetic descriptions of this unlucky affair, which so lacerated and extended the wound between the two countries, as to render all ideas of reconciliation nugatory. At length appeared in the public prints a copy of his laconic, but significant letter to one of his quondam intimate friends, Mr. Strahan, late his Majesty's law-printer, and a member of parliament for Malmsbury.

Philadelphia, July 5, 1775

"Mr. Strahan,

YOU are a member of that parliament, and one of that majority which has doomed my country to destruction.—You have begun to burn our towns, and murder our people!—Look upon your hands! —They are stained with the blood of relations!—

You and I were long friends—you are now my
enemy and I am,

    Your's,

    B. FRANKLIN."

The American contest now wore a very
serious aspect.—Being determined to persist in
their opposition to the acts of the British
parliament, is was necessary they should be
furnished with it was the means of defence. Hard
money they had little or none; and equally scanty
was their supply of arms and ammunition. In this
dilemma, the emission of a continental paper
currency was suggested. Dr. Franklin was among
the first that demonstrated the necessity of its
adoption; without which they could have made but
a short and faint resistance against the mother-
country. The first emission of three millions of
dollars took place July 25, 1775, with a promise of
redemption in three years, *as gold and silver*; and
before the Doctor left America, the latter end of
1776, they had emitted and expended upwards of
twenty-one millions, which passed as equal to
specie. How this money could be redeemed began
to puzzle Congress; and some of the members,
when the Doctor was about to depart from France,
asked his advice on the subject; he replied, "Never
mind it, we shall pay the expences of the war mostly
this way; emit your continental currency as long as
it will pay for work, paper, and lamp-black."

It is certainly fact, that the people in general, at the beginning of the contest, had no fixed plan or idea of contending for independence: the language of the public addresses and resolutions from every colony were replete with terms of loyalty to their sovereign, and with earnest desires of reconciliation; but yet it has been more than suspected that the Doctor, and a few others, extended their views to that object, and recommended such measures as had a tendency to its accomplishment.

"A man is known by his associates." The late General Lee was now in this country, and upon a footing of the strictest intimacy with the Doctor.— His active, fiery zeal led him from one colony to another, embittering and inflaming the minds of the people against the parent state; but, having less caution and command of his temper than some other crafty politicians, he would frequently divulge the secret, and openly recommend the doctrine of independence.

At length the important question was brought forward in Congress, while the Doctor was a representative for the province of Pennsylvania: It was debated several days, and met with considerable opposition. Some very able speakers appeared against; amongst whom were Mr. Dickinson, author of the Farmer's Letters; Mr. Wilson, an eminent lawyer; and Mr. Galloway; neither were all the delegates instructed as to their votes on this point; which some writers have erroneously asserted. But our Doctor stood as firm as a rock to his favourite independence; neither oratory nor argument could influence him to give up his concerted plan; and those who were opposed to it, observing the unalterable determination of their antagonists, finally agreed to the resolution.

This object being gained, ambition pointed out a new prospect to the Doctor. Well aware that the American resources principally consisted in old rags and lamp black [oil-based ink], metamorphosed into continental currency; and though the paper scheme was successful to admiration, yet as the people could not at present hear any thing of taxes, and great sums of money would be wanted to carry on their extensive military operations, there was a possibility that such a frequent emission of paper currency would induce a depreciation, and endanger the public safety.—The Doctor therefore turned his eyes once more towards Europe, as the country from whence alone the needful supplies could be procured. He accordingly obtained from Congress a Commission, as agent for the court of France, judging it a proper theatre for the display of his talents, and where in his highly-extolled philosophic reputation would probably be admired, and conciliate the affections of the nation towards him; and so it happened; for all ranks of people on his arrival, vied with each other in paying respect to this hoary-headed crafty sage. He took passage on board a ship of 16 guns, commanded by Captain Weeks, who was so fortunate as to take two prizes near Bourdeaux, which the Doctor sold for him a few days after, but not publicly, as the Americans had not yet obtained that liberty; and they arrived at Nantz the 17th December, 1776.

Shortly after his appearance at the court of France, where he was received with every mark of distinction and esteem, he with Mr. Deane his colleague, wrote several letters to Lord Stormont, the English ambassador, relative to the exchange of prisoners, but received no answer.

However, the American agents did not desist from writing and remonstrating against the treatment their people received in the prisons of England and elsewhere, but even proceeded to threaten *severe retaliation*, and observed to his lordship, "that for the sake of humanity, it was to be wished that men would endeavour to alleviate as much as possible the unavoidable miseries attending a state of war. It has been said that among the civilized nations of Europe, the ancient horrors of that state are much diminished; but the compelling men by chains, stripes and famine to fight against a new mode of barbarity, which the English nation alone had the honour of inventing."

But these and other asperities of language could not produce any other answer from the king's ambassador, than that "he received *no letters from rebels, except when they came to ask mercy.*"

Perhaps no man cherished a greater enmity to the mother country, or was more fruitful in resources to injure its Commerce and navigation, than Dr. Franklin. In conjunction with his colleague, several American privateers were privately fitted out from the ports of France; and there is little doubt but it was his advice that brought out such a number of New England privateers, cruising every where to intercept our trade. The loss of our merchants was considerable; and though we were not at war with France, yet they afforded the Americans every assistance and protection in their power. This produced a memorial to the ministers of France; couched in the following terms:

"Independent of what sovereign states owe to themselves, according to the sacred law of Nature and nations, in cases where any of their provinces may rebel; and not to mention that should the efforts of the English American colonies prove successful, the provinces appertaining to other states, might be induced to make a similar attempt; the subscribing party is instructed to represent to the enlightened ministers of France, that our colonies have nearly formed themselves into an independent and formidable empire. Should they not be timely prevented, it will by no means be difficult (considering their powerful resources of every kind) for them to attempt the conquest of other provinces in America, richer and better situated.—France and Spain have therefore every thing to apprehend for the safety of their colonies, should those of Great-Britain succeed in their designs.

"The subscribing party hopes that these reflections may induce his Most Christian Majesty not only to continue his pacific intentions at this particular juncture, but also that he may so far extend his neutrality and friendship, as to prohibit the merchants in his dominions from affording those of America (with whom they now trade openly) such vast succours as have hitherto been furnished. Above all, it is hoped that Messrs. Deane & Franklin may be restrained in those measures, which have been gradually unfolded, so as to become less equivocal. The papers annexed to this memorial will so amply display the nature and progress of Mr. Deane's negociations, that after perusal, it might reasonably be expected that he should be delivered up.

Stormont"

After the delivery of this memorial, the French minister, Comte de Vergennes, affected to appear a little shy towards Messrs. Franklin & Deane; and it was but seldom known when they were honoured with an audience: But this indifference did not continue; an event took place which stript off all disguise. The news of the surrender of the British army under General Burgoyne to General Gates, at Saratoga, October 17, 1777, arrived in France, at a time when the council of that nation was in a state of equilibrium respecting American affairs, undetermined which way to act; but the fact of this success soon turned the scale, and fixed them in their attachment to the rising states; whose splendor and reputation were now so much admired, that a gentleman just returned from making the tour of France, observed, that "from Dunkirk to Brest, from thence through Bourdeaux to Bayonne, then through Thoulouse to Marseilles, and lastly, through Lyons and Dijon to Paris," he met neither men nor women, in high or low stations, but were friends to the Americans."

The news of the defeat and captivity of General Burgoyne, was received in France with as much joy as if a victory of their own troops had been announced. Franklin, with his usual address and industry, improved the golden opportunity, and representing the resources, commerce, and population of his country, in the most advantageous point of view, so attracted the attention of the court of France to the object of his mission, that on the 16th of December, Mons. Girard, secretary of the king's council of state, waited upon the American plenipotentiaries, and informed them *by order of the king*, "that after long and full consideration of their affairs and propositions in council, it was decided, and his Majesty was determined, *to acknowledge their independence*, and make treaties with them of alliance and commerce; and that he would not only acknowledge but support their independence, by every means in his power:—That in doing this, he might possibly be soon engaged in a war, with all the expences, risque, and damage, usually attending it; yet he should not expect any compensation from them on that account, nor pretend that he acted wholly for their sakes, since besides his real good will to them and their cause, it was manifestly the interest of France, that the power of England should be diminished by their separation from it."

The treaties were concluded and signed at Paris, the 3oth of January, 1778.

Day, in the conclusion below, holds Franklin in higher esteem than most latter American historians in terms of his intellect and ability, and hence, this lends some weight to his depiction of Franklin, "our crafty doctor" as duplicitous and scheming.

An event of such magnitude and importance, and pregnant with such consequences, as enabled the revolting colonies effectually to oppose the parent state.

Thus it appeared that the same man, who had published his rules for reducing a great empire to a small one, was capable of making their application; and hence it has been remarked, that his negotiations with the court of France required uncommon abilities, and his success in the arduous work proves that during a long life, he had practically studied the philosophy of man.

France having taken a decided part in favour of America, nothing could be expected but an immediate war with England.—The declaration delivered at London by their ambassador, and the great naval preparations in every part of the kingdom, plainly indicated their design. The Sieur Girard was appointed ambassador to the New States; but before his departure, our crafty Doctor had planned a most excellent scheme for the surprize and capture of the British fleet and army, whether on the Delaware, or its borders.—The Count D'Estaing with a superior fleet was employed for this purpose, and would most certainly have effected it, if fortunately the winds and weather had not prevented.

The French admiral, meeting with bad weather, arrived too late; as the English army had evacuated Philadephia [sic], and their fleet got safe to Sandy Hook, so that he found himself fully employed the remaining part of the season, to manoeuvre and contend with one of the most able officers in the British navy.

Reflecting on the strange vicissitudes of human life, we are led (very naturally) to contemplate a striking contrast. A few years ago we saw the Britons and Americans engaged as brethren, in one common cause, and arduously endeavouring to limit and destroy the French power, in every part of the globe. We now see a transition unexpected, surprising, and unnatural! Those very people who are "flesh of our flesh and bone of our bone," uniting with our rivals and avowed enemies, and attempting to deftroy that indulgent parent from whom they had received their existence and prosperity: And all this principally brought about by the craft and agency of a self-taught philosopher and politician, who in his early years, wheeled a barrow loaded with printed papers, in the streets of Philadelphia, and got his livelihood by working at the press.

Thus do the base things of this world and things that are despised, confound the things which are mighty; probably to teach us that however extensive our empire, however great our exaltation, little causes may frustate the best concerted schemes, and that pride was never made for man!

The attachment of the French nation to America was carried, at this time, to such a degree of enthusiasm, as is difficult to be conceived: There were few persons who bore an interested part in the contest, but employed their most famous artists and first writers. But among so many characters Dr. Franklin was distinguished in a particular manner; and of the several homages that were incessantly offered to his merit, none could be more flattering than the provinces of France contending with each other, for having given birth to some of his ancestors, and endeavouring to prove by the similarity of names, that he derived his descent from among them. The following extract from the Gazette of Amiens, the capital of Picardy in France, is a convincing proof of what is here advanced:

"The king's painter at Paris," says the editor, "has lately displayed the utmost efforts of his genius, in an elegant picture, dedicated to the genius of Franklin.—Mr: Franklin is represented in it, opposing with one hand the Aegis of Minerva to the thunderbolt, which he first knew how to fix by his conductors, and with the other commanding the God of War to fight against Avarice and Tyranny; whilst America nobly reclining upon him, and holding in her hand the fasces [bundle of rods around an axe symbolizing the civic justice of Republican Rome], a true emblem of the union of the American States, looks down with tranquillity on her defeated enemies. The painter in this picture most beautifully expressed the idea of this Latin verse which has been so frequently applied to Dr. Franklin.

"Eripuit de coelo fulmen, sceptrumque tyrannis."

"The name of Franklin is sufficiently celebrated that one may glory in bearing it, and a nation pride herself in having given birth to the ancestors of a man, who has rendered his name so famous. We think ourselves entitled to dispute with the English nation, an honour of which they have rendered themselves unworthy. Franklin appears to be rather of a French than an English original. It is certain that the name of Franklin or Franquelin is very common in Picardy, especially in the districts of Vimeu and Ponthieu. It is very probable that one of the Doctor's ancestors has been an inhabitant of this country, and has gone over to England with the fleet of Jean de Biencourt, or that which was fitted out by the nobility of this province. In genealogical matters, there are bolder conjectures than this; there was at Abbeville, in the 15th and 16th century, a family of the name of Franklin. We see in the public records of the town, one John and Thomas Franquelin, woollen drapers, in 1521; this family remained at Abbe Ville till the year 1600: they have since been dispersed through the country, and there are still some of their descendants so far as Auz la Chateau. These observations are a new homage which we offer to the genius of Franklin."

It was in this year that his most Christian Majesty constituted, by letters-patent, the royal medical society of France. It consists of thirty members, all doctors of physic, and residents in Paris, of whom twenty are to be of the medical faculty of the University of that city; of sixty other members, residents in any other part of France; and of sixty other members, subjects of any other state. Besides these, the society may honour with the title of Correspondents any number of gentlemen in

France, or elsewhere.—The King was pleased to distinguish Dr. Franklin by placing his name at the head of the list of its foreign members.

Such was the manner in which the Doctor was honoured and celebrated in France; his influence also extended to the court of Spain, and diffused a favourable opinion of the American war in several other countries. Nothing was now wanting, on his part, to raise the spirits of the Americans; and his letters to his numerous correspondents were particularly written for this express purpose.

"All Europe is for you," says he in one of his epistles. "The separate constitutions of the several states are also translating and publishing here, which afford abundance of speculation to the politicians of Europe; and it is a very general opinion, that if you succeed in establishing your liberties, you will, as soon as peace is restored, receive an immense addition of numbers and wealth from Europe, by the families who will go over to participate of your privileges, and carry their estates with them. Tyranny is so generally established in the rest of the world that the prospcct of an asylum in America, for those who love liberty, gives general joy, and your cause is esteemed the cause of mankind."

Great was the Doctor's success in procuring assistance of every kind from these new allies; and in money affairs, the Congress looked up to him in every emergency. His friend Mr. Silas Deane, in a letter from Paris to Colonel William Duer of New York, represents his important services at the court of France; in the following language:

"Congress drew bills on Mr. President Laurens, as being in Holland, many months before he sailed from America; they drew on Mr. Jay long before his arrival in Spain; these bills have been honoured, and you in America have been taught to believe that it was from money received in Spain and Holland—no such thing. Those bills have been uniformly sent to Dr. Franklin for payment; even the salaries of Mr. Jay and Mr. Adams and their suits, have been drawn for on Dr. Franklin, who has paid them out of the monies received here. The agents of private states have been furnished with money for their exigencies, out of the sums granted for the support of our army; our ambassadors and agents have for some time past, cost us at least twenty thousand pounds sterling per annum. The relief of prisoners and other contingencies, more than as much more; all this has been taken from the money afforded us by France for our army.— Congress, though repeatedly advised by Dr. Franklin not to draw on him, have continued to draw without bounds, and generally without advice."

Day has penned a case for Franklin as architect of the United States of America.

From this view of affairs, it is evident that the address and abilities of this crafty politician, were of the highest consequence to the credit of congress; and that probably without him, they never could have supported the war at home, or sent any agents and commissioners abroad; but must have failed through want of the necessary resources: for how much soever America may plume herself with the ideas of Victory and Independence, yet we are sure, that without France, all her armed efforts would have proved ineffectual. It was thus, for near nine years that Dr. Franklin was engaged in the most important scenes, as minister plenipotentiary from the United States to the court of France; and having rendered his country permanent and essential services, he returned to America in the month of September, 1785, in the ship London packet, Captain Truxton.

On his arrival at Philadelphia, he was received at the wharf by a vast number of citizens who attended him to his house with acclammations of joy; whilst the discharge of cannon and the ringing of bells announced the event to the country around. The Philadelphians appeared to vie with each other in exhibiting testimonies of their esteem. The House of Assembly, the faculty of the university, and other societies, presented him with their affectionate addresses; and in October following, he was elected governor of the state of

Pennsylvania; in which office he continued to October, 1788.

Nothing could exceed the hopes formed by the people of America, from the recognition and establishment of their independence; and Dr. Franklin, during the whole contest, had by his letters and flattering representations, impressed them with the most extravagant notions of future dignity and prosperity. Fond of the whims and theories of their own brains, they expected their new democratic constitutions would become the admiration of the world: their commerce was to be as free as air, navies were to arise which would cover the ocean, and their manufacturers, aided by the numerous emigrants from Europe, were instantaneously to produce the finest fabrics. In short, all nations were to court their smiles and dread their frowns, and Great-Britain was to repeal her obnoxious navigation-act, and to sue for their alliance.

At the return of peace, these were the fond expectations of the Americans; but the Doctor on his accession to the chair of the first magistrate, found himself greatly disappointed. The state over which he presided was rent asunder with faction, and the other states of the union had lost all the credit, dignity and efficiency of government; their trade was circumscribed, and their merchants bankrupt. Amid these distresses, the resolutions and ordinances of their Congress were neglected and despised; and many began to doubt, whether there was any existing government. At length it was found requisite to call a general convention of the states, as an effort for regaining their credit, and forming a more energetic constitution. They met at Philadelphia in 1788; and Dr. Franklin appeared amongst them as one of the representatives for the state of Pennsylvania. At the conclusion of their deliberations, the Doctor is said to have delivered the following speech, in which he expresses no great approbation of the new federal system, or any sanguine expectation from its adoption; but seems to recommend it as a matter of necessity:

"Mr. PRESIDENT,

I confess that I do not entirely approve of this Constitution at present; but, Sir, I am not sure I shall never approve it: For having lived long, I have experienced many instances of being obliged by better information, or fuller consideration, to change opinions, even on important subjects; which I once thought right, but found to be otherwise. It is therefore the older I grow; the more apt I am to doubt my own judgment, and to pay more respect to the judgment of others. Most men indeed, as well as most sects in religion, think themselves in posssession of all truth, and that wherever others differ from them, it is so far an error. Steele, a Protestant, in a dedication tells the Pope, that the only difference between our two churches, in their opinions of the certainty of their doctrines, is, the

Romish church is infallible, and the church of England never in the wrong.

"But though many private persons think almost as highly of their own infallibility as that of their sect, few express it so naturally as a certain French lady, who in a little dispute with her sister said, I don't know how it happens, sister, but I meet with no body but myself that is always in the right.

'Il n'y a que mot qui a toujours raison.'

Below Franklin is quoted as predicting the American descent into a police state.

"In these sentiments, Sir, I agree to this constitution, with all its faults, if they are such; because I think a general government necessary for us, and there is no form of government, but what may be a blessing, if well administered: and I believe farther, that this is likely to be well administered for a course of years, and can only end in despotism, as other forms have done before it, when the people shall become so corrupted as to need despotic government, being incapable of any other. I doubt too, whether any other convention we can obtain, may be able to make a better constitution; for when you assemble a number of men, to have the advantage of their joint wisdom, you inevitably assemble, with those men, all their prejudices, their passions, their errors of opinion, their local interest, and their selsish views. From such an assembly, can a perfect production be expected? It therefore astonishes me, Sir, to find this system approaching so near to perfection as it does; and I think it will astonish our enemies, who are waiting with confidence to hear that our Councils are confounded, like those of the builders of Babel; and that our states are on the point of separation, only to meet hereafter for the purpose of cutting each other's throats.

"Thus I consent, Sir, to this constitution, because I expect no better; and because I am not sure that this is not the best. The opinions I have had of its errors, I sacrisice to the public good: I have never whispered a syllable of them abroad— within these walls they were born, and here they shall die. If every one of us in returning to our constituents, were to report the objections he has had to it, and endeavour to gain partizans in support of them, we might prevent its being generally received, and thereby lose all the salutary effects and great advantages resulting naturally in our favour among foreign nations, as well as among ourselves, for our real or apparent unanimity. Much of the strength and efficacy of any government in procuring, and in securing happiness to the people, depend on opinion; on the general opinion of the goodness of that government, as well as of the wisdom and integrity of its governors.

"I hope, therefore, that for our sakes, as a part of the people, and for the sake of our posterity, we shall act heartily and unanimously in recommending this constitution where-ever our influence may extend, and turn our future thoughts and endeavours to the means of having it well administered.

"On the whole, Sir, I cannot help expressing a wish, that every member of the convention who may still have objections to it, would with me, on this occasion, doubt a little of his infallibility, and to make manifest our unanimity, put his name to this instrument."

Then the motion was made for adding the last formula, viz.

"Done in convention, by the unanimous consent, &c." which was agreed to, and added accordingly.

This was the last speech the doctor ever delivered in a public capacity; but while his faculties continued in vigour, the press teemed with his admonitory political productions. Men seldom or never relinquish those studies and pursuits to which they have been early accustomed; hence we see the Rev. Mr. John Wesley, at the age of eighty-seven, preaching at Bath, and taking his annual circuit through the kingdom; and Dr. Franklin, when nearly at the same age, was busily employed in his favourite schemes, and entertained weekly *at his*

James LaFond

own house, a Society for Political and Philosophical Inquiries; so just is the observation of the poet:

Quo semel est imbuta recens, servabit odorem Testa diu.

The doctor was never distinguished as an orator; in public bodies, or private societies, he seldom troubled his audience with long speeches: He seemed always to have been careful to hide his own sentiments, but read the faces, and watched with a sedulous attention to discover those of others.

As a writer, his publications are numerous, consisting chiefly of short pieces on philosdphical, political, and economical subjects, and most of them calculated to serve some present purpose. Such is his late piece entitled "Information to those who would wish to remove to America."—The design of which is, to encourage the farmers and mechanics of Europe to emigrate to that country.

But to obviate the pernicious tendency of this performance, it becomes necessary to provide an antidote against the Doctor's emigrating instructions.—I shall therefore, as an impartial obferver, bestow a few strictures thereon, and produce the unquestionable authority of several respectable writers, by which it will appear, that the citizens of America in general are not happier than the subjects living under the benign influence and protection of the British Constitution.

The Doctor informs us, that "it cannot be worth any man's while, *who* has the means of living at home, to expatriate himself in hopes of obtaining a profitable civil office in America; and as to military offices, they are now at an end with the war, the armies being disbanded."—We perfectly coincide with this sentiment, as any man must be tinctured with some degree of insanity, to leave a certainty for uncertainty: few civil offices in America are worth the attention of a man of enterprize and genius; and, as to their military offices, long before the peace took place, they went a-begging, and could not recommend any person to the least degree of credit and reputation. In a subsequent sentence, the doctor speaks very contemptuoufly of *"birth, persons of quality, and gentlemen."*—It is true indeed, that such characters are not the most eligible for the purposes of emigration; but yet in every country, they have been and will be respected—and whether the Doctor ever made the observation or not, it is certain, that the Americans are as fond of affecting the characters of gentlemen, and persons of rank, as any people under heaven. Many of them emerging from very humble obscurity, and persons of the lowest occupations, have figured away in the cabinet and in the field; and it has been a most severe trial, perhaps worse than death, that after having tasted the sweets of distinction and military rank, the distresses and disappointments consequent to the establishment of peace, have obliged them to fall back into their former ranks, and to hide their diminished heads.

The Doctor further acquaints us, that *"with regard to the encouragements for strangers from (the American) Government, they are only what are derived from good laws and liberty."* Can any subject of the British government imagine that these young states are capable of making better laws than are existing in their own country? It may be confidently asserted that a greater security for life, liberty and property is no where generally enjoyed than in Great Britain. A British act of parliament relative to any species of property may be trusted; but will the Americans place any reliance on an act of any of their states, respecting the various emissions of their paper currency —Experience proves the contrary. —Their legislatures have all defrauded; "there is none that has done good, no not one." Ever since the peace, they have established iniquity for law, and deviated from the principles of rectitude and justice, in making such laws as violated private contracts, defrauded creditors, and cheated thousands, even their own poor soldiers, who suffered in the war, cold, nakedness, and hunger.

Soldiers and sailors [often abducted into arms] in Great Britain and America, before and after the war, were generally disarmed and defrauded of pay and released penniless, homeless and jobless into a society in which these conditions were felonies, punishable by enslavement.

It is a universal complaint that scarce a debt, contracted by the people of these states, is *punctually* discharged; but every artifice is employed to procrastinate and finally evade payment. How unhappy is the consideration that the laws and justice of a country should see fraud and knavery reduced to a science, at which they seem to wink a most hearty approbation? and it may bejustly admitted, that no people have ever afforded such astonishing proofs of a proficiency in this respect, in the short space of the last six years. This, although it should not have any evil influence on their future prospects, is pregnant with a train of mischievous effects and consequences, which are severely felt at present, and of necessity must ever attend it. It involves mechanics in ruin, merchants in difficulties, and brings perplexity and discouragement upon the honest farmer. By a perseverance in such conduct, they have rendered themselves contemptible and unworthy to be credited at home or abroad. Knaves are the pest of society, and the bane of good neighbourhood; but there being so large a portion of this class of people throughout the United States, there is a constant necessity of suspicious vigilance among all; and the ill and apparently lucrative example, makes a deplorable impression on the rising generation. By these destructive miscreants, the honest and deserving become the prey of attornies, who are in this respect a people *sui generis*, who always find their account in the dishonesty of the world. Should this fatal attachment to degenerate principles continue in America, it will of course tend to corrupt even the new federal legislature, and cause them to be equally fradulent with the states legislatures, whose neglect of distributive justice has justly merited universal abhorrence.

Day accurately predicted that the U.S.A. would become a plutocratic society in which common people were the prey of scheming attorneys.

The Doctor proceeds to describe what kind of persons they are, to whom an emigration to America may be advantageous, and what the advantages they may reason-ably expect. *"Hearty young labouring men, who understand the husbandry of corn and cattle, which is nearly the same in that country as in Europe, may easily establish themselves here. A little money saved of the good money they receive, while they work for others, enables them to buy land and begin their plantation, in which they are assisted by the goodwill of their neighbours and some credit."*

The picture drawn here of the facility with which hearty young men may establish themselves in farms and plantations, is more flattering than true. Let it be considered that the lands in America, for a considerable distance from the sea-coast, have been all taken up and occupied for many years. It is easy to perceive that any farms and plantations, in the settled parts of the country cannot be procured, but by purchase, some of them at 10 guineas per acre; and if an emigrant goes back four or five hundred miles from any market, what difficulties will he not experience, whilst felling the trees of the desert, and clearing his land for tillage?

What neighbours will he there find? I will inform him—some wretched bankrupt people, who have fled from the settled parts of the country, to be out of the reach of their creditors; others that are fugitives from the hands of justice; and others, whose lands on the sea-coast being worn out, have retreated to live in idleness by fishing and hunting, and a little tillage, much in the style and manner of Indians.—These people in general are destitute of money, and many of the comforts and conveniencies of life; cloathed in rags, they live in huts or log houses, in filth and wretchedness. It is easy to talk about money *to be* saved, the goodwill of neighbours and some credit, for the obtaining of a settlement; but in a country where money is scarcer than in any other in the world, it is no easy matter to get it; and credit is now out of the question; that benevolence and good-will which once subsisted, is quite done away—mutual confidence destroyed; and the distinctions of whig and tory, federalist and antefederalist, have taken place. The late war, and the difficulties of the present times, have embittered the minds of neighbours towards each other, and a man's foes will too often be those of his own house hold. In settlements *where* once hospitality and kindness reigned, there you will now find distrust and enmity. As to *good* money, it is almost unknown in America: —guineas, halfjoes, and other species of gold coin, are all under weight, cut, sweated, and circumcised, that it requires great circumspection, when you receive a sum of money, to prevent being cheated.

But perhaps the Doctor calls the numerous kinds of American paper-currency—*good money*. It is much to be lamented that such multitudes of people ever took it as such: greater deceptions were never practised on any nation; and thousands of helpless families will have reason, for years to come, to deplore the injury, ruin and injustice they have suffered. The text of the Doctor's instructions, in this place, might read thus:

Below Day quotes the truth that Franklin concealed, and this comical "quote" has been taken as Franklin's own.

"Hearty young husbandmen, who can endure the extremes of heat and cold, and can be daring enough to banish themselves far from civilized towns and populous cities, into desert woods and mountains, among a race of runnagates and crackers, equally wild and savage as the Indians, may emigrate to America—Poor artizans, of the necessary and useful kind, to supply those cultivators of the earth with utensils of the grosser sorts, which cannot be readily brought from Europe, may emigrate to this land of promise, where they must be very industrious, and shift hard for a living."

Below Day describes America as nothing but an economic zone for the exploitation of cheap labor, a common notion of the time that generations of American statesmen and academics attempted to cloak in a more palatable mythology of a promethean national character.

—Surely they will revere the memory of the good Doctor for such kind information; but I am persuaded that many of them, having no inclination to become *white negroes*, will exert their industry for a livelihood among their own friends, and in their native country, from a conviction that, if they leave it, *"they ne'er will see the like again."*

But we are assured, that *"all persons of moderate fortunes and capitals, who having a number of children to provide for, and are desirous of bringing them up to industry, and to secure estates for their posterity, have opportunities in America, which Europe doth not afford."*

This proposition is worthy some attention, lest families of a moderate fortune should be ruined by making the experiment here recommended.—In the first place, it is extremely troublesome and expensive for people with families to cross the Atlantic; they will be necessarily subject to many inconveniencies and dangers, with which such as have travelled are well acquainted. Their voyage to America, and the journey of several hundred miles back to the wilderness of the frontier settlements, for people of a moderate fortune cannot afford to buy land anywhere else, will almost, if not altogether, expend their *"moderate"* stock of cash. When they come there, they must build a hut or hog-house to live in, and begin to clear the land. Provisions of all kinds must be purchased at a dear rate, whilst they are employed about this; but suppose any of their family should fall sick, which is very common to people in a new climate, to what distress will they not be reduced in these frontier settlements? and it is an hundred to one, they will not be able to get a physician to assist them. Children in these back countries, so far from being brought up to industry, generally spend their time in hunting and shooting, and have little or no means of education. They are frequently to be seen running about, almost naked, in the woods of Virginia and North Carolina.

But it is surprizing the doctor should recommend America for the mechanic arts, when it is well known, that European workmen are always preferred, both for their industry and skill in business. In truth, there can be no comparison between the industry of the inhabitants of the United States and that of the people of Great Britain. What industry there is in America, is mostly to be found in the New England governments; travelling from thence to the southward, you will discover a great declension of this useful virtue, arising from the climate and manner of living. There is no country on the globe where the laborious part of the white people drink more spirituous liquors than in America. Instead of wholesome beer and cyder for their common drink, they make use of grog, a mixture of rum and water; the former in general is very indifferent; for it is either New England rum, which is called stinkabus, or new ruin of the West-India islands. A mechanic or labouring-man accustomed to this liquid fire, finds that one tumbler creates a necessity for another, so that a habit of drinking this pernicious mixture is easily and imperceptibly acquired. As this habit strengthens in a man, his industry declines, and he becomes at last enervated, and entirely devoted to rum. I have seen thousands of miserable and emaciated spectacles of this kind; and thousands are yearly destroyed by it.

The habit of rum consumption over more traditional beverages arose in English North America due to the lack of apple and grain crops throughout the 1600s, the poor shelf life of beer and cider in barrels shipped from England, and the ease of transporting rum up from the

James LaFond

West Indies as well as its stability in transport. Rum was regarded as the ruin of many a man, English, Indian and American.

Hence the American mechanics, in general, are very indolent; and, during the war, I have frequently heard the masters of mechanic trades wish they could get journeymen from Europe—for this reason, because, when first they come out, they are more industrious, and not addicted to rum: but I am sorry to add, I have sometimes heard these same masters lament, that those European journeymen were soon corrupted, and fell into this beastly vice, thereby destroying their usefulness and their lives.

I shall now corroborate the truth of the observations I have made, by quoting some American testimonies. "The Remarks of a Citizen of Philadelphia, on the Progress of Population, Agriculture, Manners and Government, in Pennsylvania, in a Letter to a Friend in England," will give us a clear idea of forming settlements in that state, which is account the first and happiest in America.—It is as follows:

"The first settler in the woods is generally a man who has outlived his credit, or fortune, in the cultivated parts of the state. His time for migrating is in the month of April: his first object is to build a small cabbin of rough logs for himself and family. The floor of this cabbin is of earth, the roof is of split logs: —the light is received through the door; and, in some instances, through a small window made of greased paper. A coarser building adjoining this cabbin affords shelter to a cow, and pair of good horses. The labour of erecting these buildings is succeeded by killing the trees on a few acres of ground near the cabbin; this is done by cutting a circle round the trees, two or three feet from the ground. The ground around these trees is then plowed, and Indian corn planted in it—the season for planting this grain is about the 20th of May; it grows generally on new ground with but little cultivation, and yields in the month of October following, from 40 to 50 bushels per acre. After the 1st of September, it affords a good deal of nourishment to his family, in its green or unripe state, in the form of what is called roasting ears: his family is fed during the summer by a small quantity of grain which he carries with him, and by fish and game. His cows and horses feed upon wild grass, or the succulent twigs of the woods. For the first year, he endures a. great deal of distress from hunger, cold, and a variety of accidental causes; but he seldom complains, or sinks under them.

—As he lives in the neighbourhood of Indians, he soon acquires a strong tincture of their manners. His exertions, while they continue, are violent; but they are succeeded by long intervals of rest: his pleasures consist chiefly in fishing and hunting: he loves spirituous liquors; and he eats, drinks and sleeps in dirt and rags in his little cabbin. In his intercourse with the world, he manifests all the art which characterizes the Indians of our country. In this situation he passes two or three years. In proportion as population increases around him, he becomes uneasy and dissatisfied. Formerly his cattle ranged at large; but now his neighbours call upon him to confine them within fences, to prevent their trespassing upon their fields of grain. Formerly he fed his family with wild animals; but these, which fly from the face of man, now cease to afford him an easy subsistence; and he is compelled to raise domestic animals for the support of his family. Above all, he revolts against the operation of laws; he cannot bear to surrender up a single natural right, for all the benefits of government; and therefore he abandons his little settlement, and seeks a retreat in the woods, where he again submits to all the toils which have been mentioned.—There are instances of many men who have broken ground on bare creation, not less than four times this way, in different and more advanced parts of the state. It has been remarked, that the flight of this class of people is always increased by the preaching of the gospel. This will not surprize us, when we consider how opposite its precepts are to their licentious manner of living. If our first settler was the owner of the spot of land which he began to cultivate, he sells it at a considerable profit to his successor; but if, as is oftener the case, he was a tenant to some rich landholder, he abandons it in debt: however, the small improvements he leaves behind him, generally make it an object of immediate demand to a second species of settler.

The man above is the quintessential American, for whom freedom means more than ease and for whom God is encountered where Man first found Him, in nature, not among polished pews abiding the platitudes of the slave masters. As will be demonstrated in Volume 12, of this series, The 13th Tribe, *the use of Christianity in English North America was primarily for the breaking of the human spirit and the making of slaves. See Cotton Mather's text* A Good Master well Served.

"This species of settler is generally a man of some property; he pays one third or fourth part, in cash, for his plantation, which consists of three or four hundred acres, and the rest in gales or installments, as it is called here; that is, a certain sum yearly, without interest, till the whole is paid.—The first object of this settler is to build an addition to his cabbin: this is done with hewed logs; his floors are made of boards, his roof is made of what is called clapboards, which are a kind of coarse shingles, split out of short oak logs: this house is divided by two floors, on each of which are two rooms; under the whole, a cellar walled with stone: the cabbin serves as a kitchen to his house. His next object is to clear a little meadow-ground, and plant an orchard of two or three hundred apple-trees:

Apple trees were important for the production of hard cider, as agriculture ruined the water supply and rum ruined the man.

his stable is likewise enlarged; and, in the course of a year or two, he builds a long barn, the roof of which is commonly thatched with rye-straw: he, moreover, encreases the quantity of his arable land; and, instead of cultivating Indian corn, he raises a quantity of wheat and rye; the latter is cultivated chiefly for the purpose of being distilled into whiskey. This species of settler by no means extracts all from the earth, which it is able and willing to give: His fields yield but a scanty increase, owing to the ground not being sufficiently plowed—the hopes of the year are often blasted by his cattle breaking through his half-made fences, and destroying his grain—his horses perform but half the labour that might be expected from them, if they were better fed; and his cattle often die in the spring from the want of provision and the delay of grass—his house as well as his farm, bear many marks of a weak tone of mind—his windows are unglazed, or, if they have any glass in them, the ruins of it are supplied with old hats or pillows. This species of settler is seldom a good member of civil or religious society: with a large portion of hereditary mechanical kind of religion, he neglects to contribute sufficiently towards building a church, or maintaining a regular administration of the ordinances of the gospel: with high ideas of liberty, he refuses to bear his proportion of the debt contracted by its establishment in our country—he delights chiefly in company, sometimes drinks spirituous liquors to excess, will spend a day or two in every week, in attending political meetings; and thus he contracts debts which, if he cannot discharge in a depreciated paper currency, compel him to sell his plantation, generally in the course of a few years, to the third and last species of settler.

What the correspondent is demonstrating in this cycle of three owners parable is that the plantation economy—the slave economy—chases out first debtors and runaways, then men with moderate means, all pushing westward away from the unfree labor economy, in which only men of means can acquire the necessary land and chattel to survive. Large amounts of labor were required to fell virgin forests and turn them into pasturage, which provided the hay which was the petroleum of the horsepower age. Few men other than Asian potentates ever had enough sons to clear 300–400 acres of old growth forest. The sons in the following example would be overseers driving gangs of slaves.

"This species of settler is commonly a man of property and good character; sometimes he is the son of a wealthy farmer, in one of the interior and ancient counties of the state—His first object is to convert every spot of ground, over which he is able to draw water, into meadow; where this cannot be done, he selects the most fertile spot on the farm, and devotes it by manure to that purpose—His next object is to build a barn, which he prefers of stone. This building is in some instances, 100 feet in front, and 40 in depth; it is made very compact, so as to shut out the cold in winter; for our farmers find that their horses and cattle, when kept warm, do not require near as much food, as when they are exposed to the cold. He uses economy likewise in the consumption of his wood: Hence he keeps himself warm in winter. His fences are every where repaired, so as to secure his grain from his own and neighbours' cattle. But further, he encreases the number of the articles of his cultivation, and instead of raising corn, wheat, and rye alone, he allots an acre or two of ground for a garden, in which he raises a large quantity of cabbage and potatoes. His newly-cleared fields afford him every year a large increase of turnips: Over the spring, which supplies him with water, he builds a milk-house; he likewise adds to the number and improves the quality of his fruit trees.—His sons work by his side all the year, and his wife and daughters forsake the dairy and the spinning wheel to share with him in the toils of harvest.—The last object of his industry is to build a dwelling-house—this business is sometimes effected in the course of his life, but is oftener bequeathed to his son, or the inheritor of his plantation—and hence we have a common saying among our best farmers, "that a son should always begin where the father left off," that is, he should begin his improvements by building a commodious dwelling-house, suited to the improvement and value of the plantation, &c.

Below, Day relates the observations of a Pennsylvania loyalist and hence that his opinions of Pennsylvania are rooted in factual experience. The path of the storied Boone clan followed the route described below, before they turned northwest across the lower Appalachians, as the Shawnee nation effectively blocked access to the Ohio Country via Western Pennsylvania as late as the 1890s, when general Sinclair's army was annihilated.

"I have only to add, says this author, upon this subject, that the emigrants from Pennsylvania always travel to the southward. The soil and climate of the western parts of Virginia, North and South Carolina, and Georgia, afford a more easy support to lazy farmers than the stubborn but more durable soil of Pennsylvania. *Here* our ground requires deep and repeated ploughing to render it fruitful; *there* scratching the ground once or twice affords tolerable crops. In Pennsylvania, the length and coldness of the winter; makes it necessary for the farmers to bestow a large share of their labour in providing for, and feeding their cattle; but in the southern states, cattle find pasture during the greatest part of the winter, in the fields or woods. For these reasons, the greatest part of the western countries of the states that have been mentioned, are settled by original inhabitants of Pennsylvania.—

Daniel Boone's family, for example, first migrated from Pennsylvania down to the Carolina back country.

During the late war, the militia of Orange County in North Carolina were enrolled, and their number amounted to 3,500, every man of whom had migrated from Pennsylvania. From this you will see, that our state (Pennsylvania) is the great out-port of the United States for Europeans; and that after performing the office of a sieve, by detaining all those people who possess the stamina of industry and virtue, it allows a passage to the rest, to those states, which are accommodated to their habits of indolence and vice."

Thus far this writer. I shall now briefly shew what Europeans may expect by emigrating to the Carolinas, that the sufferings and inconveniences arising from the climate of the country will more than over-balance any advantage they may gain. Dr. Ladd, an American poet, has given us a prospect of South Carolina, in the month of July, in the following poetical dress:

LO! wrapt in sunshine, all divinely bright,
Fair Carolina rises to the sight;
Here the hot sun, with fierce effulgent ray,
Darts from his orb *intolerable* day.
Unlike the northern beam, his fervid glow
Pays fiercer courtship to the streams below;
Hence from each stagnant pool thick vapours
rise,
Curl to the clouds, and blacken in the skies:
On such dire fogs Death rides with murky
wing,
And here thy woes, O Carolina, spring!
When vertic sun-beams wrap the mountain
heads.
And the red Dog-star's cursed venom
spreads,
Then smoke the hills; for from the marshes
round.
The curling fog invades the higher ground.
Unbless'd is he who in this luckless hour,
By dread experience proves its deathful
pow'r.

But what rash man, celestial Muses, say,
Bends o'er yon mill-clad marsh his dang'rous
way?

O stay, fond youth, no living wight can bear
The deadly influence of impoison'd air;
Stay while thy frame the rigid fibres brace,
And vermeil Health sports lovely in thy face;
Stay ere Phobera[2] thro' thy circling Veins,
Spread the dire prelude to more fatal pains:
For know, dear youth, o'er yon drear
marshes glide
The mists envenom'd miasmata[3] ride;
If in thy veins they taint the gen'rous blood,
Fair Health, adieu! and ev'ry earthly good.

Hence comes dire Tertian, Carolina's bane.
And all the haggard family of Pain:
The van pale Horror leads, and Anguish
blind;
Infernal Megrim follows close beyond.
Taste not the air, for death is in the breeze,
And the whole hydra of abhorr'd disease."

From certain knowledge I can testify to the truth of the Doctor's description, and that he has not given it too high a colouring. It is really a dreadful climate!

---

[2] The Harbingers of Disease.
[3] The Seeds of Diseases.

Below are described Irish slaves, along with some free folk of means, being imported by British interests into a two-year-old United States.

I was at Charlestown on the 1st of August, 1785; the weather at that time was remarkably hot; for Farenheit's thermometer stood at 105 degrees. At this fatal season of the year, the ship GEORGE, Captain W. Miskelly, in ten weeks from Belfast, arrived with 227 passengers on board. As these people had never breathed in so warm an atmosphere before, a considerable number of them fell sick; and, over the course of one week fifty of those unfortunate emigrants were consigned to the silent mansions of the dead.

"Immigrant" was a word used at the time used to describe voluntary and involuntary newcomers to America. See the clause on the $10 duty charged in the Constitution on "imported" "persons" or "immigrants" used interchangeably, discussed in The Greatest Lie Every Sold.]

A young gentleman, who came passenger in the ship, was so alarmed at the event, that, without delay, he took his departure from Charlestown, on board a vessel bound to Philadelphia, and from thence returned to his native country; without the least desire of seeing, or knowing anything more of the American continent.

It is certainly too little known, what a grave the southern provinces were formerly to Europeans. Multitudes emigrated annually, and the greater part soon died and were forgotten, while their mother country did not perceive its loss.

Immigrants from Scotland, at this time, would be free Scots and some of those from Ireland would have been the Scotch-Irish, who had been used to displace indigenous Irish.

Within these last thirty years, there have been more emigrants from Ireland and Scotland than from England. A few years before the late revolution, I remember the emigration, nearly at one time, of a dozen English families to the Carolinas; they were all in the prime of life, very likely people, and sanguine in their expectations of making a great landed interest—but, alas! in about five years most of them were dead, and in less than ten, they were *all* EXTINCT! It would fill a volume to relate the many dismal scenes of sickness and mortality, of which it may be truly said,

"The dead man's knell

Is there scarce ask'd, for whom: and good men's lives,

Expire before the flowers in their caps

Dying or e'er they sicken."

But let us finish this digression, and return to the Doctor's pamphlet.

"Bad examples to youth," says he, *"are more rare in Americans."* This we can by no means allow: there is less industry; and from that circumstance alone, I should be apt to infer, that youth must see more vice. In the greatest part of America which I have travelled through, I have always observed the children of the poor neglected in the article of common education; and that even some parents, in good circumstances, had no opportunity of educating their children, for want of schoolmasters of ability: This cannot be denied; and it may also be added, that if the poor put their children to learn trades, it was seldom they learnt them to any degree of perfection. The master tradesmen in America always give the preference to what they call the old country workmen; and if any of these set up for them selves, they will always advertise, and inform the public, that they came from Europe, it being a recommendation to them; so that I must be bold to aver, that America is not the country for the children of the poor, either for good examples, to learn trades, or to acquire habits of industry.

America had been, since 1585, a place that unwanted poor were "planted," not unlike unwanted waste being used to fertilize fields away from the farm house. Slave teachers, when purchased, often escaped and forged freedom documents, as described in So His Master May Have Him Again.

However, the Doctor would persuade us, that it is the land *"for piety and religion;"* but having had some opportunity of making an investigation on this head, what I shall deliver thereon, will be with the highest regard to truth. I will allow that the New-England governments *appear* to have made *some provision* for religion, in every part of their country—that many of them are strict observers of the sabbath, and regular in their attendance on the ordinances of the gospel; but of late years, there is a very visible decline among them from the simplicity and severity of their fore-fathers.

—The other governments or states, averse to any ecclesiastical establishment, can neither boast of the power or form of godliness; some of them have scarce any religion at all. Destitute of clergy, and places of worship, they are principally instructed by a few very inconsiderable sectaries. Any one acquainted with the present manners of the continent, must know that great numbers of what are *called* the better sort of people, hold religion in contempt—consider it as merely of a political nature, necessary for the good government of society. You can scarcely meet with a regular-bred physician or lawyer, who will not, to his intimate companions, profess himself a deist.

Deist, adhering to an uncommitted and abstract notion of God, not to a specific Christian church. One could expect little better in terms of religious affiliation among a people whose parents had been enslaved under the codes of the Old Testament and in which the examples of the Gospels so often cited as documents justifying slavery. For more on this see Cotton Mather's A Good Master Well Served.

Such is the present prevalence of infidelity, and such the rage for the perusal of deistical writers, that I am tempted to think, there will be a great decrease of regular learned divines among them, notwithstanding the late efforts for the establishment of Episcopacy: Many of those already ordained, have been lay teachers, taken from the Methodist Society. The translator of the Marquis De Chastellux's travels will confirm my ideas, relative to the increase of deism. In one of his notes, page 197, he says—"The truth is, that the prevalent religion of the principal inhabitants in America, and particularly to the southward, is *pure deism*, called by the name of philosophy in Europe; a spirit which has contributed in no small degree to *the revolution*, and produced their unfettered constitutions and toleration."

Among the proselytes to free-thinking, who have disgraced America, must be reckoned the famous Ethan Allen; a man whose turbulence of temper made a considerable noise at the beginning of the late contest. He was then an enthusiast, and summoned the garrison of Ticonderoga to surrender, "in the name of the Lord Jehovah and the Continental Congress."—

Being afterwards taken prisoner by the British, he gave the world a doleful history of his captivity: Since that, he has been chiefly employed in erecting a new government, called *"the State of Vermont,"* in opposition to the claims of New York and other states, and in writing his *"Oracles of Reason,"* with the evident design of subverting all divine revelation—A blessed father and instructor truly, for a new settlement, which must have greatly improved in all moral and political happiness, under the example and guidance of so resplendent a luminary!

In composing this impious work, he tells us, "he only used the bible and dictionary, and invariably endeavoured to make reason his guide," though it is well known that the greatest part of it was pilfered from the writings of a European deist.

Nothing can exceed the freedom with which this daring man has treated the most aweful and important subjects. Moses, the Saviour, and his Apostles, are considered as impostors, and the authenticity of the sacred scriptures denied in the most express terms. The feelings of every pious mind would be hurt at the rashness and ignorance of this pretender. I shall select one instance, among an hundred that might be produced, of his total inability for criticism in biblical knowledge. "Moses," says he, "in his last chapter of Deuteronomy, crowns his history with the particular account of his own death and burial.—So Moses, the servant of the Lord died there, in the land of Moab, according to the word of the Lord, and he buried him in a valley in the land of Moab, over against Beth Peor; but no man knew of his sepulchre unto this day; and Moses was an hundred and twenty years old when he died; his eyes were not dim, nor his natural force abated; and the children of Israel wept for Moses in the plains of Moab thirty days."

"This is the only historian," says Allen, "in the circle of my reading, who has ever given the public a particular account of his own death, and how old he was at that decisive period, where he died, who buried him, and where he was buried, and withal of the number of days his friends and acquaintances mourned and wept for him. I must confess, I do not expect to be able to advise the public of the term of my life, nor the circumstances of my death and burial, nor the days of the weeping or laughing of my survivors."

Had this self-taught opinionated man been conversant with the languages in which the scriptures were written, or with the common tutors on the books of Moses, he would not have made thus free with the sacred text.

"A little learning is a dangerous thing," and yet a little learning would have taught him that the last chapter of Deuteronomy was not written by Moses, but by Joshua his successor; for in the original Hebrew manuscripts, the divisions of the books, chapters, and verses, were not as we read them in our English bibles; the present form or division of the bible hath been the work of modern times.

Many religious and respectable societies in England, have been desirous to make some efforts for the civilization and instruction of the Indians; but here we see, in the internal part of the continent, among the green mountains, the principles of infidelity disseminated by an American, and the pious labours of good men ridiculed and despised. I shall take my leave of Allen, with a poetical description of his person and morals:

"ALLEN escap'd from British jail',

His tushes [teeth] broke by biting nails,

Descends from hyperborean skies,

To tell the world-*the Bible lies.*

See him on Green Hills, north afar,

Glow, like a self-inkindled star,

Prepar'd with mob-collecting club,

Black from the forge of Belzebub,

And grim with metaphysic scowl,

With quill just pluck'd from wing of owl,

As rage or reason, rise or sink,
To shed his blood, or shed his ink;
Ere yet he goes to Susquehannah,
To head new mobs, and feed with manna;
And teach the Pennsylvania quaker
High blasphemies against his Maker.
Behold him move, ye staunch divines!
This tall brow bustling through the pines;
Like some old Sachem from his den,
He treads once more the haunts of men.
All front, he seems like wall of brass,
And brays tremendous like an ass;
One hand is clench'd to batter noses,
While t'other scrawls 'gainst Paul and Moses."

But though Allen is the first who has the *honour* to write against divine revelation, on the American continent, yet there are others far more eminent than he has ever been, who have avowed similar sentiments. It has been more than whispered, that even Dr. Franklin himself was not averse to modern free-thinking; and that in his conversation with some intimates, the miracles of the Old Testament have frequently employed the sallies of his wit and humour.

This, however, is certain, that while he was employed in France, an American commissioner, in a letter to President Lawrens, charged him with deism; and that this letter was read or communicated to Congress.—In private life this philosopher was not exempted from the little imperfections and weaknesses of human nature: irregular in his addresses to the Cyprian goddess, the legal partner of his bed Complained of infidelities. It is well known, he had mistresses plenty; and there are several living testimonies of his licentious amours.—A gentleman of Philadelphia, who was very intimate with him, has frequently told the following anecdote: that walking some years since in an afternoon, near the doctor's house, he perceived a quarrel between two females before his door. On approaching nearer, he found that one of them was the doctor's housekeeper, and the other a comely washerwoman, who had been also honoured with his intimate acquaintance: the one was in place, the other *cashiered*; and therefore it could be no wonder they had no great esteem for each other. The contest was sharp both in words and blows; the streets re-echoed with their shrieks, and their caps flew in pieces; while the Doctor, from a window, beheld the battle, and laughed most heartily.—*Nemo mortalium omnibus horis sapit*; and philosophers have their frailties like other men.

The two women would have been unfree, one a happy slave in her master's house and the other a bonded out slave jealous of Franklin's new slave girl. In the course of this 13-volume investigation it has been found that many unfree female laborers become wives, adopted daughters and even free wage-earning employees. Women and girls were rarer than male slaves by margins ranging from 20-1 to 2-1 depending on the province and period and fared that much better, rarely attempting to escape as we shall see in the statistical study of escaped Marylanders at the end of this book.

In converse with his friends and acquaintance, the Doctor was affable and obliging, and frequently indulged himself in relating entertaining and laughable anecdotes, which were not lost for want of gathering. Possessing strong mental abilities, a collection of his common sayings would form an intellectual banquet: his letters to his correspondents were full of them; and in these instructive compositions, his pithy aphorisms appeared "like apples of gold in pictures of silver."

Several years before his death, he was afflicted with the gravel; but in the beginning of April, 1790, he was seized with a feverish indisposition, without any particular symptoms attending it, till the third and fourth day, when he complained of a pain, in his left breast; which increased, till it became extremely acute, attended with a cough and laborious breathing. In this way he continued till the 17th, when, with resignation to the divine will, he took his leave of this transient state of existence, aged 85.

The following is an epitaph written by himself, long before his death:

The B O D Y

of

BENJAMIN FRANKLIN, printer,

Like the cover of an old book,

Its contents worn out,

And stripped of its lettering and gilding,

Lies here, food for the worms;

Yet the work shall not be lost,

For it shall (as he believed) appear once more,

In a new

And most beautiful edition,

corrected and revised

By the Author.

The E N D.

Plantation Fugitives

Maryland Runaway Servants, 1728–75

The following compilation has been done of runaway servant ads, which I took a look at for the first half of the Plantation America series, providing some contextual footnotes. The overall record is stilted first by the late introduction of printing in Plantation Maryland and secondly by war. The academic purview of the archive I use refuses to take into account ongoing Caucasian slavery under the Continental Congress and later the United States, post 1775. We can only hope that during the war between the Mercantile Slave Mother and the overseers of her plantations, that many men made their way west out of bondage.

The reader will find raw numbers at the end of each period with bookending events.

Cold months are defined as October through April, making seven months with freezing nighttime temperatures in 18th century Maryland.

Thefts were usually of clothing, household goods and sometimes horses and boats, predominantly items necessary for survival.

Specific items of value may be mentioned just before the theft entry. For a more detailed treatment, see *So His Master May Have Him Again* and *So Her Master May Have Her Again.*

Als. indicates an alias.

An additional name on the line indicates the owner of the runaway property.

Through this period in Maryland, negroes sometimes lacked names and rarely had a surname, with the common usage of the day like so: Mister Smith's Negro, Negro John, etc.

Unidentified listings would be people who ran away as soon as they were purchased and were definitely not indented servants, but some other type of undocumented chattel. Another likely explanation was that such men had been caught without freedom papers and had been appropriated after refusing to give their names, or their names not being registered by the time of their escape.

The following information has been adapted from the Runaway White Boy Register (Archives) which is a Maryland State Archive compiled from three Maryland periodicals: *Dunlop's Maryland Gazette, Maryland Gazette* and *Maryland Journal and Baltimore Advertiser.* The advertisements are listed by date.

The reader will find six distinct periods, arranged before the data was compiled, in order to assess social correlations to runaway rates:

Running away is a measure of servile discontent. Likewise, posting a paid advertisement for the recovery of the runaway is a measure of master class will to control, so an increase in runaway advertisements indicates that both servant discontent and master will were increasing, though in uncertain proportions. The act of running away is the measure, not the number of persons running away, so that repeat listings of prolific runaways like William Beale and a handful of others denote an increase in the social schism between master and slave.

The category "shackled" in the summation tables tallies the number of runaways who were beaten, tortured or chained enough for it to gain a noticeable mention. The shackled listing, in the end, is a measure of servile misery and masterly will.

The non-Caucasian listings do not represent accurately the number of colored folk fleeing bondage but rather the willingness to pay for advertising to recover them. It was assumed that a black person was a slave unless he could prove otherwise. While poor whites were suspected of being escaped slaves, blacks were assumed to be so, placing less need on advertisements, as the slave catcher could simply target any black at large and be relatively certain they had a bountiful captive.

Apprentice listings represent a higher order of slave, a person who was voluntarily bound by himself or his parent to a master. The running away of apprentices—such as Benjamin Franklin in 1725–1727—is therefore a prime indication of the weakening social bonds.

Before my editor compiles the relevant statistics, I will make the following predictions, which will be addressed in the summation, to be written by her:

1. Due to increased populations of former slaves, including family relations, as time went on, it would be easier for an Irishman or an Englishman to run away and hide among his own. Much of the logic for switching chattel to wildly more expensive African imports had to do with this consideration.

2. Increased printing capacity would simply make more runaways known to the historian after 1725.

3. With the end of the Beaver Wars and the tensions building between France and England, Indian alliances began to deteriorate, reducing the number of Indian warriors available to act as slave catchers. This increased population pressure on Indian Tribes also encouraged the adoption of runaways into tribal bodies.

4. If the brutality in Virginia in the 1670s and 1850s is any indication, as the servile European population became more restless and sought out the above opportunities to free themselves, the masters, who had invested money in these people, would logically become more brutal as time went on.

Notes

1. Escaped white female slaves habitually took two to three changes of clothes with them, all such clothes belonging to the master, for slaves did not own the clothes they wore and were often barefoot. To runaway shoed and clothed was to be a thief as well.

2. Iron works, such as the Merchant's Mill in Occoquanva, Virginia, and other hellish places to be enslaved, were founded and operated by a Quaker, with Quakers and

other such "peaceful" Congregationalists being the largest owners of white slaves in 18th century English America.

3. If a hired man ran away, he was still in breach of contract and then might be recaptured and sold to pay off the remainder of his contract, service owed rendered into a sale price.

4. An apprentice was treated no differently than a transport, a convict, a redemptioner, an indenture or a negro and had no rights other than to have his beatings limited to 30 lashes.

5. People fitted with iron collars were generally so treated for being chronic runaways.

Plantation Fugitives I

Inception: December 1728 through November 1734

1. Manning, John, 24–31 Dec. 1728
2. Hancock, John als. Anderson, 7–14 Jan. 1728/9
3. Unidentified tools, theft, 22–29 Apr. 1729
4. Unidentified tools, theft, 22–29 Apr. 1729
5. Anderson, John, 29 April to 6 May 1729
6. Edge, Edward, 29 April to 6 May 1729
7. Heath, Robert, 3–10 June 1729
8. Brooks, John, 3–10 June 1729
9. Wood, John als. Charles Oglesby theft, 17–24 June 1729
10. Lamb, Thomas missing teeth, 24 June to 1 July 1729
11. Davis, Samuel, 8–15 July 1729
12. Barry, Eleanor, 8–15 July 1729
13. Jones, John (?), 15–22 July 1729
14. Hancock, John als. Anderson, theft, 19–26 May 1730
15. Smith, William, 19–26 May 1730
16. Pain, Richard, 7–16 June 1730
17. Taylor, Sarah, theft, 24 Nov. to 1 Dec. 1730
18. English, Richard, 15–22 Dec. 1730
19. Evans, John, thefts, 26 Jan. to 2 Feb. 1732/3
20. Lang, James, 21–28 Dec. 1733
21. Lee, Edward als. Mortimer, 12–19 July 1734
22. Tyzard, John, 26 July to 2 Aug. 1734

23. Howard, Thomas, theft, 26 July to 2 Aug. 1734
24. Unidentified property of John Gardner, theft, 26 July to 2 Aug. 1734
25. Berry, John, Anne Arundel County, property of Benjamin Tasker, iron collar and handcuffs, 25 Oct. to 1 Nov. 1734
26. Ward, Christopher, 25 Oct. to 1 Nov. 1734
27. Abel, Thomas, 25 Oct. to 1 Nov. 1734

Interlude

There is a lack of advertisements for the following period from 1734 through 1743. To fill the gap, I have included a portion of a chronology found at (Manual On-Line).

1727, Sept. Maryland Gazette, first newspaper in the Chesapeake, published by William Parks at Annapolis (until 1734).

1727-1731. Benedict Leonard Calvert, governor.

1729. Baltimore Town established by charter.

1730. Sotweed Redivivus, by Ebenezer Cook (c.1665-c. 1732), published (Annapolis).

1731. Baltimore Company began ironmaking on Patapsco River. [See Benjamin Tasker, 1734, iron master, above]

1731-1732. Samuel Ogle, governor.

1732. Salisbury Town laid out by commissioners.

1732. Establishment of boundary line with three lower counties of Pennsylvania, which later became Delaware.

1732-1733. Charles Calvert, governor.

1733-1742. Samuel Ogle, governor.

James LaFond

This author cannot determine why there is a gap in the runaway white slave record from 1734 to 1745.

Plantation Fugitives II

Peak Plantation: 1745 to 1749

1. Unidentified, 7 June 1745
2. Unidentified Negro, 7 June 1745
3. Barker, James, 14 June 1745
4. Eagleston, John Smith Prother, theft, 28 June 1745
5. Galloway, John, Queen Anne's, Hinson Wright, saddle bridle, theft, 5 July 1745
6. Hogan, Dominick, Patapsco Iron Works, Benjamin Tasker, theft, iron collar, 5 July 1745
7. Jolly, Matthew Patapsco Iron Works Benjamin Tasker, theft, 5 July 1745
8. Kirk, Henry, Patapsco Iron Works, Benjamin Tasker, theft, about 20-years old, 5 July 1745
9. Gee, John, 19 July 1745
10. Sullivan, Daniel, Samuel Smith, 26 July 1745
11. King, Thomas, theft, 26 July 1745
12. Maccoy, Alexander, 26 July 1745
13. Mills, Edward, 2 Aug. 1745
14. Piercy, Elizabeth, 23 Aug. 1745
15. Powell, John als. Charles Lucas,
16. William Robert, 30 Aug. 1745
17. Baley, John, 13 Sept. 1745
18. Queenborough, Samuel, 13 Sept. 1745
19. Haviaghton, William, 4 Oct. 1745
20. Dowling, James, 18 Oct. 1745

21. Barrett, Joan als. Judith, 18 Oct. 1745
22. Murry, John, 25 Oct. 1745
23. Bateman, John, 8 Nov. 1745
24. Perie, Alexander, 6 Dec. 1745
25. Nouks (Noaks), Gilbert, 11 Feb. 1746
26. Smith, Joseph, 4 Mar. 1746
27. Millar, John, 4 Mar. 1746
28. Lylis, James, 4 Mar. 1746
29. Wood, Thomas als. John Wilson, 18 Mar. 1746
30. Skidmore, Baldwin, 29 Apr. 1746
31. Unidentified Woman theft, 27 May 1746
32. Sterlock, John, thefts, 27 May 1746
33. Venabell, James, thefts, 27 May 1746
34. Smith, Charles, 17 June 1746
35. Conner, Edmund, 24 June 1746
36. Tenby, Edward, 8 July 1746
37. Wood, John, 15 July 1746
38. Jennings, John, Virginia, 5 Aug. 1746
39. Macgee, Owen, 2 Sept. 1746
40. Shortel, James, 2 Sept. 1746
41. M'Craw, Daniel, 30 Sept. 1746
42. Ross, John, 30 Sept. 1746
43. Haily, Thomas, 30 Sept. 1746
44. Burn, William, theft, 13 Jan. 1747
45. Conner, Roger, 27 Jan. 1747
46. Hyde, John, 17 Mar. 1747
47. Chapman, James, 7 Apr. 1747
48. Holten, William, 21 Apr. 1747
49. Silver, John, 28 Apr. 1747
50. Esmey, Samuel, 26 May 1747
51. Charleton, Edward, 16 June 1747
52. Ramsden, Edward, 16 June 1747
53. King, Thomas, 16 June 1747

54. Philips, James, 16 June 1747
55. Black, Michael, 16 June 1747
56. Unidentified property of James Reid, 16 June 1747
57. Unidentified property of James Reid, 16 June 1747
58. Macguire, James, 30 June 1747
59. Meuley, John, 30 June 1747
60. Flack, John als. Evans, 18 Aug. 1747
61. Charlton, Edward, 30 Sept. 1747
62. Williams, Francis, 30 Sept. 1747
63. Flack, John als. Evans, 14 Oct. 1747
64. Griffin, John, 21 Oct. 1747
65. Barnes, Margaret als. Hopping Peg, 11 Nov. 1747
66. Fletcher, Thomas, 24 Feb. 1748
67. Cooke, Richard, 2 Mar. 1748
68. Carter, Edward, 6 Apr. 1748
69. O'Neal, Henry als. Harry M, 13 Apr. 1748
70. Unidentified, theft, 13 Apr. 1748
71. Crampton, Benjamin, 20 Apr. 1748
72. McKeddie, Daniel, Virginia, theft, 15 June 1748
73. Camm, William, 6 July 1748
74. Bowing, Edmund, 20 July 1748
75. Charlton, Edward, 27 July 1748
76. Tomlin, John, 7 Sept. 1748
77. Lawrence, Richard, 7 Sept. 1748
78. Stokes, Robert, 14 Sept. 1748
79. Purfield, John, theft, 21 Sept. 1748
80. Kent, John, theft, 21 Sept. 1748
81. Key, John, 2 Nov. 1748
82. Woodley, John, 3 May 1749
83. Benem, William, 24 May 1749

84. Philips, John als. Gorman, 13 Sept. 1749

85. Dundess, James, 15 Nov. 1749

86. Eltheridge, Francis, 13 Dec. 1749

Plantation Fugitives III

Eve of the French and Indian War 1750–1753

1. Brown, Charles als. Burgess, 24 Jan. 1750
2. Sheats, John, 31 Jan. 1750
3. Burman, William, theft, 21 Feb. 1750
4. Wallace, Michael, 21 Feb. 1750
5. Davis, John, 18 Apr. 1750
6. Old, John als. Wood, 18 Apr. 1750
7. Jones, James, 9 May 1750
8. Waite, Richard, 9 May 1750
9. Unidentified, 9 May 1750
10. Maxfield, John, David Ross, 16 May 1750
11. Hennisse, John, Baltimore, John Paca Jr. saddle bridle, thefts, 6 June 1750
12. Corrier, John, Kent Island, Nicholas Clouds, 13 June 1750
13. Sedgewick, John, Anne Arundel C, Charles Griffith, iron collar, 20 June 1750
14. King, John, 4 July 1750
15. Unidentified, 11 July 1750
16. Davis, John, 18 July 1750
17. Dannison, George, 18 July 1750
18. Coise, John, 18 July 1750
19. Gardner, James, 18 July 1750
20. Herrile, Francis, 1 Aug. 1750
21. Wood, Robert, 1 Aug. 1750
22. Guinn, John, 1 Aug. 1750
23. Stocks, Henry, thefts, 29 Aug. 1750

24. Edwards, Philip, 3 Oct. 1750
25. Warnett, Michael, 14 Nov. 1750
26. Sullivan, Daniel, 14 Nov. 1750
27. Handley, William, 21 Nov. 1750
28. Duncaster, Benjamin, 5 Dec. 1750
29. Serr, John, 19 June 1751
30. Jones, Edward, 19 June 1751
31. Gulliver, Edward, 3 July 1751
32. Johnson, John, 3 July 1751
33. McCain, Roger, 3 July 1751
34. Flarerty, Darby, 3 July 1751
35. Wisendon, Robert, 10 July 1751
36. Hore, William, 10 July 1751
37. Maples, John, 31 July 1751
38. Craft, James, 7 Aug. 1751
39. Unidentified, 16 Oct. 1751
40. Sherlock, Ralph, 20 Nov. 1751
41. Cranwell, Joseph, 27 Nov. 1751
42. Negro Joe, 12 Mar. 1752
43. Day, Henry, 19 Mar. 1752
44. Ferrill, Francis, 9 Apr. 1752
45. Nailles, John, 9 Apr. 1752
46. Monk, James, theft, 30 Apr. 1752
47. Turner, Samuel, theft, 30 Apr. 1752
48. Cockland, Michael, 14 May 1752
49. M'Coy, Robert, 28 May 1752
50. Ray, Thomas, theft, 4 June 1752
51. Steer, George, theft, 4 June 1752
52. James, Samuel, Annapolis, James Steuart, 2 July 1752
53. Hollingshoo, Michael als. Holsboo, Patapsco Iron Works, Charles Carroll, theft, 9 July 1752

54. Kilburn, Reuben, Baltimore Town, James Cary, 9 July 1752

55. Wood, James, Baltimore, Charles Ridgely, 16 July 1752

56. Sherwood, Henry, Baltimore, Charles Ridgely, theft, 16 July 1752

57. Jebb, John, 23 July 1752

58. Robertson, Thomas, 23 July 1752

59. Eccland, George, Bladensburg, Christopher Lowndes, iron collar, 30 July 1752

60. Frances, John, Bladensburg, Christopher Lowndes, 30 July 1752

61. Barrett, Richard, 27 Aug. 1752

62. Selvan, William, 27 Aug. 1752

63. Cooke, John, 14 Sept. 1752

64. Kervan, Michael, 14 Sept. 1752

65. Hughes, William, 28 Sept. 1752

66. Fitzgerald, John, 26 Oct. 1752

67. Johnstone, John, 16 Nov. 1752

68. Gilpin, Thomas, 16 Nov. 1752

69. Brown, Thomas, 14 Dec. 1752

70. Taylor, Samuel, 22 Feb. 1753

71. Cunningham, James, theft, 1 Mar. 1753

72. Kelly, Thomas, theft, 1 Mar. 1753

73. Barneby, John, apprentice, 8 Mar. 1753

74. M'Donald, John, apprentice, 8 Mar. 1753

75. Starkie, Thomas, theft, 22 Mar. 1753

76. Morris, Thomas, theft, 22 Mar. 1753

77. Jones, James, theft, 5 Apr. 1753

78. Beall, William, theft, 19 Apr. 1753

79. Blackwood, Hamilton, theft, 19 Apr. 1753

80. Brown, Thomas, 26 Apr. 1753
81. Welsh, John, theft, 26 Apr. 1753
82. Beall, William, 17 May 1753
83. Godfrey, George, 17 May 1753
84. Williams, John, 17 May 1753
85. Archer, John, 24 May 1753
86. Weldon, John, 24 May 1753
87. Smith, Thomas, 24 May 1753
88. Dennison, John, theft, 7 June 1753
89. Dennison, Hannah, theft, 7 June 1753
90. Williams, Philip, 14 June 1753
91. Gibbons, Henry, 14 June 1753
92. Dennis, Rowland, theft, 5 July 1753
93. Bare, George, 5 July 1753
94. Reynolds, John, apprentice, 12 July 1753
95. Beall, William 5th time, 28 June 1753
96. Starkie, Thomas, 28 June 1753
97. Sweeting, Nathaniel, 28 June 1753
98. Hughes, Richard, theft, 19 July 1753
99. Griffin, Lewis, theft, 19 July 1753
100. Kemp, William, 19 July 1753
101. Weldon, John, 2 Aug. 1753
102. Mills, Thomas, theft, 2 Aug. 1753
103. Knight, Thomas, theft, 2 Aug. 1753
104. Young, Anne, 2 Aug. 1753
105. Davis, Joseph, theft, 2 Aug. 1753
106. German, Edward, theft, 2 Aug. 1753
107. Mahoney, Darby, 9 Aug. 1753
108. Allen, George, 9 Aug. 1753
109. Combs, Bartholomew, theft, 16 Aug. 1753
110. Illett, Francis, theft, 16 Aug. 1753
111. Corbett, Peter, theft, 16 Aug. 1753

112.Lowry, Nicholas, 16 Aug. 1753

113.Richardson, Joseph (same as Joseph Rylan) 21-years old, 16 Aug. 1753

114.Fox, John, 30 Aug. 1753

115.Macfall, James, theft, 30 Aug. 1753

116.M'Koy, Robert, theft, 6 Sept. 1753

117. Gordon, John, 20 Sept. 1753

118.Rylan, Joseph (same as Joseph Richardson) 21-years old, 20 Sept. 1753

119.Hackett, John, theft, 4 Oct. 1753

120. French, Michael, Baltimore, John Hall & Jacob Giles, theft, 18 Oct. 1753

121.Branann, James, Baltimore, John Hall & Jacob Giles, theft, 18 Oct. 1753

122. Tader, Henry, Baltimore, John Hall & Jacob Giles, 18 Oct. 1753

123. Ellis, Thomas, Kent Island, Thomas Day, iron collar, 15 Nov. 1753

Plantation Fugitives IV

The French and Indian War: 1754–1763

This was a 10-year conflict associated with the European Seven Years War

1. Alexander, Daniel, Marsh Creek, William Boyd, 22 Nov. 1753
2. Bond, Peter, theft, 31 Jan. 1754
3. Taylor, William, 7 Feb. 1754
4. Roberson, James, 7 Feb. 1754
5. Hoafman, Martin, theft, 14 Feb. 1754
6. Northwood, William, theft, 14 Mar. 1754
7. Nichols, Nathaniel, theft, 14 Mar. 1754
8. Henry, John, 14 Mar. 1754
9. Flack, John, 11 Apr. 1754
10. Richards, George, 18 Apr. 1754
11. Parker, Thomas, 25 Apr. 1754
12. Wilcox, Walter, 25 Apr. 1754
13. M'Clean, Ellin, 25 Apr. 1754
14. Finneling, Nicholas, thefts, 25 Apr. 1754
15. Murphy, James, thefts, 25 Apr. 1754
16. Hamilton, Archibald, 30 May 1754
17. Whorton, Robert, 30 May 1754
18. Shefield, Is, Anne Arundel County, 30 May 1754
19. Ross, William, theft, 4 July 1754
20. Whealor, Jonathan, 22 Aug. 1754

21. Dale, George, 29 Aug. 1754
22. Cansday, Charles, 29 Aug. 1754
23. Oulton, John, Baltimore Iron Works, Charles Carroll, steel collar, 5 Sept. 1754
24. Watkinson, Francis, 5 Sept. 1754
25. Lord, James, 3 Oct. 1754
26. McGoyn, James, 10 Oct. 1754
27. Edwards, John, theft, 12 Dec. 1754
28. Cady, John, theft, 12 Dec. 1754
29. Griffith, John, 19 Dec. 1754
30. Musprate, Thomas, 30 Jan. 1755
31. King, John, theft, 20 Feb. 1755
32. Dunken, James, theft, 20 Feb. 1755
33. Johnson, Thomas, 13 Mar. 1755
34. Francis, James, theft, 20 Mar. 1755
35. Large, James, theft, 3 Apr. 1755
36. Kenley, William, apprentice, 8 May 1755
37. Sherlard, Nathaniel, thefts, 8 May 1755
38. Smith, Patrick, 15 May 1755
39. Hammond, Thomas, apprentice, 22 May 1755
40. Freeman, William, 5 June 1755
41. Horseburg, Robert, thefts, 19 June 1755
42. Griffith, George, thefts, 19 June 1755
43. Simmonds, Thomas, thefts, 3 July 1755
44. Unidentified, thefts, 3 July 1755
45. Doiel, Philip, 17 July 1755
46. Harling, Richard, 17 July 1755
47. Lovit, George Henry, theft, 24 July 1755
48. Ryley, Dennis, 24 July 1755
49. Carey, Peter, 14 Aug. 1755

50. Matthews, Abraham, 4 Sept. 1755
51. Miller, John Lewis from Norfolk, Virginia, 11 Sept. 1755
52. Unidentified woman from Norfolk, Virginia, 11 Sept. 1755
53. Collins, John als. Jack Ketch "speaks as if he was half-choak'd" 1 Sept. 1755
54. Cage, Samuel, theft, 11 Sept. 1755
55. Gale, John, 18 Sept. 1755
56. Dyton, Thomas, 18 Sept. 1755
57. Cooper, John als. Benjamin Birch, 2 Oct. 1755
58. Mallone, Daniel, 2 Oct. 1755
59. Norclift, William, 9 Oct. 1755
60. Nun, James, 9 Oct. 1755
61. Crouch, Henry, 9 Oct. 1755
62. Holland, Thomas, apprentice, 9 Oct. 1755
63. Bond, Peter, theft, 16 Oct. 1755
64. Orrick, Charles, apprentice, 6 Nov. 1755
65. Aldridge, Thomas, 13 Nov. 1755
66. Emmatt, Thomas, 27 Nov. 1755
67. Sabrey, Leighton, 27 Nov. 1755
68. Thompson, William, 27 Nov. 1755
69. Garvay, Alexander, theft, 4 Dec. 1755
70. Prather, John, 18 Dec. 1755
71. Jarvis, Richard als. Garner/Gidden, 18 Dec. 1755
72. Dallamore, Henry, 3 thefts, 15 Jan. 1756
73. Ivory, Thomas, 25 Mar. 1756
74. Carter, Nathaniel, 15 Apr. 1756
75. Ungra, Michael, 27 May 1756
76. Hubber, Andreas, 27 May 1756

77. Macey, William, theft, 3 June 1756
78. Jefferson, Thomas, theft, 3 June 1756
79. Moffatt, John, theft, 3 June 1756
80. Fossett, Henry, 10 June 1756
81. Bradford, Edward, 17 June 1756
82. Murphey, James, 8 July 1756
83. Pane, Michael, 22 July 1756
84. Tingy, George, 2 Sept. 1756
85. Barns, John, theft, 30 Sept. 1756
86. Henderson, John, 7 Oct. 1756
87. Harris, Edward, theft, 21 Oct. 1756
88. Bower, Michael, 16 Dec. 1756
89. Vanhouse, Mantish, 7 Apr. 1757
90. Kennedy, Thomas, 7 Apr. 1757
91. Unidentified, 4 Aug. 1757
92. Luster, William, 18 Aug. 1757
93. Williams, Robert, 1 Sept. 1757
94. M'Clain, Peter, theft, 15 Sept. 1757
95. Love, Charles, 29 Sept. 1757
96. Sayer, Anne, 6 Oct. 1757
97. Maples, John, 29 Dec. 1757
98. Williams, John, 19 Jan. 1758
99. Patridge, Joseph, 19 Jan. 1758
100. Mulatto Isaac Cromwell, 23 Feb. 1758
101. Green, Anne, 23 Feb. 1758
102. Williams, Henry, 6 Apr. 1758
103. Jackson, John, 11 May 1758
104. Jackson, Mary, 11 May 1758
105. Wells, John, 5 Oct. 1758
106. Muller, Francis, 22 Mar. 1759
107. Nicles, Martin, 22 Mar. 1759
108. Philips, Samuel, 28 June 1759
109. Mulatto Thomas Williams, 19 July 1759

110. Smith, Lawrence, 26 July 1759
111. Wiggan, Richard als. Farmer, Baltimore, John Tayloe, irons on neck and one leg, 6 Sept. 1759
112. Cantwell, Edward, apprentice, 13 Sept. 1759
113. Yeates, Joshua, apprentice, 13 Sept. 1759
114. Unidentified, 15 Nov. 1759
115. Stephenson, William, 24 Apr. 1760
116. Waller, Edmund als. James Edmons, 7 Aug. 1760
117. Bowman, Daniel, 4 Sept. 1760
118. Ash, James, 18 Dec. 1760
119. Aulder, Thomas, 5 Feb. 1761
120. Anderson, John, thefts, 16 Apr. 1761
121. Gossitt, Mary, theft, 16 Apr. 1761
122. Park, James, 23 Apr. 1761
123. Macgilly, Thomas, 28 May 1761
124. Macgilly, Mrs., 28 May 1761
125. Burrows, John, 11 June 1761
126. Dixon, Mary, 2 July 1761
127. Williams, William, 16 July 1761
128. Williams, Thomas, 16 July 1761
129. Earley, Margaret, 30 July 1761
130. Mace, John, 11 Mar. 1762
131. Mobs, Philip, theft, 15 Apr. 1762
132. Scott, Jacob, 22 Apr. 1762
133. Taubert, William Augustus, thefts, 8 July 1762
134. Milborn, John, from Occaquan Iron Works, Virginia, 16 Sept. 1762
135. Edwards, Tise, 16 Sept. 1762
136. Jones, James, about 17-years old, 16 Sept. 1762

137. Brookes, William, 21 Oct. 1762
138. Payne, John als. Cowley als. Monday als. Weaver, 21 Oct. 1762
139. Wickonton, David, hired, 4 Nov. 1762
140. Murdo, William, theft, apprentice, 4 Nov. 1762
141. Downy, Samuel, 9 Dec. 1762
142. Wickenden, David, 6 Jan. 1763
143. Henry, Jonathon, 20 Jan. 1763
144. Kellock, Mary, 3 Feb. 1763
145. Clark, Richard, apprentice, 10 Mar. 1763
146. Collins, John als. Thomas Lockier, Baltimore, Josias Slade, 26 May 1763
147. Daley, John, 2 June 1763
148. Wickenden, David, Baltimore, Alexander Wells, iron collar, 16 June 1763
149. St. Lawrence, Ambrose Anne Arundel Thomas Rutlays, 23 June 1763
150. Carroll, William als. Stanley, London-Town, William Brown, 23 June 1763
151. Payne, John, Virginia, Richard Bowis, late of Maryland, 7 July 1763
152. Watts, Thomas, Turkey-Island, George Steuart, 7 July 1763
153. Unidentified, 14 July 1763
154. Robinson, Owen, 4 Aug. 1763
155. Stinsicomb, Thomas, apprentice, 11 Aug. 1763
156. Conner, Thomas, thefts, 18 Aug. 1763
157. Britt, Patrick, 25 Aug. 1763
158. Moran, Mary, 25 Aug. 1763

159. Collins, John als. Thomas Locker, 25 Aug. 1763
160. Riston, Zachariah, apprentice, 8 Sept. 1763
161. Bryan, John, 29 Sept. 1763
162. Davis, John, 29 Sept. 1763
163. Henry, James als Molison, 27 Oct. 1763

Plantation Fugitives V

Interwar Years: 1764–1772

1. Wickeden, David, 5 Jan. 1764
2. Skinner, Sarah, 19 Jan. 1764
3. Clark, James, 26 Jan. 1764
4. Hurd, James als. Barnett Baltimore Thomas Owings iron collar; "has also Runaway from his Bail, in several Actions" 2 Feb. 1764
5. Williams, James, 16 Feb. 1764
6. Pinamore, John, thefts, 8 Mar. 1764
7. Paterson, Basil, theft, 12 Apr. 1764
8. Morgan, John, theft, 12 Apr. 1764
9. McKeen, Roger, 12 Apr. 1764
10. Farrow, James, 19 Apr. 1764
11. Laha, Priscilla, 19 Apr. 1764
12. Burch, Thomas, theft, 19 Apr. 1764
13. Smith, George, 3 May 1764
14. Woods, George, 3 May 1764
15. Simpson, Thomas, 3 May 1764
16. Scrivener, George, 24 May 1764
17. Kanare, William, 24 May 1764
18. Gillhespy, Joseph, 31 May 1764
19. Williams, James, 14 June 1764
20. Abdell, John, 14 June 1764
21. Rose, Peter, 14 June 1764
22. Donerly, Patrick, 12 July 1764
23. Lasher, Henry, 19 July 1764
24. Gouge, Richard, 9 Aug. 1764

25. Unidentified, 9 Aug. 1764
26. Unidentified, 9 Aug. 1764
27. Unidentified, 9 Aug. 1764
28. Unidentified, 9 Aug. 1764
29. Unidentified, 16 Aug. 1764
30. Ward, John, 16 Aug. 1764
31. Diggan, Patrick, thefts, 16 Aug. 1764
32. Todd, John, 13 Sept. 1764
33. Bacon, Joseph Neale, 13 Sept. 1764
34. Verdiman, Jacob, 27 Sept. 1764
35. Grussely, Peter, theft, 4 Oct. 1764
36. Connant, William, 22 Nov. 1764
37. Parker, John, theft, 29 Nov. 1764
38. Wilkins, John, 29 Nov. 1764
39. Thackfield, William, 7 Mar. 1765
40. Gibbons, George, 7 Mar. 1765
41. Hulet, William, 7 Mar. 1765
42. Watkins, John, 4 Apr. 1765
43. Wilkins, John, 11 Apr. 1765
44. Moalton, James, 11 Apr. 1765
45. Milme, Robert, 18 Apr. 1765
46. Fisher, George, 2 May 1765
47. Cain, John als. Farrill, theft, 16 May 1765
48. Mathews, Jacob, 27 June 1765
49. M'Donald, Hugh Cecil John Read, theft, "small" iron collar; about 17-years old, 4 July 1765
50. Hearly, Timothy, 18 July 1765
51. Shepherd, John, theft, 18 July 1765
52. Dent, Joseph, 1 Aug. 1765
53. Roden, Joseph, 1 Aug. 1765
54. Somerwell, John, 1 Aug. 1765

55. Lovewell, Richard, 1 Aug. 1765

56. Fulleralleary, Edward, 15 Aug. 1765

57. Dixon, James, theft, 22 Aug. 1765

58. Chalmers, John, 5 Sept. 1765

59. Cooke, Philip, theft, 5 Sept. 1765

60. More, George, 5 Sept. 1765

61. Taylor, John, theft, 5 Sept. 1765

62. Fagin, Garret, 12 Sept. 1765

63. Burrough, George, 12 Sept. 1765

64. Gorman, John, 3 Oct. 1765

65. Aliseram, James Henry, 10 Oct. 1765

66. Green, Samuel, 30 Jan. 1766

67. Payne, William, Dorchester, William Ennals, 10 Apr. 1766

68. Sertain, James, Baltimore, John Dorsey, iron collar; formerly a convict servant, 24 Apr. 1766

69. Williams, John, Kent, John Bolton, theft, 24 Apr. 1766

70. Lewis, John, Queen Anne's, John Bennett, theft, 24 Apr. 1766

71. Smith, Joseph, Charles County, John Semple, about 19-years old, 24 Apr. 1766

72. McClene, Thomas als. Ohan, 1 May 1766

73. Billington, William, 8 May 1766

74. Kean, William, 15 May 1766

75. Sullivane, Daniel, 5 June 1766

76. Williamson, George, 12 June 1766

77. Firth, William, theft, 26 June 1766

78. Leary, John, theft, 26 June 1766

79. Russell, James, theft, 26 June 1766

80. Rolings, John, theft, 26 June 1766
81. Dent, Joseph, theft, 26 June 1766
82. Garraughty, John, 7 Aug. 1766
83. Dial, Francis, 14 Aug. 1766
84. Holmes, Thomas, theft, 2 Oct. 1766
85. George, William, theft, 2 Oct. 1766
86. Strictfoot, Matthias, 27 Nov. 1766
87. Evans, Guy, apprentice, 1 Jan. 1767
88. M'Daniel, James, theft, 19 Feb. 1767
89. Norman, John, theft, 19 Feb. 1767
90. Whitton, John, 5 Mar. 1767
91. Fachy, Patrick, 5 Mar. 1767
92. Lacey, Catherine als. Dunn, theft, 16 Apr. 1767
93. Fachy, Patrick, Baltimore, Charles Ridgely Jr., theft, iron collar, 30 Apr. 1767
94. Chappel, John, theft, 4 June 1767
95. Butler, Edward, theft, 11 June 1767
96. Craig, Michael, 11 June 1767
97. Grimshaw, Edmond, 18 June 1767
98. Hardy, John, 18 June 1767
99. Piles, Basil, 25 June 1767
100. Griffith, Anne, married to man in Philadelphia, 16 July 1767
101. Hatton, William als. Jackson, 1 Oct. 1767
102. Chapman, Thomas, 1 Oct. 1767
103. Smith, Samuel als. Simmonds, 1 Oct. 1767
104. Biggs, William, 12 Nov. 1767
105. Cooke, William, 10 Dec. 1767
106. Eagan, Edward, 31 Dec. 1767
107. Hennis, David, apprentice, 21 Jan. 1768

108. Lamb, John, 18 Feb. 1768
109. Throp, Thomas, 18 Feb. 1768
110. Byrne, Thomas, 10 Mar. 1768
111. Hawkes, Thomas, 10 Mar. 1768
112. Hatton, William als. Jackson, 10 Mar. 1768
113. Chapman, Thomas, 10 Mar. 1768
114. Johnston, James, 19 May 1768
115. Clark, James, 26 May 1768
116. Conway, Sarah, 2 June 1768
117. Jones, Thomas, theft, 2 June 1768
118. Stewart, William, 23 June 1768
119. Murray, Mary, 21 July 1768
120. Theodore, Leray, 28 July 1768
121. Welch, Richard, 1 Sept. 1768
122. Dilladd, George, 20 Oct. 1768
123. Williams, Charles, 27 Oct. 1768
124. Cyas, John, 3 Nov. 1768
125. Blanch, William, 3 Nov. 1768
126. Mulatto Philip Gray, 17 Nov. 1768
127. Smith, William, 17 Nov. 1768
128. Berrage, John, 17 Nov. 1768
129. Coreshil, Thomas, 22 Dec. 1768
130. Cooke, William, 5 Jan. 1769
131. Denny, Peter, thefts, 19 Jan. 1769
132. Quin, John, 2 Feb. 1769
133. Coreshil, Thomas, 2 Feb. 1769
134. Allen, John, 9 Feb. 1769
135. Carr, Hannah, 16 Mar. 1769
136. Owings, John, 6 Apr. 1769
137. Shepherd, William, 6 Apr. 1769
138. Evans, John, theft, 13 Apr. 1769
139. Barber, John, theft, 13 Apr. 1769
140. Williams, Henry, thefts, 13 Apr. 1769

141. Adair, William, theft, 13 Apr. 1769
142. Whateley, William, 13 Apr. 1769
143. Winter, John, 20 Apr. 1769
144. Thomas, Daniel, 22 June 1769
145. Child, James, 22 June 1769
146. Thompson, Henry, 22 June 1769
147. Kean, Mathew, theft, 29 June 1769
148. Rourke, Con als. James Campbell, 29 June 1769
149. Murphy, Daniel, 6 July 1769
150. Carthy, Timothy, 6 July 1769
151. Alan, Charles, theft, 20 July 1769
152. Alan, Joseph, 20 July 1769
153. Burrage, John, 27 July 1769
154. Kenning, Samuel, 27 July 1769
155. Larkin, Andrew, 10 Aug. 1769
156. Scott, Alexander, 17 Aug. 1769
157. Adams, John, 24 Aug. 1769
158. Bishop, Joseph, 24 Aug. 1769
159. Keen, Richard, apprentice, 12 Oct. 1769
160. Mulatto Charles Fenton, 2 Nov. 1769
161. Mulatto Humphry Hill, 9 Nov. 1769
162. M'Critch, Daniel, 16 Nov. 1769
163. Cavendish, George, 16 Nov. 1769
164. White, Thomas, 4 Jan. 1770
165. Taylor, James, 18 Jan. 1770
166. Goodwin, John, 1 Feb. 1770
167. Murphy, Edward, 1 Feb. 1770
168. Loney, Edward, 1 Feb. 1770
169. M'Carty, James, 1 Feb. 1770
170. Niness, William, 1 Feb. 1770
171. Dorrovan, Daniel, 26 Apr. 1770
172. Taylor, John, 26 Apr. 1770

173. Miller, Joseph, 17 May 1770
174. Fossett, John, 17 May 1770
175. Cullen, Joan (male), 24 May 1770
176. Riley, Patrick, 24 May 1770
177. Lacy, Hugh, 24 May 1770
178. Hughs, John, 24 May 1770
179. Plain, William, 14 June 1770
180. Harrison, William, 14 June 1770
181. Dodd, Charles, 14 June 1770
182. Johnson, John, 14 June 1770
183. Robinson, William, 14 June 1770
184. Inkley, William, 14 June 1770
185. White, John, theft, 21 June 1770
186. Joseph, Henry, theft, 21 June 1770
187. Marshall, Joseph, theft, 21 June 1770
188. Moor, Joseph als. Joseph Simon, 28 June 1770
189. Ager, Thomas, 28 June 1770
190. Kelly, Thomas, theft, 28 June 1770
191. Holaway, James, 12 July 1770
192. Keith, Andrew, 26 July 1770
193. MacDonald, Daniel, 26 July 1770
194. Riley, Bell, 26 July 1770
195. Ball, Henry, 26 July 1770
196. Murdock, John, theft, 2 Aug. 1770
197. Evans, Arthur, theft, 9 Aug. 1770
198. Downs, John, 16 Aug. 1770
199. Warren, Richard, 16 Aug. 1770
200. Gwynn, Mansfield Lewis, 16 Aug. 1770
201. Squires, Daniel, 16 Aug. 1770
202. German, Hugh, theft, 16 Aug. 1770
203. Bentley, Thomas, 13 Aug. 1770
204. Dowling, Patrick, 27 Sept. 1770
205. Thomson, Isaiah, 27 Sept. 1770

206. Cravan, Lawrence, 11 Oct. 1770
207. Jackson, William, 11 Oct. 1770
208. Fletcher, John, 18 Oct. 1770
209. Heavey, Daniel, 8 Nov. 1770
210. Kelly, Peter, 10 Jan. 1771
211. Bawden, William Henry, theft, 7 Feb. 1771
212. Stanton, Adam, 7 Feb. 1771
213. Gorman, John, 7 Mar. 1771
214. Glanding, John, 14 Mar. 1771
215. Hall, James, 4 Apr. 1771
216. Routlidge, James, 20 June 1771
217. Worgar, John, 20 June 1771
218. Mealy, Roger, 20 June 1771
219. Bryan, Thomas, 20 June 1771
220. Bullin, Luke, 4 July 1771
221. Milson, Abraham, 4 July 1771
222. Milson, Susanna, 4 July 1771
223. Langley, William, 11 July 1771
224. Townsend, Thomas, theft, 18 July 1771
225. Jolly, John, 18 July 1771
226. Francis, James, 25 July 1771
227. Tippins, George, 25 July 1771
228. Stephens, Oliver, Annapolis, Mrs. Howard 2nd escape, 1 Aug. 1771
229. Lutts, Philip, Pennsylvania, about 18-years old, 1 Aug. 1771
230. Grayham, John, 8 Aug. 1771
231. Burns, Hugh, 8 Aug. 1771
232. Phillips, Thomas, 15 Aug. 1771
233. Conner, Timothy, 15 Aug. 1771
234. Gouldsboury, Michael, 15 Aug. 1771
235. Henderson, James, 15 Aug. 1771

236. Duffey, Nill (male), 29 Aug. 1771
237. Redmond, Andrew, 12 Sept. 1771
238. O'Brien, John, 12 Sept. 1771
239. Philips, Thomas, 26 Sept. 1771
240. Conner, Thomas, Frederick Jacob Windrode, 10 Oct. 1771
241. Winters, John, Anne Arundel, Ephraim Howard, 10 Oct. 1771
242. Johnson, John, Baltimore, John Heeston & John Kayton, 31 Oct. 1771
243. Berns, Thomas, Baltimore, John Heeston & John Kayton, 31 Oct. 1771
244. Leetch, Solomon, Baltimore, John Heeston & John Kayton iron collar, 31 Oct. 1771
245. Fields, Roger, 21 Nov. 1771
246. Lee, William, 28 Nov. 1771
247. Langley, William, 12 Dec. 1771
248. Angess, William Daniel, 26 Dec. 1771
249. Royston, James, theft, 16 Jan. 1772
250. Osborn, Walter, theft, 16 Jan. 1772
251. Rylot, Edward, thefts, 5 Mar. 1772
252. Pollard, John, thefts, 5 Mar. 1772
253. Bissey, John, thefts, 5 Mar. 1772
254. Norris, William, thefts, 5 Mar. 1772
255. Witmore, Henry, thefts, 5 Mar. 1772
256. Elton, Thomas, 16 Apr. 1772
257. Hughs, William, had been whipped & pilloried at PG Co. Ct., 16 Apr. 1772
258. Dunlop, Andrew, 30 Apr. 1772
259. Cummins, Robert, 21 May 1772
260. Jones, Richard, 21 May 1772
261. Matthews, John, 4 June 1772
262. Clark, Mary, 4 June 1772

Plantation Fugitives VI

The Eve of Revolution: 1773–1775

Can runaway records in Maryland give an indication of increased social stress prior to the Revolution? If so, then this would suggest parallels with Bacon's Rebellion a century earlier. Or was the unrest in Plantation America only related to the strained relations with the mother country, as standard histories suggest?

1. Willard, Edward, 7 Jan. 1773
2. Wharton, Robert, 21 Jan. 1773
3. Clark, James, Kent Island, James Martin, (iron) collar round neck, 18 Feb. 1773
4. Roper, James, 6 May 1773
5. Fitzpatrick, Bryan, 13 May 1773
6. Shane, Arthur, apprentice, 27 May 1773
7. Stackabout, William, 15 July 1773
8. Shane, Cornelius, 15 July 1773
9. Humphreys, Edward, Baltimore, James Baker, 19 Aug. 1773
10. M'Carty, Owen, Baltimore, 20 Aug. 1773
11. Johnson, William, Baltimore, apprentice, thefts, 20–28 Aug. 1773

12. Hollingsworth, John, Baltimore, 20–28 Aug. 1773

13. Leary, Jeremiah, Baltimore, 20–28 Aug. 1773

14. Meredith, Thomas, handcuffs; had run away before; escaped again before they got him home, 20–28 Aug. 1773

15. Wallis, Hector, Prince George's, 28 Aug. to 4 Sept. 1773

16. Samuel, Prince George's, 28 Aug. to 4 Sept. 1773

17. Howell, Nicholas, Patuxent Iron Works, 28 Aug. to 4 Sept. 1773

18. Hogg, Thomas, Patuxent Iron Works, 28 Aug. to 4 Sept. 1773

19. Dangerfield, Samuel, Baltimore broke open store, 9–18 Sept. 1773

20. Tuff, Thomas, Baltimore, 9–18 Sept. 1773

21. M'Guier, Daniel als. Gilmer Baltimore, 18–25 Sept. 1773

22. Magrath, William Baltimore, 18–25 Sept. 1773

23. Hoskins, Thomas, 23 Sept. 1773

24. Bennett, Hooper, Charles Richard Lee, 19-years old, 30 Sept. 1773

25. Unidentified, 30 Sept. 1773

26. Fitzpatrick, Barnard, Bladensburg, 9–16 Oct. 1773

27. White, John, Tulip Hill, 9–16 Oct. 1773

28. Bryant, Robert, Tulip Hill, 9–16 Oct. 1773

29. Parsons, John, Tulip Hill, 9–16 Oct. 1773

30. Pendergast, Richard, Frederick, 9–16 Oct. 1773

31. Doyle, Thomas, Baltimore, 16–23 Oct. 1773

32. Fitzpatrick, Barnard, 28 Oct. 1773
33. Garland, James, 4 Nov. 1773
34. Black (Block), Richard, 6–13 Nov. 1773
35. Dickinson, James, Baltimore, 13–20 Nov. 1773
36. Valliant, Robert, Dorset, 20–27 Nov. 1773
37. Fogaty, John, 27 Nov. to 9 Dec. 1773
38. Sadler, Richard, 27 Nov. to 9 Dec. 1773
39. Sawyer, Charles, 27 Nov. to 9 Dec. 1773
40. M'Kain, Hugh, Frederick, 27 Nov. to 9 Dec. 1773
41. Smith Sarah, 9 Dec. 1773
42. Hateley, Ralph, Baltimore, 9–18 Dec. 1773
43. Unrick, Rosannah, Baltimore, 9–18 Dec. 1773
44. Hall, Thomas, 16 Dec. 1773
45. Anderson, Joseph, theft, 16 Dec. 1773
46. Cockle, John, 16 Dec. 1773
47. Driver, John, 16 Dec. 1773
48. Murphy, Edward Kent, 30 Dec. 1773–1778 Jan. 1774
49. Burk, Tobias, Kent "his left leg is very sore", 30 Dec. 1773–1778 Jan. 1774
50. Green, James, Baltimore, apprentice, 20 Jan. to 10 Feb. 1774
51. Quelch, William, thefts, 27 Jan. 1774
52. Corker, Timothy, 10 Feb. 1774
53. Walsh, John, 10 Mar. 1774
54. Merchant, John, Baltimore, 10–31 Mar. 1774
55. Diar, James, Frederick, iron collar, 10–31 Mar. 1774
56. Payne, Richard, Baltimore, 10–31 Mar. 1774

57. Baxter, Barney, Baltimore, 10–31 Mar. 1774

58. Foster, John, 10–31 Mar. 1774

59. Ward, William, Baltimore, 10–31 Mar. 1774

60. M'Inerhency, Thomas, 17 Mar. 1774

61. Franey, John, Baptist Dilla, 24 Mar. 1774

62. Hujen, Hugh als. M'Can, theft, 31 Mar. 1774

63. Young, George, 7 Apr. 1774

64. Saddler, Richard, 7 Apr. 1774

65. Wakefield, John, 7 Apr. 1774

66. Sprotson, Croasdale, 7 Apr. 1774

67. Farrow, Robert, 14 Apr. 1774

68. Burke, Festus, George Town, William Deakins Jr., iron collar, 28 Apr. 1774

69. Bready, Thomas, theft, 19 May 1774

70. M'Coy, Nicholas, Baltimore, 28 May 1774

71. Carney, Winney, Baltimore, 28 May 1774

72. Jennings, Joseph, Elk Ridge Furnace, 28 May 1774

73. Gough, John, Elk Ridge Furnace, 28 May 1774

74. Ball, John, Elk Ridge Furnace, 28 May 1774

75. Woolford, John, Elk Ridge Furnace, 28 May 1774

76. Sanders, William, 9 June 1774

77. Nisbett, John, theft, 9 June 1774

78. Reed, Henry, theft, 9 June 1774

79. White, John, 9 June 1774

80. Gregory, Thomas, 9 June 1774

81. Skipper, Isaac, 9 June 1774

82. Coomb, John, Frederick, 11-18 June 1774
83. Wallace, William, 16 June 1774
84. King, Thomas, 16 June 1774
85. Easton, Thomas, 16 June 1774
86. Breaton, Thomas, 16 June 1774
87. Columbine, Thomas, 16 June 1774
88. Fowler, Thomas, Cumberland, 18 June to 2 July 1774
89. M'Mahon, John, Frederick, 18 June to 2 July 1774
90. Curly, Bridget Frederick, 18 June to 2 July 1774
91. Allen, George, 23 June 1774
92. Allen, John, 23 June 1774
93. Bawn, William, 30 June 1774
94. Riley, James, 30 June 1774
95. Ennis, Patrick, 30 June 1774
96. Clifford, Thomas, 30 June 1774
97. Lindsey, James, 30 June 1774
98. Sutton, Thomas, 30 June 1774
99. Welsh, Thomas, Baltimore, 2–9 July 1774
100. Cookmar, James, theft, 7 July 1774
101. Powis, Samuel, 14 July 1774
102. Williams, Edward, 14 July 1774
103. Brown, James, 14 July 1774
104. Murphey, William, 14 July 1774
105. Stone, Thomas, 14 July 1774
106. Bryan, John, 14 July 1774
107. Spriggs, Thomas, 21 July 1774
108. Porter, Benjamin, 21 July 1774
109. Breaton, Thomas, 11 Aug. 1774
110. Boswell, Henry, Baltimore, 24 August 1774

111. Linnaham, Darby, Baltimore, 24 August 1774
112. Walch, Nicholas, Baltimore, 24 August 1774
113. M'Ginley, James, Anne Arundel, 24 August 1774
114. Riley, Owen, 25 Aug. 1774
115. Kennedy, Daniel, 15 Sept. 1774
116. Trayner, Simon, 15 Sept. 1774
117. Painter, Thomas, Harford C, Alexander Cowan, 15 Sept. 1774
118. Justice, Charles, Frederick C, 21 Sept. 1774
119. Lawson, Ralph, Frederick C, 21 Sept. 1774
120. Bean, Edwin, theft, 22 Sept. 1774
121. Willson, John, 22 Sept. 1774
122. Smith, John, 22 Sept. 1774
123. Griffith, William, Anne Arundel C, James Elder, 20- years old, 6 Oct. 1774
124. George, William, Dorsey's Forge, Samuel Dorsey Jr. & Edward Norwood, iron collar, 6 Oct. 1774
125. Burnham, Solomon, Dorsey's Forge, Samuel Dorsey Jr. & Edward Norwood, iron collar, 6 Oct. 1774
126. Chapman, Samuel, Dorsey's Forge, Samuel Dorsey Jr. & Edward Norwood, 6 Oct. 1774
127. Murray, James, Harford C, 26 Oct. 1774
128. Joyce, Thomas, Harford C, 26 Oct. 1774
129. Johnson, John, theft, 3 Nov. 1774
130. Driscol, Matthew, theft, 3 Nov. 1774
131. Blundell, Charles, theft, 3 Nov. 1774

132. Fisher, Joseph, theft, 10 Nov. 1774

133. Creamer, Patrick, theft, 10 Nov. 1774

134. Booth, William, theft, 10 Nov. 1774

135. Wilson, John, 17 Nov. 1774

136. Mills, Robert, 17 Nov. 1774

137. Bell, James, 17 Nov. 1774

138. Fell, George, 30 Nov. 1774

139. Mills, Robert, 1 Dec. 1774

140. Bell, James, 1 Dec. 1774

141. Mags, Thomas, Kent I, 19 Dec. 1774

142. Coughlen, John, Baltimore, 26 Dec. 1774

143. Callagan, Thomas, Harford C, 26 Dec. 1774

144. Carrel, William, Frederick C, 2 Jan. 1775

145. Powel, James, 5 Jan. 1775

146. Unidentified, 26 Jan. 1775

147. Thompson, Joseph Zachariah, 9 Feb. 1775

148. Daime, John, 23 Feb. 1775

149. Buchanan, Peggy, 16 Mar. 1775

150. Burges, Thomas, 16 Mar. 1775

151. Mulatto Will Adams, 16 Mar. 1775

152. Connally, William, 23 Mar. 1775

153. Smith, John, Baltimore, 29 Mar 1775

154. Low (?), Joseph, 30 Mar. 1775

155. Cerbie, John, 30 Mar. 1775

156. Mulatto James Mason, Frederick C, 5 Apr. 1775

157. Megrah, John als. Christian, Baltimore, 5 April 1775

158. Carney, Nicholas, Baltimore, 5 Apr. 1775

159. Davis, John, 6 Apr. 1775

160. Manis, Francis, 20 Apr. 1775
161. Delany, John, 20 Apr. 1775
162. Ramage, John, Baltimore, 26 Apr. 1775
163. Spears, Thomas, 27 Apr. 1775
164. Webster, William, 27 Apr. 1775
165. Cooper, Joseph, Frederick C, 10 May 1775
166. Curly, Dominick, Baltimore, 24 May 1775
167. Sladers, Thomas, Frederick C, 30 May 1775
168. Colebert, Simon, Frederick C, 30 May 1775
169. Blackhead, Anthony, Frederick C, 30 May 1775
170. Compton, William, Baltimore, 31 May 1775
171. Love, William, Baltimore, 31 May 1775

172. Jackson, Thomas als. Stevens, Baltimore, May 1775
173. Hendly, Patrick, Baltimore, 31 May 1775
174. Gee, John, Snowden's Iron Works, 1 June 1775
175. Wilson, James, Snowden's Iron Works, 1 June 1775
176. Jackson, William, Baltimore, 7 June 1775
177. Barrett, Francis, Patapsco Neck, Charles Ridgely, theft, iron collar, 8 June 1775
178. Hain, Job, Kent I, 27 June 1775
179. Craston, Joseph als. Richard Dudley, Frederick C, 27 June 1775
180. Gee, George, Cumberland, 27 June 1775
181. Kelly, Peter als. Peirce Burn, 15 June 1775

182. Hill, Richard, Baltimore, 5 July 1775
183. Broadfield, William, Baltimore, 11 July 1775
184. Hall, William, Baltimore, 12 July 1775
185. Fisbay, William, Baltimore, 12 July 1775
186. Windless, Martin, Baltimore, apprentice, 18 July 1775
187. Dermont, Henry, Baltimore, 18 July 1775
188. Linney, John, Baltimore, 19 July 1775
189. Hays, John als. Maw, Anne Arundel C, 19 July 1775
190. Hays, Elinor, Anne Arundel C, 19 July 1775
191. Smith, John, Baltimore, 19 July 1775
192. M'Avoy, Christopher, 20 July 1775
193. Rork, Hugh, Baltimore, 25 July 1775
194. Simpson, Rachel, 25 July 1775
195. Murray, Lewis, Baltimore thefts, 25 July 1775
196. Humphreys, Thomas, Baltimore, thefts, 25 July 1775
197. Humphreys, Thomas, Baltimore, 26 July 1775
198. Hill, Daniel, Georgetown, 26 July 1775
199. Davis, Samuel, Georgetown, 26 July 1775
200. Thompson, Mary, Georgetown, 26 July 1775
201. Place, James, Baltimore, 2 Aug. 1775
202. Norris, William, iron collar and

darbies on legs, 2
Aug. 1775

203. Bessy, John, iron
collar and darbies
on legs, 2 Aug. 1775

204. Hall, William,
Baltimore, 2 Aug.
1775

205. Osborn, James,
Baltimore, 2 Aug.
1775

206. Hain, Job, 3 Aug.
1775

207. Humphreys,
Thomas, theft, 3
Aug. 1775

208. Bishop, George,
theft, 10 Aug. 1775

209. Ormsby, James,
theft, 10 Aug. 1775

210. Kettle, William,
theft, 10 Aug. 1775

211. Richards, Edward,
10 Aug. 1775

212. Skinner, Jane, 10
Aug. 1775

213. Hain, Job, 10 Aug.
1775

214. Quaty, Archibald
D, 15 Aug. 1775

215. Whitby, Jonathan,
17 Aug. 1775

216. Humphreys,
Thomas,

Baltimore, 3 thefts,
23 Aug. 1775

217. Ward, George,
Frederick C, 23
Aug. 1775

218. Casey, Peter,
Frederick C, 23
Aug. 1775

219. Mulatto Richard
Bute, 29 Aug. 1775

220. Humphreys,
Thomas, 31 Aug.
1775

221. Holmes, James, 7
Sept. 1775

222. Butler, Patrick,
Frederick C, 12
Sept. 1775

223. Scott, John, Talbot
C, 12 Sept. 1775

224. Unidentified
Woman, Talbot C,
12 Sept. 1775

225. Bower, Casper,
Baltimore, 13 Sept.
1775

226. Bear, Valentine,
Baltimore, 13 Sept.
1775

227. Turner, Thomas,
Frederick C, 13
Sept. 1775

228. Mahony, John, Baltimore, 20 Sept. 1775

229. Hennesey, Dennis, Baltimore, 20 Sept. 1775

230. Arnold, Richard, Baltimore, 20 Sept. 1775

231. Brown, Luke, Baltimore, 26 Sept. 1775

232. Taylor, Andrew, Baltimore, 26 Sept. 1775

233. Night, John, Harford C, 26 Sept. 1775

234. Colson, John, 28 Sept. 1775

235. Greenwell, John, apprentice, 28 Sept. 1775

236. Sterling, Jane, Baltimore, 4 Oct. 1775

237. Murgee, Turrance, Frederick, 4 Oct. 1775

238. Redman, Patrick, Elk Ridge, 11 Oct. 1775

239. Mulatto Thomas Duglass, Elk Ridge, 11 Oct. 1775

240. Irvin, John, 12 Oct. 1775

241. Jones, William, 12 Oct. 1775

242. Cammil, Robert, theft, 9 Nov. 1775

243. Knot, Randal, theft, 9 Nov. 1775

244. Gould, Thomas, Baltimore, 22 Nov. 1775

245. Summers, John, Baltimore, 22 Nov. 1775

246. Jones, John, Baltimore, 22 Nov. 1775

247. Kennedy, Judeth, Baltimore, 28 Nov. 1775

248. Wilson, George, theft, 5 Dec. 1775

249. Bloxham, Matthew, Baltimore, 19 Dec. 1775

Thoughts on the Eve of Revolution

Runaways are more likely to come from outlying areas and be participants in mass breakouts from the various iron works, which were hellish facilities. As Maryland industrialized and employed African slaves in crop production, white slaves were finding themselves, like Meshach Browning 20 years later, in frontier zones at the very time the British authorities were discouraging immigration to the frontier. The fabric of society was being pulled tight.

Statistical Summary

The tables below give a summary of the numbers of runaways advertised in each period, along with other observations, including the time of year (cold or warm weather months), whether thefts were also listed in the advertisements, male, female and non-Caucasian runaways, and whether the runaway was described as an apprentice, or shackled.

	I	II	III	IV	V	VI	Total
Total Runaways Reported	27	86	123	163	286	249	934
In Cold Months*	13	35	41	74	101	100	364
In Warm Months	14	51	82	89	185	149	570
Thefts	8	14	35	45	59	24	185
Male	25	82	121	152	275	241	896
Female	2	4	2	11	11	8	38
Unidentified	3	6	3	5	5	3	25
Non-Caucasian	-	2	1	2	3	4	12
Apprentice	-	-	3	10	4	4	21
Shackled	1	1	3	5	6	12	28
Years in Period	7	5	4	10	9	3	38
Runaways per year	3.9	17.2	30.8	16.3	31.8	83.0	24.6
Shackled per year	<1	<1	<1	<1	<1	4.0	<1

* Cold weather runaways were primarily observed in spring rather than autumn or winter

The same facts are presented below as percentages. We can see a decided preference for running during warmer months, and that the overwhelming majority of runaways were men. Trends are less clear in other observations.

	I	II	III	IV	V	VI	Total
In Cold Months	48%	41%	33%	45%	35%	40%	39%
In Warm Months	52%	59%	67%	55%	65%	60%	61%
Thefts	30%	16%	28%	28%	21%	10%	20%
Male	93%	95%	98%	93%	96%	97%	96%
Female	7%	5%	2%	7%	4%	3%	4%
Unidentified	11%	7%	2%	3%	2%	1%	3%
Non-Caucasian	0%	2%	1%	1%	1%	2%	1%
Apprentice	0%	0%	2%	6%	1%	2%	2%
Shackled	4%	1%	2%	3%	2%	5%	3%

Societal Friction Graphs

Unfree labor, particularly unfree Caucasian labor, as it was more highly skilled in cities and towns and was used to push the frontier, was the core of the Plantation Era economy. Turmoil among the slave class equaled economic uncertainty according to its severity, and, more importantly, was an indication of the strength of the social mechanisms of control.

Servile Desperation

Servile Desperation is defined as cold month escapes combined with thefts. This is an indication of how difficult it was for a slave to escape, taking extreme chances in the winter and having to steal supplies for survival, likely indicating that free folk were unlikely to assist or harbor the runaway

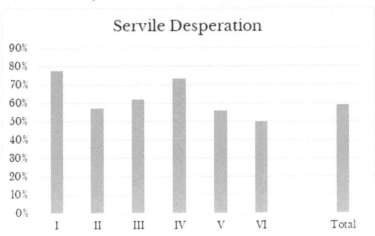

Master Brutality

Master Brutality is defined as runaways who were shackled combined with one-tenth of male runaways. One-tenth of male runaways were estimated by the author as repeat offenders, indicating extraordinary motivations for running.

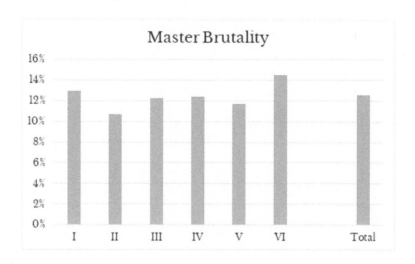

Social Instability

Social Instability is defined as apprentices, non-Caucasian and unidentified runaways during a period. Black slaves or servants were generally less likely to runaway, as were apprentices, therefore, their willingness to risk running away indicates a weakening confidence in their own status and increased general instability.

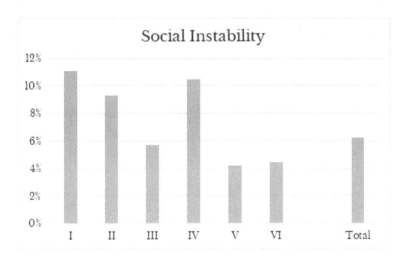

Appendices

Reviews of Secondary Sources

Editor's note: about half of the videos reviewed below had been removed in the year or so that has passed from writing to publication. Some were copyright violations and some were hosted on channels that have been censored. Where possible, I have created citations that should allow the interested reader to locate the films.

'Dangerous Disaffection' -- *American Negro Slave Revolts* by Herbert Aptheker, 1943, Columbia University Press, New York, 409 pages

Researched as part of a thesis in the 1930s and reprinted for the last time in 1968 in support of the Civil Rights Movement, *American Negro Slave Revolts*, when read closely, is not likely to support any modern notion that descendants of African-American slaves might peacefully cohabitate with whites or each other in agrarian, industrial or postmodern cities.

Despite Aptheker's passionate belief that American blacks possessed a higher level of humanity and yearned equally for freedom to their white contemporaries, this reader has found his record to be a gold mine. The very class of whites, roundly dismissed as having no agency whatsoever [poor whites] under the plantation system by Aptheker, are brought to life nonetheless, as the lurking ghosts present yet unacknowledged by the author. Aptheker is commendable in his inclusion of the story of Caucasian servitude, largely unwittingly, as his focus is on the plight of blacks and elite whites only, keeping with the modern liberal narrative that working whites are non-entities in American history, which is merely the story of elite white avarice and heavenly black martyrdom.

I have annotated this valuable book and will use it to place white servitude in context at the conclusion of this work.

However, Aptheker makes a good case that negro servile unrest had three primary causes:

1. The crucial precondition was a local increase of negroes compared to whites, caused by A) poor white migration away from desertified land and blighted cities and B) the importation of large bodies of African immigrants by elite whites based in and out of English America [often English and Dutch]. Aptheker makes it clear that the mass importation of African slaves beginning in 1680

almost immediately turned such areas of English America into seething cauldrons of discontent, from which poor whites migrated into hostile Indian lands rather than remain as unemployed laborers and unpaid slave catchers, causing a destabilizing racial imbalance.

2. The accelerant of discontent was industrialized agriculture, which made rural work increasingly harsh, combined with the concentration of blacks in increasingly large plantations and in urban areas such as Charleston, South Carolina, New York and New Orleans, which were centers of unrest and where black-on-black violence was the rule, not the exception.

3. Severe and frequent economic depressions were the immediate catalysts, without which uprisings would not have been significant, meaning that the plantation system [the foundation of all of the English-American colonies] was doomed to failure due to its own intrinsic economic unsustainability and extreme social inequity.

Although Aptheker thought he was writing an indictment of American black chattel slavery, he penned an indictment of the entire American system, which was and is the plantation system, crucial to which is the ideal of population replacement [which was the reason for the birth of the system in 16th century Ireland].

Aptheker's survey further proves that the only exclusively black uprisings requiring military-level responses were committed by tribal maroons and/or under strong mystical leaders like Nat Turner and that most plots that got beyond the planning stage featured white specialists and/or leaders.

By combining the dense information in Aptheker's survey with my chronology in America in Chains, I will be able to present a comprehensive history of underclass revolts against the American Plantation System from 1620 through 1860.

Thanks to reader Gene Gibson for the thoughtful gift of this book.

'Yellow Dogs'

Always in a Hole: Life in a Pennsylvania Coal Town During the Great Depression and World War II, Arthur Vincent Ciervo, Chapter 4, pages 53–60

The Coal and Iron Police, sent into the small mining towns of Pennsylvania the year after the Civil War, later worked with the Pinkerton Detective Agency to break unions. In 1922 alone, in Pennsylvania, there were 1,807 strikes. In Pittsburg, there were 500–600 private police, heavily armed with clubs and weighing between 200 and 250 pounds. As far back as the 1860s, these brutal overseers would use their horses to prevent women from speaking to each other on the street.

It is no accident that as soon as the agrarian South, with its outdated system of agricultural slavery, was defeated, the U.S. Senate began enacting laws to bring back the type of brutal white slavery that Plantation America had been founded and run on from 1607 through the 1830s. There is quite an irony to the fact that full-blown, race-based black chattel slavery was only in existence (as we are taught, it was from 1606 through 1865) for two generations before the war that abolished it, and as soon as this system was abolished, the old white slavery was retooled for industry. Police in industrial America were the retooled overseers of the plantation era, a brutal thug dedicated to bullying the wives of miners and beating and killing the miners themselves. Do keep in mind that these miners were effectively held hostage in isolated mountain villages and were not paid through most of the 70-year period of this trafficking in human families, a period almost precisely as long as the African Chattel period in the South, which ran from 1804 to 1865, to give way to the 1865–1933 stage of predominantly white industrial slavery in the North.

It should be noted that the later form of agrarian slavery fed the earlier industrial model, with coal mines and factories in the British Isles devouring about 10,000 men, women and children per year, through the process of refining the cotton of America in the factories of Great Britain.

The 1922 committee investigating Coal and Iron Police stated:

"...They are very large men; most of them weighing from 200 to 250 pounds. They are heavily armed and carry clubs usually designed as a "blackjack."

As late as the 1980s, two white men, brothers I knew, were beaten to death by cops using blackjacks.

"Everywhere your committee visited they found victims of the coal and iron police who had beaten up and were still carrying scars on their faces and heads from the rough treatment they received."

The two watershed years in private police brutality against predominantly white ethnic labor were 1866, with laws authorizing companies with police powers over their employees, and in 1900, with the increased government backing of industrial interest ties to American imperial aspiration, requiring coal-fueled ships of coal-forged steel.

According two witnesses of police activity around Pittsburg:

"Deputy sheriffs are simply bums, ward heelers and City Hall loafers."

"When there was violence Yellow Dogs" [police] with clubs would crack miners on the head and let them lay there."

Again, the word crack comes to mind, seeming to have alternated meaning from generation to generation in the form of the cracker, first the man who was cracked with a whip or club and then later referring to he who did the cracking. Indeed, in Pennsylvania of 1977, teachers in my middle school beat children with paddles [of the same design previously used to discipline and kill servants] and we called it "cracking."

'A Snake'

The Company Store, *Always in a Hole* by Arthur Vincent Ciervo, pages 77–88

"Saint Peter, don't call me
Because I can't go.
I owe my soul to the company store."
-Tennessee Ernie Ford, *16 Tons*

"It's not but slavery, comrades,
To mine this precious coal
It takes away your manhood
And it's tiresome to your soul."

-Harry Rager

The information on miner's pay and mining town economics comes mostly from the later period in the early 1900s, but the proportions do not seem to have been affected by inflation over the decades. Indeed, mining unions fought more for the reversal of pay reductions than for the increased pay I saw when I was a kid in Pennsylvania. In the 1970s, coalminers made great money, but the jobs were going away, being mechanized. The grandfathers of those men were terrorized industrial slaves, whose families were often—especially early on—held hostage in company towns, policed by goons who had such methods as driving their horses between two speaking women and beating the children of miners who violated the 9 p.m. town curfew.

Not only did companies have the authority to hire their own police but to issue currency as well!

The currency was only redeemable at the company store, but the company money was only worth 3 for every 5 government dollars. Many miners never made any money. The entire system was an updated version of the time-slave system upon which this nation was founded, by which a person never escaped an imposed debt cycle and would forever have to resell himself to an owner, until he no longer had value and was then consigned to starvation and the elements. A miner was paid in "scrip" credit that could only be paid back into the company system. The result, for many miners, of their wives and children buying on their credit while they were in the mine was that they got paid with a "snake," a squiggly line that indicated that no scrip was owed the miner.

Working for a credit line? Does that sound familiar?

Some miners were threatened if they took their scrip elsewhere, traded it for cash to people that wanted goods only available at the company store and then used it for buying elsewhere:

"Joe, we've treated you right. Now that you have a little bit of money, you're going to the Jew store. This is not right."

-Vesta Pennsylvania Mine Foreman to Joe Budzanoski, 1920s.

Pennsylvania, the Quaker slave colony, sanctioned the sale of more Irish than any other English-American province, and that province alone, when it became a State, decided not to archive the evidence of its crimes for posterity. That lack of remorse, Quaker pioneering of the American correction system and the natural resources of that coal-rich state, positioned it well for pioneering industrial slavery.

The America Boat

Varg Vikernesdiscusses how ostracism was used to get rid of criminals from Norway and ship them to America: emptying asylums, poor houses and jails. (Vikernes)

Another White Slavery Find

From Our Pennsylvania Researcher

James,

I ran across a reference to this book the other day (Tenzer). It looks as though it would be filled with some relevant data in regards to white slavery, etc. Unfortunately, I haven't seen a copy that retails for anything less than $999. Did find the intro, which has only made me more curious.

Here's the intro (adpowellblog).

Take care down there. Hope to catch you at some point when things slow down a bit.

-Nero the Pict

This is news to me, Sir.

I will place it in the end notes of *Cracker-Boy* and read and annotate the introduction for the print release.

-James

James LaFond

'Deserted by Their Home Governments'

White Slavery Video Resource [Now deleted by YouTube, and I don't have the title—Sorry!]

Note the tale of the Icelandic traitor at 15:00 of the video. This traitor was a "servant" [always meaning slave in pre-20th century settings]. The fact is, that raids by slavers into Europe as well as by pirates into American ports and colonies, which were often facilitated by the practice of the target society of keeping slaves, were a sure method for insuring an internal enemy in time of war. The video is an excellent lesson in what happens when a people give up their martial heritage and responsibility to defend themselves—or has it taken from them by their government. The discussion of English and Dutch pirates switching alliances to Islam, so that they continue their piratical ways after Spain made peace with Holland and England is excellent and on point.

This is a very good documentary, recommended by Deuce.

Colony of the Damned

Video Sources for White Slavery in Plantation America and Penal Australia (Reid), (Wright), (Beresford) [and one more video deleted from YouTube]

Devil's Island and *Black Robe* reflect two drastically different colonial roles played by the French government over the centuries, which are important to understand to place the English-American plantation experience in context, as English America was at first bordered to south and north by French colonies, and no fewer than five frontier wars were fought between French and English frontiersmen.

The two videos on Australia—one rosy-hued and deluded from the modern liberal perspective and one more on the mark—may give the reader a better idea of what early American settlements were like, as Australia was largely settled with convict labor because the United States refused to accept any more white servants from England beginning in 1804, a deadline that was set in 1787.

AMERICAN GULAG

James LaFond

The Province Which Held More Whites in
Bondage than Any Did Not Save the Records
(Pennsylvania)

One expects the fiendish Quaker state
hierarchs to label all white slaves and servants as
"Indentured," but for them to trash their records
speaks unwritten volumes.

"INDENTURED   SERVANTS: The
Pennsylvania State Archives does not hold records
of indentured servants.   This bibliography was
compiled by Mary F. Schoedel, November 1, 2006,
for   the   Pennsylvania   State   Archives.   For
information about and records of such individuals,
consult the following books:"

The Indentured Project

I was thinking about the indentured project.
Of course, Pennsylvania never kept records of the
blot upon its honor. Have you tried the state
archives of Rhode Island or Vermont?

Rhode Island was big in the whaling and slave
trades (not to mention privateering). It also had a
quasi-rebellious streak running through it. They
didn't call it Rogue Island for nothing. Vermont,
was the same way in many respects, even prior to

the Green Mountain boys of Ethan Allen's time. Remember that they were an independent republic for a while. I feel like the state governments of these areas might be more amenable to actually keeping documents/testimonies of indentureds on hand...Just an idea.

-Nero the Pict

I will pursue these suggestions as soon as I am done with servant records in 17th century Virginia. Thank you so much for your help and support on this project.

'The Bodies of Lower Sort Men'

Project Muse: An Excerpt

Some Ivory Tower eggheads are actually looking into white slavery as a serious business.

Below is a sample of analysis from the project, which seems to have gathered weight due to the vast online traffic in ancestry searches. (Newman)

"By describing runaways in terms of property, often alongside advertisements for livestock, and by caricaturing them in ways that degraded African Americans, Irish, German, and native-born white Americans, masters defined, evaluated, and objectified their slaves and servants. Yet the advertisements and the descriptions they contain serve to illustrate that impoverished men and women who did not enjoy legal ownership of the labor of their bodies or even their very bodies, nonetheless strove to refashion and redefine their bodies, thereby reasserting control over them. More than anything else, runaway advertisements tell stories about battles over the bodies of lower sort men and women..."

White Cargo Reviewed at American Thinker

The Forgotten History of Britain's White Slaves in America

James, once again you are on the cutting edge of societal evolution. Awareness of history of white slavery in Colonial (plantation) America is going more mainstream. At least, such awareness is expanding in the conservative/Alt-Right blogosphere, which is where the real news is these days. Enjoy! (Levy)

The Forgotten History of Britain's White Slaves in America

July 28, 2017

By Janet Levy

"Slavery in America, typically associated with blacks from Africa, was an enterprise that began with the shipping of more than 300,000 white Britons to the colonies. This little known history is fascinatingly recounted in White Cargo (New York University Press, 2007). Drawing on letters, diaries, ship manifests, court documents, and government archives, authors Don Jordan and Michael Walsh detail how thousands of whites endured the hardships of tobacco farming and lived and died in bondage in the New World.

"Following the cultivation in 1613 of an acceptable tobacco crop in Virginia, the need for labor accelerated. Slavery was viewed as the cheapest and most expedient way of providing the necessary work force. Due to harsh working conditions, beatings, starvation, and disease, survival rates for slaves rarely exceeded two years. Thus, the high level of demand was sustained by a continuous flow of white slaves from England, Ireland, and Scotland from 1618 to 1775, who were imported to serve America's colonial masters..."

Note: In 1617, white boys were already being weighed on scales against the tobacco used to purchase them. The British government moved to enable mass deportation in 1618, and in 1619, 20 blacks were sold to over 5,000 whites, and three years later, the local Indian tribes—heavily stocked with runaway white slaves, almost wiped out the Virginia colony. This was the first mixed-race class war of the modern age and it is buried beneath a layer of lies and a veil of silence.

Read more at The American Thinker, but before you do, what happened in 1676?

That's right, the biggest white slave uprising since Spartacus, with most of the blacks and all of the Indians fighting on the side of the slave masters.

Might this have had something to do with the huge influx of 5,000-plus blacks a year, where previously as few as 20 a year might be bought by the rich as house slaves?

'The Vast Underbelly'

The Horrific World of England's Workhouse & The Children Who Built Victorian Britain (S. Chu), (Macaulay)

These documentaries do not reach as far back as the era of brutal servitude during which the American Colonies were founded as slave plantations for the extraction of natural resources. However, coming at the tail end of the iconic institutions central to British Society—that being child slavery, with millions involved in the selling of their own children and the stealing of others' children—one does catch a glimpse at the horror that was once a child's life in an age only hinted at by Dickens and denied by all.

Joes

A Chattel Coin from the Plantation Era

I found a good reference for exchange rates and currency use in the plantation era: (Michener).

"Among the most important of these coins were the Portuguese Johannes and moidore (more formally, the moeda d'ouro) and the Spanish dollar and pistole. The Johanneses were gold coins, 8 escudos (12,800 reis) in denomination; their name derived from the obverse of the coin, which bore the bust of Johannes V. Minted in Portugal and Brazil, they were commonly known in the colonies as "joes." The fractional denominations were 4-escudo and 2-escudo coins of the same origin. The 4-escudo (6,400 reis) coin, or "half joe," was one of the most commonly used coins in the late colonial period."

There is a conversion table on that page from 1771.

-Lynn

James LaFond

Thank you, Lynn. This is a priceless—of course the pun is intentional—resource on this matter. Below is but one paragraph that indicates the confused monetary landscape in Plantation America. Later on, the authors go on to note that P. T. Barnum once had difficulty purchasing a piece of fruit, as he was operating on a Connecticut pence and the seller on a New York pence scale.

"The units of account in colonial times were pounds, shillings, and pence (1£ = 20s., 1s. = 12d.). These pounds, shillings, and pence, however, were local units, such as New York money, Pennsylvania money, Massachusetts money, or South Carolina money and should not be confused with sterling. To do so is comparable to treating modern Canadian dollars and American dollars as interchangeable simply because they are both called "dollars." All the local currencies were less valuable than sterling. A Spanish piece of eight, for instance, was worth 4 s. 6 d. sterling at the British mint. The same piece of eight, on the eve of the Revolution, would have been treated as 6 s. in New England, as 8 s. in New York, as 7 s. 6 d. in Philadelphia, and as 32 s. 6 d. in Charleston (McCusker, 1978)."

Below is a repost of the monetary table from *So His Master May Have Him Again*.

What You Bought Your Boys With

18th Century Currency & Coinage and Unfree Labor Costs

-Pence [English, penny]; 12 pence = 1 shilling

-Shilling [English] = 1 day's wage

-Dollar [Spanish, silver peso "piece of eight"] = 4 shillings & 6 pence

-Pistole [Spanish, gold dubloon] = 18 shillings

-Pound [English] = 20 shillings

-Guinea [English, coin] = 21 shillings

The pound was a unit of measurement and was not represented by a minted coin, making the pistole the de facto capital coin; the guinea was used as a pound coin, though it was rare in the colonies.

The colonial administrations of the Plantation provinces were not permitted to coin their own currency.

The pistole was the primary medium of exchange in Virginia from 1700 to 1750. Usually a century-old Spanish coin, but sometimes a French gold Louis d'or, minted in the late 17th century, it was highly sought.

The term "shill," as in a paid advocate, comes ultimately from the shilling.

Three shillings were sometimes termed a "bob."

Servant Cost

-A shilling was the basic value of a laborer's day wage at the beginning of the period in the 1600s.

-The purchase price of a servant was a median of 15 pounds, or 300 shillings.

-The reward price of a servant ranged from 20 to 200 shillings [up to 5 pounds].

-A servant served for 7 years, for just over 300 days per year, including Sabbaths and holidays, bringing 3,500 days of labor to his owner.

-A man who buys a servant to ditch for 7 years would typically pay 300 shillings.

-A man who paid a ditcher by the day would expend 3,500 shillings over the same period.

-If a free man hired a ditcher and competed with a servant speculator for a ditch-digging contract, his single day laborer would cost him more than a servant speculator's crew of 10!

-Peter Williamson was sold for 16 pounds.

-African slaves sold for 25–100 pounds, with a median that seemed to be about 50 pounds, or 2,000 shillings, meaning a slave owner would have a hard time competing with a servant speculator but would still have much cheaper labor than a contractor paying a free wage laborer.

-The problem with servant speculation was runaways, expressed in reward costs and newspaper subscriptions, if the servant was recovered, which were paid for by the servant, who had time added to his term to compensate.

-Ultimately, the prime factors that turned the elite from servant speculation to slave owning were: homebred slaves cost nothing, then lived at the place of their birth, making them less likely to flee than the kidnapped, convicted and indebted servants who had preceded them.

Food is not calculated in the labor comparisons. However, servants and slaves usually ate nothing but water and corn, and were therefore more cheaply fed than cattle.

Eating Slave Girls in Jamestown

A Footnote to *Cracker-Boy*

"The delightful (and dastardly) secrets of the birth of America: Inside the colonial site of Jamestown, where starving English settlers feasted on rats and even other HUMANS. (Milton)

-The Mail on Sunday's Giles Milton toured the archaeological site of Jamestown in the state of Virginia.

The ancient human skull of a young female revealed she had been likely been eaten by her fellow settlers.

James LaFond

It's the setting for an epic new series, Jamestown, which tells the story of the women who arrived in 1619."

These dozen women were sold as "wives" to a population of elite brutes who had been working, beating, raping and killing boys for a decade. When the "Indians" rose up to wipe these fiends out three years later, many—and possibly most—of those Indians were escaped white slaves, named as "rogues" or "Vagabonds" in surviving journals. In the same year, 20 blacks would be sold, brought up from Barbados. The best estimate for the number of white male children sold in Jamestown that year is 3,000, only 150 of whom would be alive five years later. This researcher is willing to wager that the fate of these white boys, the majority population of human chattel in early Virginia, will be overlooked as the fate of the 32 people who matter in the modern mind's eye is examined in some dramatic detail.

'Buried with a Dead Dog'
The History of Ireland: Parts 1–3

Early Ireland was much more complex than commonly believed, and, in their perch above the

Western Ocean, the Irish preserved a great wealth of European culture and primordial savagery in uneasy concourse. (Conolly)

The Rape of the Abbess of Kildare

The medieval Irish, beginning with its traitor kings, who castrated and blinded enemies, raped holy women and buried the enemy with dogs, were the nastiest of their age, buying English slave boys since the 1000s, and seem to have a well-earned place in the mercantile hell of the future British Empire. Alice the Vicious, the Norman hell-bitch who killed 70 men to avenge the death of her lover, is a favorite.

Cromwell was such a savage that he had a garrison commander beaten to death with his own wooden leg and gave orders that men, women and children would be killed with clubs to save bullets. Cromwell began the systematic extermination and deportation of the Irish.

Of the west of conquered Ireland, one English lord said, "There is not water enough to drown a man, wood enough to hang him, nor earth enough to bury him."

Scattered into Exile

The Christian Wars of Europe, between Catholic and Protestant, found fertile ground in Ireland, and the solution of "the Plantation" was the first modern experiment in social engineering. Of course, in this documentary the slaves sold into American bondage are called settlers, but they were not. The term settler comes from English moving to Ireland to enslave Irish natives. But when those Irish slaves were shipped to America, in retrospect, we apply the term settler to them, associating it with their movement rather than their condition. The term *Planter*, however says it all, a planter of people.

The holocausts of the 1620s and 1630s are skipped, overshadowed as they were by the savagery of Cromwell's protectorate of the 1650s and 1660s. Again, our vantage is chronologically clouded and hopelessly backward looking.

"We have been your slaves all this time..." says one Irish rebel in the 1640's Ulster Rising.

So, it is there if you look.

There is scant information—in this documentary—on the enslavement of the Irish. However, the savagery of the Protestant–Catholic conflict in the British Isles well explains how Catholics became the standard slave of early North America.

The coverage of American immigration completely skips the Irish slaves and focuses on the Scots-Irish immigrants who displaced the escaped Irish slaves of Plantation America.

'He Sold Me for $415'

Bangladesh's Biggest Brothel - 101 East (A. J. News)

The description given by the kidnapped woman beginning at 2 minutes is very similar to most of what can be gleaned from the records of "indentured servants" in Plantation America.

Parents fall on hard times.

The parent or parents or an acquaintance take advantage of the young person seeking work and sell them.

Then, the buyers watch over the slave in a state of paranoia that she will escape before her debt is paid off.

What amazes is that although this happens to millions of women and children around the world annually and news organizations are willing to cover it, Americans, more heavily brainwashed than most human cattle, insist that their country did not begin by such means, and that American slavery was purely race-based.

And so, the greatest lie of our time remains buoyant in the sewer stream of the American narrative.

Bibliography

About Americans (Alt Right Edition). Dir. Varg Vikernes. Perf. Varg Vikernes. 2017. https://www.youtube.com/watch?v=9J482O3 DrWY.

adpowellblog. *The Forgotten Cause of the Civil War: A New Look at the Slavery Issue by Lawrence R. Tenzer*. 15 June 2014. https://adpowellblog.wordpress.com/2014/0 6/15/the-forgotten-cause-of-the-civil-war-a-new-look-at-the-slavery-issue-by-lawrence-r-tenzer/. 18 February 2019.

Archives, Maryland State. *Runaway Servants, 1728-1775 — 1 by Date of Advertisement*. Chart. Annapolis: Maryland State Archives, n.d. https://msa.maryland.gov/megafile/msa/spe ccol/sc2900/sc2908/000001/000822/pdf/c hart108.pdf.

Bangladesh's Biggest Brothel, 101 East. Dir. Al Jazeera News. Perf. Al Jazeera News. 2017. Television.

Bergreen, Laurence. *Over the Edge of the World: Magellan's Terrifying Circumnavigation of the Globe*. New York: HarperCollins Publishers Inc., 2004.

Bible, New International Version. n.d.

Black Robe. Dir. Bruce Beresford. Perf. Lothaire Bluteau. 1991. Film.

Boucher, Jonathan. "Runaway Slave Ad." *Virginia Gazette* 1 June 1769. http://www2.vcdh.virginia.edu/gos/search/relatedAd.php?adFile=sg69.xml&adId=v1769061615.

Brockenbrough, John. "Runaway Slave Ad." *Virginia Gazette* 15 June 1769. http://www2.vcdh.virginia.edu/xslt/servlet/XSLTServlet?xml=/xml_docs/slavery/ads/rg69.xml&xsl=/xml_docs/slavery/ads/display_ad.xsl&ad=v1769060388.

Brown, Deneen L. "Hunting down runaway slaves: The cruel ads of Andrew Jackson and 'the master class'." *Washington Post* 1 May 2017. https://www.washingtonpost.com/news/retropolis/wp/2017/04/11/hunting-down-runaway-slaves-the-cruel-ads-of-andrew-jackson-and-the-master-class/?utm_term=.136ee67a0425.

Buchan, W. *DOMESTIC MEDICINE CHAP. XIV. OF INTERMITTING FEVERS, OR AGUES.* 10 November 1785. Electronic. 9 February 2019. <https://www.americanrevolution.org/medicine/med14.php>.

Carter, Charles. "Runaway Slave Advertisement." *Virginia Gazette* 4-11 March 1736 (1737): 2-3. Electronic. <http://www2.vcdh.virginia.edu/xslt/servlet/XSLTServlet?xml=/xml_docs/slavery/ads/rg37.xml&xsl=/xml_docs/slavery/ads/display_ad.xsl&ad=v1737030006>.

Children Who Built Victorian Britain. Dir. Christina Macaulay. Perf. Jane Humphries. 2010. Television, BBC Four.

Colonies of the Condemned. Dir. Bob Reid. Perf. Jim Seibert. 2002. Television, Discovery Channel.

Costa, Tom. *The Geography of Slavery in Virginia.* 2005. 24 12 2018. <http://www2.vcdh.virginia.edu/gos/explore.html>.

Davies, C.S.L. "Slavery and Protector Somerset; The Vagrancy Act of 1547." *Economic History Review, The* (1966): 17. Electronic copy.

Day, Thomas Esq. *Memoirs of the late Dr. Benjamin Franklin: with a review of his pamphlet, entitled "Information to those who would wish to remove to America.".* London: A. Grant, 1790. https://books.google.com/books?pg=PA3&id=qp9WAAAAcAAJ#v=onepage&q=wilmer&f=false.

Dunglison, Robley. *Medical Lexicon, A Dictionary of Medical Science.* Philadelphia: Blanchard and Lea, 1865. http://www.civilwarmedicalbooks.com/A_Dictionary_of_Medical_Science.html.

Ellefson, C. Ashley. *Private Punishment of Servants and Slaves in Eighteenth-Century Maryland, The.* Cortland, NY: Archives of Maryland, 2010. Electronic.

—. *Seven Hangmen of Colonial Maryland*. Cortland, NY: Archives of Maryland, 2009. Electronic.

Flood, Chevalier W.H. Grattan. *IRISH EMIGRATION TO THE AMERICAN COLONIES, 1723 TO 1773*. Ed. Cathy Joint Labath. 1927. Electronic. 4 February 2019. <http://www.celticcousins.net/ireland/earlye migration.htm>.

French, Robert. "To George Washington from Robert French, 24 April 1789." *National Archives, Founders Online*. St. Croix, 24 April 1789. Electronic. 28 January 2019. <https://founders.archives.gov/documents/ Washington/05-02-02-0108>.

General Court Responds to Runaway Servants and Slaves (1640). General Court of Colonial Virginia. 22 July 1640. Electronic Copy. <https://www.encyclopediavirginia.org/Gen eral_Court_Responds_to_Runaway_Servan ts_and_Slaves_1640>.

Guerra, Francisco. *The Pre-Columbian Mind*. Seminar Press Limited, 1971.

Hawkins, David. "Runaway Slave Ad." *Poughkeepsie Journal* 10 June 1788. http://genealogytrails.com/ny/orange/news _slavery.html.

Heinegg, Paul. *FREE AFRICAN AMERICANS OF VIRGINIA, NORTH CAROLINA, SOUTH CAROLINA, MARYLAND AND DELAWARE*. 2001. 24 12 2018.

<http://www.freeafricanamericans.com/East
_Indians.htm>.

Hening, William Waller. *Hening's Statutes at Large.*
Torrance: Spradlin, Freddie L., 1823.
Electronic copy.
<http://vagenweb.org/hening/index.htm>.

Hoffman, Michael E. *Unz Review, The.* 18 July 2018.
10 January 2019.
<http://www.unz.com/article/whites-in-
servitude-in-early-america-and-industrial-
britain/>.

Horrific World of England's Workhouses, The. Dir.
Simon Chu. Perf. Jim Carter. 2013.
Television.

Johnston, Benjamin. "Runaway Slave Ad." *Virginia
Gazette* 20 October 1774.
http://www2.vcdh.virginia.edu/gos/search/r
elatedAd.php?adFile=sg74.xml&adId=v17741
01944.

Kinard, June,. "Maryland Colonial Census, 1776."
Provo: Ancestry.com Operations Inc., 2000.

Levy, Janet. "The Forgotten History of Britain's
White Slaves in America." *American Thinker*
28 July 2017.
https://www.americanthinker.com/articles/2
017/07/the_forgotten_history_of_britains_
white_slaves_in_america.html.

Manual On-Line, Maryland. *A Guide to Maryland
and its Government.* Annapolis, MD, 29 June
2018.

https://msa.maryland.gov/msa/mdmanual/
01glance/chron/html/chron17.html.

Martin, Anthony. "Runaway Slave Ad." *Virginia Gazette* 21 February 1771.
http://www2.vcdh.virginia.edu/gos/search/r
elatedAd.php?adFile=rg71.xml&adId=v17710
20540.

Maryland State Archivist. *Archives of Maryland*. Annapolis: State of Maryland, 1637-1664. Electronic copy.
<http://aomol.msa.maryland.gov/html/volu
mes.html>.

Michener, Ron. *Money in the American Colonies*. 8 June 2003.
http://eh.net/encyclopedia/money-in-the-
american-colonies/. 19 February 2019.

Milton, Giles. "The delightful (and dastardly) secrets of the birth of America: Inside the colonial site of Jamestown, where starving English settlers feasted on rats and even other HUMANS." *Daily Mail* 5 August 2017.
https://www.dailymail.co.uk/travel/article-
4763702/Giles-Milton-explores-canabalism-
Jamestown-Virginia.html#ixzz4ovka0ol6.

Mitchell, John, William Lynn and Charles Dick. "Runaway Slave Advertisement." *Virginia Gazette* 7-14 August 1746. Electronic.
<http://www2.vcdh.virginia.edu/gos/search/
relatedAd.php?adFile=sg46.xml&adId=v1746
081417>.

Mittelberger, Gottlieb. *Journey to Pennsylvania in the Year 1750 and Return to Germany in the Year 1754*. Philadelphia, Pennsylvania: German Society of Pennsylvania, 1898.

New Castle, County. "Runaway Slave Ads." *Essex Gazette, and others* 1769-. http://genealogytrails.com/del/newcastle/news_slavery.html.

Newkirk, Charles. "Runaway Slave Ad." *The National Advocate* 8 November 1816. http://genealogytrails.com/ny/orange/news_slavery.html.

Newman, Simon P. *Embodied History: The Lives of the Poor in Early Philadelphia*. 1 January 2014. https://muse.jhu.edu/chapter/783851. 18 February 2019.

News, Ireland Old. *REDEMPTIONERS and INDENTURED SERVANTS*. n.d. Electronic. 4 February 2019. <http://irelandoldnews.com/History/runaways.htm>.

Penn., Gazette. "Runaway Slave Advertisement." *Pennsylvania Gazette* Various Various 1751-1771. Electronic. <http://www.irelandoldnews.com/History/runaways2.htm>.

Pennsylvania, State of. *Indentured Servants*. 1 November 2006. https://www.phmc.pa.gov/Archives/Research-Online/Pages/Indentured-Servants.aspx. 18 February 2019.

Pickering, Danby. *Statutes at Large from the 32d Year of King Henry VIII to the 7th Year of King Edward VI Inclusive*. Vol. V. Cambridge: Joseph Bentham, 1763. CIX vols. Electronic copy. 17 January 2019. <https://archive.org/details/statutesatlarge24 britgoog/page/n273>.

Rossiter, F.M. *The Torch of Life*. Eugenics Publishing Group, 1939.

Short History of Convict Australia. Dir. Ian Wright. Perf. Ian Wright. 1998. Television, Discovery Channel.

Spence, Jonathan D. *Question of Hu, The*. New York: Vintage Books, 1988.

Springston, Chuck. *Population of the 13 Colonies 1610-1790*. 28 October 2013. Electronic. 3 February 2019. <http://www.yttwebzine.com/yesterday/201 3/10/28/75757/population_13_colonies_char t>.

Tenzer, Lawrence. *The Forgotten Cause of the Civil War: A New Look at the Slavery Issue*. Manahawkin, NJ: Scholars' Publishing House, 1997. Paperback.

The History of Ireland, Parts 1 - 3. Dir. Mike Conolly. Perf. Fergal Keane. 2011. Film.

Trails, Geneology. *Geneology Trails, Harford County, Maryland*. 22 January 2019. Electronic. 22 January 2019.

<http://genealogytrails.com/mary/harford/a
ssociationoffreemen.html>.

Wiseman, Samuel. *Book of Record*. Lexington
Books, 2009.

Wray, Robert. "Runaway Slave Ad." *The Adams
Centinel* 20 May 1801.
http://genealogytrails.com/penn/adams/ne
wspaper.html.

Zane, Isaac. "Runaway Slave Ad." *Virginia Gazette*
22 November 1776.
http://www2.vcdh.virginia.edu/gos/search/r
elatedAd.php?adFile=vg1776.xml&adId=v177
6112099.

Made in the USA
Coppell, TX
27 November 2021